FINDER'S GUIDE NUMBER ONE

KITS & PLANS

Joseph Rosenbloom

OLIVER PRESS
WILLITS, CALIFORNIA

Library of Congress Card Number   73-92459

ISBN   0-914400-00-2

First Printing January 1974
Second Printing July 1974
Third Printing December 1974
Fourth Printing April 1975

OLIVER PRESS
1400 Ryan Creek Road
Willits, California 95490

CONTENTS

HOW TO USE KITS AND PLANS

Kits & Plans consists of two main indexes: a MASTER INDEX and a COMPANY INDEX. The MASTER INDEX is a list of products alphabetically arranged. If you are looking for a kit or plan for a specific product, first check for the product in the MASTER INDEX. The MASTER INDEX will then tell you which company or companies offer the specific product. Next, check the COMPANY INDEX to find out more about each company listed. The COMPANY INDEX offers information about each company, the range of its products, whether it offers kits or plans or both, as well as details about its catalog. If the description of a company sounds interesting, by all means write to the company directly. Only the company itself can provide final, authoritative information about its products and prices. Don't hesitate to write to more than one company, if more than one company provides the specific product in which you are interested. In this way you can compare before you buy.

MASTER INDEX

DUCK decoys
  Craftplans
  Minnesota Woodworkers
     Supply Co.
  Wilson-Allen Corp.
DULCIMERS (See also Hammered
     dulcimers)
  Albert Constantine and Son, Inc.
  Craftsman Wood Service Co.
  The Dulcimer Shoppe
  Here, Inc.
  Hughes Co.]
  The String Shop
DUNE buggies
  IECO
  K & P Mfg.
  J. C. Whitney & Co.

Now that you are ready to use <u>Kits & Plans,</u> a word about service, shortages and prices. Rapidly rising prices is a painful fact of modern life. Suppliers of kits and plans are suffering from this malady like everyone else. Since it takes time to prepare, print and distribute catalogs, prices are often outdated by the time they are received. Only the companies themselves can give you a firm price at any specific time. Then there is the matter of a critical shortage of various supplies. The manufacturers or distributors of kits and plans are affected by shortages as are other businesses and this sometimes results in delayed deliveries. Finally, as most everyone must have noted by now, the United States Postal Service is, to put it mildly, not what it used to be. For these reasons, patience and understanding may be necessary in dealing with the suppliers and manufacturers of kits or plans during these trying days.

COMPANY INDEX

HUGHES CO.
8665 West 13th Ave.
Denver, Col. 80215

PRODUCTS:

Balalaikas	Irish harps
Dulcimers	Lyres, ancient Greek
Guitars	Sitars
Hammered dulcimers	Thumb pianos (West African instruments)

Kits for making your own folk musical instruments, and save considerable money thereby. Thus a completed balalaika costing $37.00 (model B32M3) can be bought in kit form for $8.85, or a dulcimer completed (model M37M4) costing $29.95 can be bought in kit form for $11.95. Savings for other instruments and models are comparable. Instruments can be made by the amateur without special tools or skills. The assembly time varies from 4 to 5 hours for a small dulcimer to 40 or 50 hours for a guitar. Special school discounts for lots of 3 or more.

Illustrated catalog free

INTRODUCTION

More and more people are building things for themselves today. Is there any wonder? The grim facts of runaway inflation are making a shambles of our lives. One way to combat the high cost of things is to make them yourself. You can thereby save money, often half or even more. You can also get a great deal of satisfaction and pleasure by working with your own two hands. The suppliers of kits and plans are offering more and more products for the more and more people who want to do things for themselves. This book lists over 4,000 products to be made from kits or plans. There is something here for every taste and level of skill.

The major problem is: how to find out "who" makes "what" kit or plan. Let us say, by way of example, that you are interested in building a rolltop desk. First, you might scan the ads in your favorite build-it-yourself magazine. Your chances of finding a lead for this type of desk is a hit-or-miss proposition at best. Not all the companies offering kits or plans for a rolltop desk advertise in that particular magazine. And even if the companies did so advertise, the ad might not specifically mention rolltop desks. Perhaps the ad simply reads "furniture" or "desks". Well, you might decide next to take your chances and write to the most likely companies. Here again the question is "iffy". It is most unlikely that by reading any one magazine you can find all or nearly all of the companies supplying such kits or plans so that you could pick out the best one for what you have in mind. Try another magazine? O. K. Then another, if you still aren't quite satisfied? Fine. But this process could be bothersome and time-consuming.

This guide to the kits and plans world is essentially an attempt to ease the problems faced by anyone who wants to find out "who" makes "what". Those companies which supply kits and plans have been located and identified. Their catalogs have been analyzed and their projects or products have been broken down into useful categories. Now, if you want to find out who makes kits or plans for rolltop desks, it is a simple matter of consulting the index. Refer to the companies indicated by the index, and the kits or plans will be listed for you. There is also information in this guide about the companies' catalogs. We have tried to solve the problem of finding out "who" makes "what" kit or plan by doing much of the preliminary, time-consuming work for you.

PREFACE

This guide to the kits and plans world is based on information taken directly from the catalogs of more than 400 companies. The guide consists of two parts: MASTER INDEX, an alphabetic listing of projects or products by subject and, COMPANY INDEX, a list of suppliers arranged alphabetically. The COMPANY INDEX describes the suppliers, their products, and gives information about catalogs. To find out who makes a particular kit or plan, consult the MASTER INDEX first. The index will then direct you to those companies offering the kits or plans in which you are interested. To find out more about the companies and their catalogs, consult the COMPANY INDEX.

Only companies with catalogs or an acceptable equivalent are included in this guide, with rare exceptions. The term "plan" as used here includes blueprints, assembly instructions, or any other information which clearly assists the builder in the completion of a project. As defined here, with few exceptions, "kits" refer to groups of parts or components which when put together using a plan, result in a completed object. A mere collection of things like "screwdriver kits" or "spark plug kits" are excluded.

No responsibility is assumed for any claims made by the suppliers of kits or plans about their products or services. Prices stated in this guide are intended to be illustrative only. Prices are subject to change without notice by the suppliers of kits and plans themselves. The model making and the handicraft world are omitted from this guide, regrettably. These fields would require separate books in themselves to deal with them in any adequate way.

It is hoped that subsequent revisions of this guide will remedy such unintentional errors as might occur, and that frequent revisions will keep the guide abreast of the everchanging, fast-moving world of kits and plans.

MASTER INDEX

1

Jurca Plans
K & S Aircraft Supply
Landis G. Ketner
The Lacey M-10 Co.
E. Littner
Monnett Experimental Aircraft
Mooney Mite Aircraft
Henry Francis Parks Laboratory
Pazmany Aircraft Corp.
Popular Mechanics, Dept. CO
J.R. Scoville
Jerry Smith
Southern Aeronautical Corp.
Dorothy Spezio
Stephens Aircraft Co.
Stewart Aircraft Corp.
Stolp Starduster Corp.
Sturgeon Air Ltd.
The Teenie Co.
Turner Aircraft and Engineering
Bill Warwick
Western Aircraft Supplies
AIRPLANES, antique
Experimental Aircraft Association, Inc.
Jurca Plans
Herb Rayner
Redfern & Son
Replica Plans
Stolp Starduster Corp.
Sturgeon Air Ltd.
AIRPLANES, biplane
Experimental Aircraft Association, Inc.
Javelin Aircraft Co., Inc.
K & S Aircraft Supply
Meyer Aircraft
Mong Sport
Barney Oldfield Aircraft Co.
Replica Plans
Science & Mechanics Publishing Co.
Shober Aircraft Enterprises
Smith Miniplane
Steen Aero Lab
Stolp Starduster Corp.

Sturgeon Air Ltd.
ALL terrain cycles (ATC's)
Heald, Inc.
C.F. Struck Corp.
ALL terrain vehicles (ATV's)
Brown's Motorsports
Mechanix Illustrated
C.F. Struck Corp.
ALPHABET patterns
Albert Constantine and Son, Inc.
Craftplans
Minnesota Woodworkers Supply Co.
ALTERNATOR power source
B-UR-O Company
Creative Products
AMPHIBIANS
Anderson Aircraft Corp.
Explorer Aircraft Co.
Flight Dynamics, Inc.
Osprey Aircraft
Spencer Amphibian Air Car
Volmer Aircraft
AMPLIFIERS, four channel (see Four channel amplifiers)
AMPLIFIERS, guitar
Heath Company
H.J. Knapp Co.
Henry Francis Parks Laboratory
AMPLIFIERS, ham
Heath Company
AMPLIFIERS, mono
Electronic Aids
Heath Company
AMPLIFIERS, vacuum tube (see Vacuum tube amplifiers)
ANIMAL barns
Hammond Barns
ANTIQUES (see Airplanes, antique, Automobiles, antique, Pistols, antique, Rifles, antique)
ANVILS
Casting Specialities
APARTMENTS/income producing units
L.M. Brunier & Assoc., Inc.

Custom Builders Corp.
Garlinghouse Co., Inc.
Hexagon Housing Systems, Inc.
Home Building Plan Service
Modular Concepts, Inc.
National Plan Service
Standard Homes, Co.
APPLIANCE testers
  Bigelow Electronics
  Digiac Corp.
  Eico Electronic Instrument
    Co., Inc.
  Lafayette Radio Electronics
  Trigger Electronics
ARMOIRES
  Craft Patterns Studio
ARROWS
  Bingham Archery
  Craft Patterns Studio
  Finneysports
  Herter's, Inc.
  Kittredge Bow Hut
ASSAYERS, metal (see Metal
  assayers)
ATOMIC energy laboratory
  Edmund Scientific Co.
ATTACK delay units
  Paia Electronics, Inc.
ATTICS
  Craft Patterns Studio
AUDIO generators
  Eico Electronic Instrument
    Co., Inc.
  Heath Company
  Lafayette Radio Electronics
  Phase Corp.
AUTOMOBILES (see also Cars)
AUTOMOBILES, antique
  Mechanix Illustrated
  Popular Science Plans Division
AUTOMOBILES, midget (motor-
  ized)
  Braco Mfg. Co.
  Brown's Motorsports
  Craftplans
  Gilliom Mfg. Co.
  Mechanix Illustrated
  Minnesota Woodworkers
    Supply Co.

Popular Mechanics, Dept. CO
Science & Mechanics Publish-
  ing Co.
C. F. Struck Corp.
AUTOMOTIVE equipment (see
  under following subjects)
  Alternator power source
  Burglar alarms, automobile
  Battery chargers, automotive
  Cab-to-camper intercoms
  Engine analyzers
  Engine stands
  Ignition analyzers
  Ignition, capacative discharge
  Jeep/Scout repowering
  Steam engines, auto
  Tachometer & dwell angle
    meters
  Tachometers
  Timing lights
  Tune-up meters
  Voltage regualtors
  Windshield wiper controllers
AWNINGS
  Craft Patterns Studio
BACKPACKS
  Frostline, Inc.
BAJA bugs/buses
  Miller Havens Enterprises
BALALAIKAS
  Hughes Co.
BANCIMERS (dulcimer fretted
  banjos)
  Here, Inc.
  The String Shop
BANJOS
  The Guitar Center
  Here, Inc.
  The String Shop
BAR generators (see Color bar
  generators)
BARBECUE carts
  Better Homes and Gardens
  Craft Patterns Studio
  U-Bild Enterprises
  Western Wood Products Asso-
    ciation
BARBECUE dining sets
  Craft Patterns Studio

U-Bild Enterprises
BARBECUE pits
    Craft Patterns Studio
    Sakrete, Inc.
    U-Bild Enterprises
BARN homes
    Yankee Barns, Inc.
BARNS (see also Animal barns,
    Barn homes, Horse barns)
    Hammond Barns
    National Plan Service
    Popular Mechanics, Dept. CO
    Popular Science Plans Division
    U-Bild Enterprises
    Vermont Log Buildings, Inc.
BARS
    American Plywood Association
    Better Homes and Gardens
    Craft Patterns Studio
    Furn-A-Kit, Inc.
    Furniture Designs
    Minnesota Woodworkers
      Supply Co.
    U-Bild Enterprises
    Yield House
BASEMENT remodelling
    Better Homes and Gardens
    Craft Patterns Studio
BATTERY chargers
    Digiac Corp.
    Edmund Scientific Co.
    Eico Electronic Instrument
      Co., Inc.
    Graymark Enterprises, Inc.
    Heath Company
    McGee Radio Co.
    Technical Writers Group
BATTERY chargers, automotive
    Digiac Corp.
    Heath Company
BATTERY testers
    Bigelow Electronics
    Eico Electronic Instrument
      Co., Inc.
    Lafayette Radio Electronics
    Trigger Electronics
BEACHER marine railways
    Reimann & Georger, Inc.

BEDS, geodesic-chrome steel
    dome
    Dome East
BEDS/headboards (see also Bunk
    beds)
    American Plywood Association
    Bedford Lumber Co.
    Cohasset Colonials - by Hagerty
    Albert Constantine and Son,
      Inc.
    Craft Patterns Studio
    Designer Kits, Inc.
    Furniture Designs
    Old South Pattern Co.
    Stanley Tools
    U-Bild Enterprises
BELLS, brass
    Germaco
BELL sensors, remote
    Totaltron Laboratory
BENCHES
    Cohasset Colonials - by Hagerty
    Craft Patterns Studio
    Furniture Designs
    Shaker Workshops
    Stanley Tools
    U-Bild Enterprises
    Western Wood Products Asso-
      ciation
    Yield House
BENCHES, storage
    Old South Pattern Co.
BENDING brakes
    Science & Mechanics Publish-
      ing Co.
BICYCLES, motorized
    BAT-RE-BIKE Co.
    Plans
    Schmieder Motors
BIKE racks, car top
    U-Bild Enterprises
BIPLANES (see Airplanes)
BIRD call imitators
    Lafayette Radio Electronics
BIRD houses (see also Martin
    houses)
    Craft Patterns Studio
    Held Products
    Mastercraft Plans

BIRD houses/feeders
  Craftplans
  Minnesota Woodworkers
    Supply Co.
  T.C. Industries
  U-Bild Enterprises
BIRD songsters, electronic
  Paia Electronics, Inc.
BLACK light
  Edmund Scientific Co.
  Graymark Enterprises, Inc.
  Lafayette Radio Electronics
BLOCK planes
  Germaco
BOATS/boating equipment (see
    under following subjects)
  Canoes
  Can-yaks (combination canoe
    and kayak)
  Catamarans
  Cruisers
  Ferro-cement boats
  Houseboats
  Hovercraft, see VEHICLES
  Hydroplanes
  Ice boats
  Inboards
  Kayaks
  Outboards
  Paddle-wheel boats
  Playaks
  Pontoon Boats
  Rowboat type (rowboats, prams,
    dinghies, etc.)
  Runabouts
  Sailing, cruising
  Sailing, day sailers
  Side-wheelers
  Steamboats
  Stern-wheelers
  Submarines
  Submarines, historic (the
    "Monitor")
  Trimarans
  Workboats/ commercial boats
BOATS, children's
  Science & Mechanics Publish-
    ing Co.
  Smug Harbor Boat Works

U-Bild Enterprises
BOATS, equipment
  Beacher marine railways
  Depth sounders
  Docks/piers
  Fender boards
  Flying bridges
  Foghorns/hailers
  Fuel vapor detectors
  Hydrofoils
  Lifts, boat
  Marine engine conversions
  Marine engines, steam
  Ports, boat
  Rafts
  Ramps, boat
  Sails/sail gear
  Storages, boat
  Tachometers
  Trailers, boat
BONGOS, electronic
  Eico Electronic Instrument
    Co., Inc.
  Lafayette Radio Electronics
BOOK easels/stands
  Yield House
BOOKCASES
  Bedford Lumber Co.
  Better Homes and Gardens
  Cohasset Colonials - by Hagerty
  Craft Patterns Studio
  Furn-A-Kit, Inc.
  Furniture Designs
  Giles & Kendall
  Old South Pattern Co.
  Stanley Tools
  U-Bild Enterprises
  Yield House
BOOKENDS
  Stanley Tools
BOOTS, down
  Carikit
  Frostline, Inc.
BOWS
  Bingham Archery
  Craft Patterns Studio
  Kittredge Bow Hut
BRAINWAVE machines
  Extended Digital Concepts

BREAKFAST nooks
  Craft Patterns Studio
  U-Bild Enterprises
BROADCASTERS, neighborhood
  Digiac Corp.
  Lafayette Radio Electronics
  Technical Writers Group
BROWSING bins (display matted
      works)
  Dryad Press
BUFFETS
  Better Homes and Gardens
  Albert Constantine and Son,
      Inc.
  Craft Patterns Studio
  Furniture Designs
  Stanley Tools
  U-Bild Enterprises
BULLDOZERS, garden/suburban
  C.F. Struck Corp.
BUNK beds
  American Plywood Association
  Better Homes and Gardens
  Craft Patterns Studio
BURGLAR alarms, automobile
  Howard
  Informer Alarm Supplies Co.
  King Research Labs, Inc.
  Lafayette Radio Electronics
  McGee Radio Co.
  Pem Enterprises
  Totaltron Laboratory
BURGLAR/fire alarms, home or
      business
  Creative Products
  Edmund Scientific Co.
  Eico Electronic Instrument
      Co., Inc
  Graymark Enterprises, Inc.
  Heath Company
  Howard
  Informer Alarm Supplies Co.
  King Research Labs, Inc.
  Lafayette Radio Electronics
  McGee Radio Co.
  Mountain West Alarm Supply
      Co.
  Olson Electronics
  Pem Enterprises

  Protecto Alarm Sales
  Radio Shack
  TPC (Theft Prevention Co.)
  Trigger Electronics
CABANAS
  U-Bild Enterprises
CABINETS
  American Plywood Association
  Better Homes and Gardens
  Craft Patterns Studio
  Furn-A-Kit, Inc.
  Old South Pattern Co.
  Western Wood Products Asso-
      ciation
CABINETS, collectors/curio
  Albert Constantine and Son,
      Inc.
  Craft Patterns Studio
  Furniture Designs
  Minnesota Woodworkers
      Supply Co.
  Old South Pattern Co.
  U-Bild Enterprises
CABINETS, file (see File cabinets)
CABINETS, fishing gear
  American Plywood Association
  Minnesota Woodworkers
      Supply Co.
  Western Wood Products Asso-
      ciation
CABINETS, gun/rifle
  American Plywood Association
  Bedford Lumber Co.
  Better Homes and Gardens
  Albert Constantine and Son,
      Inc.
  Craft Patterns Studio
  Craftplans
  Furniture Designs
  Minnesota Woodworkers
      Supply Co.
  U-Bild Enterprises
  Western Wood Products Asso-
      ciation
  Yield House
CABINETS, kitchen
  Craft Patterns Studio
CABINETS, medicine
  Yield House

6

CABINETS, oversized (for artists, photographers)
 Dryad Press
CABINETS, paperback
 Yield House
CABINETS, phonographic record
 Craft Patterns Studio
 U-Bild Enterprises
 Yield House
CABINETS, recipe
 Yield House
CABINETS, sewing
 Bedford Lumber Co.
 Craft Patterns Studio
 Minnesota Woodworkers
  Supply Co.
 U-Bild Enterprises
CABINETS, spice
 Albert Constantine and Son,
  Inc.
 Craft Patterns Studio
CABINETS, stero/hi-fi
 Bedford Lumber Co.
 Better Homes and Gardens
 Craft Patterns Studio
 Furn-A-Kit, Inc.
 Furniture Designs
 Giles and Kendall
 Old South Pattern Co.
 Jerry Sanford
 Stanley Tools
 U-Bild Enterprises
 Yield House
CABINETS, tie
 Yield House
CABINETS, tool (see Tool cabinets)
CABINETS, TV
 Craft Patterns Studio
 U-Bild Enterprises
 Yield House
CABINS/cottages
 American Plywood Association
 Bellaire Log Cabin Mfg. Co.
 Bloch Brothers
 Craft Patterns Studio
 Custom Builders Corp.
 Garlinghouse Co., Inc.
 Hexagon Housing Systems, Inc.

Home Building Plan Service
Home Planners, Inc.
International Homes of Cedar
Lindal Cedar Homes
Mechanix Illustrated
Modular Concepts, Inc.
National Log Construction of
 Montana
National Plan Service
Shelter-Kit, Inc.
U-Bild Enterprises
CABINS, log
 Bellaire Log Cabin Mfg. Co.
 Bloch Brothers
 Custom Builders Corp.
 Fab-A-Log of Washington
 Garlinghouse Co., Inc.
 Mills Cabin Mills, Inc.
 National Log Construction of
  Montana
 Northern Products, Inc.
 Vermont Log Buildings, Inc.
 Ward Cabin Co.
CAB-TO-CAMPER intercoms
 Heath Company
CADDIES, garden
 U-Bild Enterprises
CALCULATORS, electronic
 Heath Company
CALIBRATION oscillators
 Phase Corp.
CAMERA equipment (see Contact
  printers, Enlarger meters,
  Enlargers, Flash units,
  Timers, photo)
CAMERAS obscura
 Edmund Scientific Co.
CAMP kitchens (see Kitchens,
  camp)
CAMPERS
 Comstock Camper and Trailer
  Supply
 Craft Patterns Studio
 Glen L. Recreational Vehicles
 Luger Camper Kits
 Mechanix Illustrated
 Trail-R-Club of America
 U-Bild Enterprises
 J.C. Whitney & Co.

CAMPERS, car-top
    Science & Mechanics Publish-
        ing Co.
CAMPERS, folding
    American Plywood Association
    Popular Science Plans Division
    Science & Mechanics Publish-
        ing Co.
CAMPERS, tent (see Tent campers)
CAMPING (see under following
        subjects)
    Backpacks
    Bike racks, car-top
    Boots, down
    Campers, car-top
    Campers, folding
    Kitchens, camp
    Jackets, down
    Luggage carriers, car-top
    Mitts, down
    Pants, down
    Parkas
    Picnic equipment
    Ponchos
    Sleeping bags
    Sweaters, down
    Tent campers
    Tents
    Trailers, campers, mobile
        homes, see VEHICLES
    Vests, down
CAN-YAKS (combination canoe &
        kayak)
    Glen L. Marine
CANDELABRAS
    Casting Specialties
    Germaco
CANDLESTICKS
    Casting Specialties
    Germaco
CANE/rush furniture
    Cohasset Colonials - by Hagerty
    Albert Constantine and Son,
        Inc.
    Furniture Designs
    Newell Workshop
    H.H. Perkins Co.
    Sarin Handicrafts
    Yield House

CANOES (see also Can-yaks)
    James Bliss & Co., Inc.
    Folboat Corp.
    Mechanix Illustrated
    Outdoor Sports
    Popular Science Plans Division
    Quicksilver Boats
    Science & Mechanics Publish-
        ing Co.
    Sportscraft Co.
    C.F. Struck Corp.
    Taft Marine Corp.
    Trailcraft, Inc.
CANOPIES, geodesic dome
    Geodesic Domes
CAPACITOR substitution boxes
    Bigelow Electronics
    Eico Electronic Instrument
        Co., Inc.
    Heath Company
    Lafayette Radio Electronics
CAPACITOR testers
    Eico Electronic Instrument
        Co., Inc.
    Heath Company
    Lafayette Radio Electronics
    McGee Radio Co.
CARD tables (see Tables, card)
CARPORTS
    American Plywood Association
    Better Homes and Gardens
    L.M. Brunier & Associates,
        Inc.
    Craft Patterns Studio
    U-Bild Enterprises
CARRIERS (see Luggage carriers)
CARS (see also Automobiles)
CARS, electric (see Electric cars)
CARS, sport
    Bradley Automotive
CARS/trucks, toy
    Craft Patterns Studio
    Craftplans
    U-Bild Enterprises
CARTS (see also Barbecue carts,
        Push carts)
CARTS, hostess, chrome steel
    Designer Kits, Inc.

CARTS, hostess/tea
  Better Homes and Gardens
  Albert Constantine and Son,
    Inc.
  Furniture Designs
  Old South Pattern Co.
  Stanley Tools
  U-Bild Enterprises
CATAMARANS
  John Brandlmayr, Ltd.
  Canadian Multihull Services
  Clark Craft Boat Co.
  W. M. Cookson
  Glen L. Marine
  International Catamarans
  Mechanix Illustrated
  Polynesian Catamaran Sail-
    boats
  Popular Mechanics, Dept. CO
  Taft Marine Corp.
CEDAR chests
  Bedford Lumber Co.
  Giles & Kendall
  Yield House
CELLOS
  International Violin Co.
CHAIRS
  Cohasset Colonials - by Hagerty
  Albert Constantine and Son,
    Inc.
  Craft Patterns Studio
  Furn-A-Kit, Inc.
  Minnesota Woodworkers
    Supply Co.
  Old South Pattern Co.
  U-Bild Enterprises
CHAIRS, captain's
  Albert Constantine and Son,
    Inc.
  Furniture Designs
  Old South Pattern Co.
  Yield House
CHAIRS, chrome steel
  Designer Kits, Inc.
CHAIRS, kang-chi (oriental temple)
  Old South Pattern Co.
CHAIRS, ladderback
  Cohasset Colonials - by Hagerty
  Albert Constantine and Son, Inc.

H. H. Perkins Co.
Savin Handicrafts
Shaker Workshops
Yield House
CHAIRS, rocking
  Cohasset Colonials -by Hagerty
  Craft Patterns Studio
  Furniture Designs
  Old South Pattern Co.
  H. H. Perkins Co.
  Savin Handicrafts
  Shaker Workshops
  Stanley Tools
  U-Bild Enterprises
CHALETS
  American Timber Homes, Inc.
  Bellaire Log Cabin Mfg. Co.
  L. M. Brunier & Associates,
    Inc.
  Cedar Homes Mfg. Corp.
  Custom Builders Corp.
  Fab-A-Log of Washington
  Garlinghouse Co., Inc.
  Home Planners, Inc.
  International Homes of Cedar
  Mills Cabin Mills, Inc.
  Modular Concepts, Inc.
  National Plan Service
  Northern Products, Inc.
  Nor-Wes Trading Ltd.
  Vermont Log Buildings, Inc.
  Ward Cabin Co.
CHART recorders
  Heath Company
CHEMICAL formulas/projects
    (see Formulas, chemical)
CHEST of drawers
  Bedford Lumber Co.
  Cohasset Colonials -by Hagerty
  Furniture Designs
  Old South Pattern Co.
  Stanley Tools
CHEST on chests
  Furniture Designs
CHESTS (see also Cedar chests)
  Bedford Lumber Co.
  Cohasset Colonials - by Hagerty
  Craft Patterns Studio
  Old South Pattern Co.

Shaker Workshops
Stanley Tools
CHESTS, apothecary
Yield House
CHESTS, machinists (see Machi-
nists chests)
CHESTS, tool (see Tool chests)
CHESTS, toy (see Toy chests)
CHESTS, utility (see Utility
chests)
CHIFFOROBES
U-Bild Enterprises
CHILDREN'S things (see under
following subjects)
Boats, children's
Bunk beds
Carnival rides
Cars/trucks, toy
Cradles
Cradles, colonial
Cribs
Doll furniture
Doll houses
Furniture, children's
hobby horses
Kitchen's, children's
Kites
Merry-go-rounds
Mobiles
Play houses
Play houses, geodesic dome
Playpens
"Potty" rockers, colonial
Puppet theatres
Rocking toys
Sand boxes
Science toys
Slotless racing
Swings
Toy chests
Toys
Toys, educational (tell time,
add, etc.)
Toys, geodesic dome
Toys, musical (using Swiss
musical movements)
Trains/locomotives, play
Tricycles
Wading pools

CHOPPERS (motorcycle)
American Motorsport Mfg.
California Choppers
Custom Cycle Delight, Inc.
North American Imports
Wheel Specialties
CHRISTMAS decorations
Albert Constantine and Son,
Inc.
Craft Patterns Studio
Craftplans
Mastercraft Plans
Minnesota Woodworkers
Supply Co.
U-Bild Enterprises
CHRISTMAS tree stand
Casting Specialties
CHROME steel furniture
Designer Kits, Inc.
Furn-A-Kit, Inc.
CIRCUIT testers
Lafayette Radio Electronics
McGee Radio Co.
Trigger Electronics
CLAMPS (see Miter clamps)
CLAVICHORDS
J. Witcher-Ancient Instruments
CLOCKS, weather instruments,
(thermometers, barometers,
etc.)
Craft Products Co.
H. DeCovnick & Son, Inc.
Mason & Sullivan
Old Bedford Clock Co.
CLOCKS, cuckoo
JHS Enterprises
Selva Company
Yield House
CLOCKS, decor
Albert Constantine and Son,
Inc.
Craft Patterns Studio
Craftplans
Craft Products Co.
Gaston Wood Finishes
House of Clermont
Mason & Sullivan
Minnesota Woodworkers
Supply Co.

Newport Enterprises
Selva Company
CLOCKS, digital
Technical Writers Group
CLOCKS, grandfather
Albert Constantine and Son,
Inc.
Craft Patterns Studio
Craftplans
Craft Products Co.
Craftsman Wood Service Co.
H. DeCovnick & Son, Inc.
Mason & Sullivan
Minnesota Woodworkers
Supply Co.
Science & Mechanics Publish-
ing Co.
Stanley Tools
Yield House
CLOCKS, grandmother
Albert Constantine and Son,
Inc.
Craft Patterns Studio
Craftplans
Craft Products Co.
H. DeCovnick & Son, Inc.
Mason & Sullivan
Stanley Tools
CLOCKS, period
Albert Constantine and Son,
Inc.
Craft Patterns Studio
Craftplans
Craft Products Co.
H. De Covnick & Son, Inc.
Mason & Sullivan
Minnesota Woodworkers
Supply Co.
Newport Enterprises
Old Bedford Clock Co.
CLOCKS, school
Craft Patterns Studio
Craft Products Co.
H. De Covnick & Son, Inc.
Mason & Sullivan
CLOCKS, synchronomes (master
clocks)
Caldwell Industries

CLOCKS, wooden wheel
Caldwell Industries
Albert Constantine and Son,
Inc.
Craftplans
Craft Products Co.
Held Products
Herter's, Inc.
Minnesota Woodworkers
Supply Co.
Selva Company
Thomas Woodcraft
Yield House
CLOSETS
American Plywood Association
Better Homes and Gardens
Craft Patterns Studio
U-Bild Enterprises
Western Wood Products Asso-
ciation
Yield House
COBBLERS benches
Minnesota Woodworkers
Supply Co.
CODE oscillators
Bigelow Electronics
Eico Electronic Instrument
Co., Inc.
Electronic Aids
GC Electronics
Graymark Enterprises, Inc.
Heath Company
H.J. Knapp Co.
Lafayette Radio Electronics
Progressive Edu-Kits, Inc.
COFFEE tables (see Tables,
coffee)
COIN cleaners
Creative Products
COLONIAL style furniture
Bedford Lumber Co.
Cohasset Colonials - by Hagerty
Albert Constantine and Son,
Inc.
Craft Patterns Studio
Craftplans
Furniture Designs
Mechanix Illustrated

Old South Pattern Co.
Yield House
COLOR bar generators
Eico Electronic Instrument
Co., Inc.
Lafayette Radio Electronics
McGee Radio Co.
COLOR computers
Heath Company
COLOR organs
Bigelow Electronics
Digiac Corp.
Edmund Scientific Co.
Eico Electronic Instrument
Co., Inc.
Graymark Enterprises, Inc.
Howard
Lafayette Radio Electronics
Radio Shack
Technical Writers Group
Trigger Electronics
COMMODES
Mechanix Illustrated
Stanley Tools
COMPRESSORS
Casting Specialties
COMPUTERS
Edmund Scientific Co.
Lafayette Radio Electronics
Technical Writers Group
CONNESTOGA wagon settees
U-Bild Enterprises
CONTACT printers
Mechanix Illustrated
CORNER shelves
Furniture Designs
Old South Pattern Co.
CORRALS (see Horse corrals)
COTTAGES (see Cabins/cottages)
COUCHES, chrome steel
Designer Kits, Inc.
Furniture Design
CRADLES
Craft Patterns Studio
U-Bild Enterprises
CRADLES, colonial
Albert Constantine and Son,
Inc.
Craft Patterns Studio

Furniture Designs
Old South Pattern Co.
U-Bild Enterprises
CREDENZAS
Furniture Designs
CRIBS
Craft Patterns Studio
Furniture Designs
Minnesota Woodworkers
Supply Co.
CROSSBOWS
Crossbowman
CRT testers
Eico Electronic Instrument
Co., Inc.
Lafayette Radio Electronics
CRUISERS
David D. Beach, Naval Archi-
tect
John Brandlmayr, Ltd.
George Calkins
Clark Craft Boat Co.
Glen L. Marine
Viktor Harasty
International Amateur Boat
Building Society
Nils Lucander
Luger Boat Kits
Mechanix Illustrated
George E. Meese
Edwin Monk & Son
Harold H. Payson
Romack Marine
Samson Marine Design, Ltd.
Seven Seas Press
T. L. Sinclair, Jr.
Texas Dory Boat Plans
U-Bild Enterprises
Alexander W. Vetter
CRYSTAL frequency time stand-
ards
Environmental Products (EPD)
CUCKOO clocks (see Clocks,
cuckoo)
CUE racks
Craft Patterns Studio
T. C. Industries
U-Bild Enterprises
Yield House

CUPBOARDS
    Cohasset Colonials -by Hagerty
    Furniture Designs
    Old South Pattern Co.
    Shaker Workshops
    Stanley Tools
    Yield House
CUPOLAS
    Craft Patterns Studio
    U-Bild Enterprises
    Yield House
CW rigs
    Heath Company
DANISH/Scandinavian furniture
    Furn-A-Kit, Inc.
    Furniture Designs
DECADE capacitance boxes
    Eico Electronic Instrument
        Co., Inc.
    Heath Company
DECADE resistance boxes
    Eico Electronic Instrument
        Co., Inc.
    Heath Company
DECKS
    Better Homes and Gardens
    California Redwood Associa-
        tion
    Western Wood Products Asso-
        ciation
DECORATIONS (see Christmas
    decorations, Easter decora-
    tions)
DECOYS (see also Duck decoys)
    Carv-A-Coy
    Decoys Unlimited
DELAY units (see Attack delay
    units)
DENS
    Craft Patterns Studio
    U-Bild Enterprises
DEPTH sounders
    Heath Company
    Henry Francis Parks Labora-
        tory
    Radio Shack
DESK organizers
    Yield House

DESKS
    Bedford Lumber Co.
    Better Homes and Gardens
    Cohasset Colonials -by Hagerty
    Albert Constantine and Son,
        Inc.
    Craft Patterns Studio
    Craftplans
    Furniture Designs
    Minnesota Woodworkers
        Supply Co.
    Mechanix Illustrated
    Old South Pattern Co.
    Stanley Tools
    U-Bild Enterprises
    Western Wood Products Asso-
        ciation
    Yield House
DESKS, chrome steel
    Designer Kits, Inc.
DESKS, roll top
    Design Craftsman
    Furniture Designs
    Mechanix Illustrated
    Yield House
DIGITAL clocks (see Clocks,
    digital)
DINETTES
    Craft Patterns Studio
DINING room sets
    Furn-A-Kit, Inc.
    U-Bild Enterprises
DINING tables (see Tables, dining)
DISPLAY cases
    Charlie F. & Others
    Yield House
DISPLAY panels (art display,
    bulletin Board, etc.)
    Dryad Press
DISTORTION boosters
    Heath Company
DISTORTION meters (see Harmo-
    nic distortion meters)
DIVIDERS, room (see Room divi-
    ders)
DOCKS/piers
    Huck Finn, Inc.
    Reimann & Georger, Inc.
    Supercraft Products

13

DOG houses
  Craft Patterns Studio
  Crest Kennel Co.
  Hammond Barns
  Shettel-Way Innovations
  U-Bild Enterprises
DOG houses, automatic heated
  Technical Writers Group
DOG kennels
  American Plywood Association
DOLL furniture
  Craftplans
  U-Bild Enterprises
DOLL houses
  Better Homes and Gardens
  Craft Patterns Studio
  Craftplans
  Minnesota Woodworkers
    Supply Co.
  U-Bild Enterprises
  Yield House
DOMES (see Geodesic domes)
DOOR knockers
  Germaco
DORMERS
  Craft Patterns Studio
DRAFTING tables
  Dandyplans
DRESSERS
  Craft Patterns Studio
  Furniture Designs
  Stanley Tools
  Yield House
DRILL presses
  Caldwell Industries
  Casting Specialties
  Gilliom Mfg. Co.
DROP-leaf tables (see Tables,
    drop-leaf)
DRUMS, electronic
  Paia Electronics, Inc.
DRY sinks
  Craft Patterns Studio
  Furniture Designs
  Old South Pattern Co.
  Stanley Tools
DUCK decoys
  Craftplans

Minnesota Woodworkers
    Supply Co.
  Wilson-Allen Corp.
DULCIMERS (see also Hammered
    dulcimers)
  Albert Constantine and Son,
    Inc.
  Craftsman Wood Service Co.
  The Dulcimer Shoppe
  Here, Inc.
  Hughes, Co.
  The String Shop
DUNE buggies
  IECO
  K & P Mfg.
  J.C. Whitney & Co.
DWELL meters (see Tachometer
    & dwell angle meters)
EARPHONES/headphones
  Bigelow Electronics
  Radio Shack
EASELS (see Book easels)
EASTER decorations
  Craft Patterns Studio
ECHO units
  Technical Writers Group
EIGHT track players conversion
    to eight track players/re-
    corders)
  Sound Four Enterprises
EIGHT track players/recorders
  Heath Company
ELECTRIC cars
  Seecom
ELECTRONICS (see under follow-
    ing subjects)
  Amplifiers, mono
  Amplifiers, ham
  Appliance testers
  Audio generators
  Battery chargers
  Battery testers
  Bird call imitators
  Broadcasters, neighborhood
  Calculators, electronic
  Calibration oscillators
  Capacitor substitution boxes
  Capacitor testers
  Circuit testers

14

Code oscillators
Color bar generators
CRT testers
CW rigs
Decade capacitance boxes
Decade resistance boxes
Earphones/headphones
Eight track players conversion
    to eight track players/re-
    corders
Eight track players/recorders
Espionage/surveillance devices
Electronic switches
Faradohm bridges/analyzers
Four channel stero adapters
Four channel stero amplifiers
FM-DM'ers
FM stero generators
FM tuners
Frequency meters
Frequency meters, digital
Grid-dip meters
Harmonic distortion meters
Impedence bridges
Intercoms
Intermodulation analyzers
Jammers
Keyers, electronic
Line voltage monitors
Linear amplifiers
Microphones, FM wireless
Motor/speed controllers
Multimeters
Multiplex FM stereo adaptors
Multi-signal tracers
PA systems
Phase comparative analyzers
Phonograph/radio combinations
Phonographs, portable
Phonographs, stereo
Power generators
Power suppliers, AC-DC
Power suppliers, DC-AC
Power suppliers, regulated/
    variable
Radar
Radar detectors
Radios, aircraft monitor
Radios, AM

Radios, FM
Radios, portable
Radios, short wave
Radios, sun powered
Radios, transistor
Radios, weather/police
R-C bridges
R-C substitution boxes
Receivers, CB/SW
Receivers, ham
Remote controls/switches
Resistance substitution boxes
RF signal generators
Rotating speaker simulators
Selenium rectifiers
Semiconductor curve tracers
Signal generators
Signal probes/tracers
Sine/square wave generators
Sirens
Spectrum analyzers, electronic
Station consoles, ham
Stereo/hi-fi, amplifiers
Stereo/hi-fi, compact systems
Stereo/hi-fi preamplifiers
Stereo/hi-fi, receivers
Stereo/ hi-fi, speakers
Stereo/hi-fi, tuners
Sweep/marker generators
Telephone amplifiers
Telephone transmitters, wire-
    less
Time base generators
Transceiver testers
Transceivers, CB/ham/single-
    banders
Transformer/yoke testers
Transistor-diode curve testers
Transistor testers
Transmitters, ham
Transmitters, phone/CW
Transmitters, FM wireless
Triggered pulse generators
Tube testers
TV cameras
TV commercial eliminators
TV remote controls
TV sets, black & white
TV sets, color

TVOM's
TVM's
TV vector monitors
Ultrasonic cleaners
Utility function oscillators
Vacuum tube amplifiers
Volometers
VOM's
VTVM's
Walkie-talkies
Watt inverters
Wattmeter/SWR bridges
ELECTROSTATIC generators
  Science & Mechanics Publish-
    ing Co.
ELEVATORS, home
  J.P.F.
END tables (see Tables, end)
ENGINE analyzers
  Eico Electronic Instrument
    Co., Inc.
  Lafayette Radio Electronics
  Radio Shack
  Trigger Electronics
ENGINE conversions (see Marine
    engine conversions)
ENGINE stands
  Crower Cams & Equipment Co.
ENGINES, gasoline
  Caldwell Industries
  Lancer Engineering
  Mechanix Illustrated
  Montessa Motors, Inc.
ENGINES, jet
  EMG Engineering Co.
ENGINES, motorcycle
  Montessa Motors, Inc.
ENGINES, railroad, midget (see
    Railroad engines, midget
    (motorized))
ENGINES, steam (see also Marine
    engines, steam)
  Caldwell Industries
  H.P.K. Models
  Lancer Engineering
  Semple Engine Co., Inc.
ENGINES, steam, auto
  Reliable Industries, Inc.

ENLARGER meters
  Howard
ENLARGERS
  Mechanix Illustrated
ENVIRONMENTS, geodesic dome
  Dome East
ESPIONAGE/ surveillance devices
  Howard
  Trigger Electronics
ESP tests
  Edmund Scientific Co.
  Howard
ETAGERES, chrome steel
  Designer Kits, Inc.
  Furn-A-Kit, Inc.
ETAGERES, plastic
  Rohm and Haas Co.
EXERCISE machines
  U-Bild Enterprises
EXPERIMENTAL/scientific pro-
    jects (see under following
    subjects)
  Atomic energy laboratory
  Bird songsters, electronic
  Brainwave machines
  Chart recorders
  Coin cleaners
  Collimeters
  Computers
  Crystal frequency time standards
  Digital displays
  Drug and narcotic identification
    kits
  Electrostatic generators
  ESP tests
  Fiber optics
  Formulas, chemical
  Frequency counters
  Geiger counters
  Gold/silver recovery units
  Hearing aids
  Holography
  Infra-red detectors
  Insect traps, electronic
  Lasers
  Lie detectors
  Light detectors
  Metal assayers
  Missile trackers

Noise pollution eliminators
("pink" noise)
Oscilloscope, dual trace switches
Oscilloscopes, triggersweeps
Oscilloscopes/vectorscopes
Photoelectric relays
Pollution testers
Pregnancy testers
Radar
Polygraphs, see Lie detectors
Remote writers
Revolution counters (optical
tachometers)
Science fair projects
Sex determining kits
Sleep inducers, electronic
Solar furnaces
Sound intensity meters
Sound telescopes
Sound transmission over light
beams
Spectroscopes
Steam whistles, electronic
Surveying transits
Synthesizers, surf
Synthesizers, wind
Synthesizers, wind chimes
Tic-tac-toe machines
Treasure/metal locators
Voice operated relays/switches
Weather stations
X-ray fluorscopes
FARADOHM briadges/analyzers
Eico Electronic Instrument
Co., Inc.
FENCES
American Plywood Association
Brinkman Mfg. & Fence Co.,
Inc.
California Redwood Associa-
tion
Craft Patterns Studio
Craftplans
National Plan Service
Western Wood Products Asso-
ciation
FENDER boards
James Bliss & Co., Inc.

FERRO-cement boats
Jay R. Benford & Associates,
Inc.
Clark Craft Boat Co.
Romack Marine
Samson Marine Design, Ltd.
Seven Seas Press
FIBER optics
Edmund Scientific Co.
Lafayette Radio Electronics
Radio Shack
FIGURES (see Markers/signs/
figures)
FILE cabinets
Better Homes and Gardens
Yield House
FIRE alarms (see Burglar/fire
alarms, home or business)
FIREPLACE mantels
Craft Patterns Studio
FIREPLACE sets
Germaco
FIREPLACES, outdoor
Craft Patterns Studio
Craftplans
FISH locators/spotters
Heath Company
Howard
Radio Shack
FISHING lures/jigs/sinkers
Aspen Lures
Finnysports
Fireside Angler, Inc.
Herter's, Inc.
E. Hille-The Angler's Supply
House
Lure-Craft Mfg. Co.
Midland Tackle Co.
Netcraft, Inc.
Walmsley's Tackle
FISHING, plastic worms
Lure-Craft Mfg. Co.
FISHING rods
Aspen Lures
Finnysports
Fireside Angler, Inc.
Herter's, Inc.
E. Hille-The Angler's Supply
House

Midland Tackle Co.
Netcraft, Inc.
FLASH units, electronic
    Plasma Systems
FLOORING, parquet
    Wood-Mosaic Corp.
FLY tying kits
    Fireside Angler, Inc.
    Genes Tackle Shop
    Herter's, Inc.
    E. Hille-The Angler's Supply
        House
    Netcraft, Inc.
    Raymond C. Rumpf & Son
FLYING bridges
    Rickborn Industries, Inc.
FM-DX'ers
    Paia Electronics, Inc.
FM stereo generators
    Heath Company
FM tuners
    Dynaco, Inc.
FOGHORNS/hailers
    Heath Company
FORMULAS, chemical
    Joseph H. Belfort
    Creative Products
    Deeprock Mfg. Co.
FOUNTAINS
    Rain Jet Corp.
FOUR wheel drive conversion to
        tracked vehicles
    Imagineering Associates, Inc.
FOUR channel stereo adaptors
    Eico Electronic Instrument
        Co., Inc.
    Heath Company
    Technical Writers Group
    Trigger Electronics
FOUR channel stereo amplifiers
    Carston Studios
    Heath Company
FRAMES (see Picture frames)
FREQUENCY counters
    Environmental Products (EPD)
    Heath Company
    Technical Writers Group
FREQUENCY meters
    Heath Company

Technical Writers Group
FREQUENCY meters, digital
    Micro-Z Electronics Systems
FUEL vapor detectors
    Heath Company
FURNITURE (see under following
        subjects)
    Armoires
    Bars
    Beds/headboards
    Beds/headboards, chrome
        steel
    Beds, geodesic dome
    Benches
    Benches, storage
    Book easels/stands
    Bookcases
    Bookends
    Bookshelves
    Breakfast nooks
    Breakfronts
    Buffets
    Cabinets
    Cabinets, collectors/curio
    Cabinets, fishing gear
    Cabinets, gun/rifle
    Cabinets, medicine
    Cabinets, paperback
    Cabinets, phonograph record
    Cabinets, recipe
    Cabinets, sewing
    Cabinets, stereo/hi-fi
    Cabinets, spice
    Cabinets, tie
    Cabinets, TV
    Cane/rush furniture
    Carts, hostess/tea
    Carts, hostess/tea, chrome
        steel
    Cedar chests
    Chairs
    Chairs, captain's
    Chairs, Kang-Chi (oriental
        temple)
    Chairs, ladderback
    Chairs, rocking
    Chest on chests
    Chest of drawers
    Chests

Chests, apothecary
Chifforobes
Chrome steel furniture
Colonial style furniture
Commodes
Corner shelves
Couches, chrome steel
Credenzas
Cupboards
Danish/Scandanavian furniture
Desk organizers
Desks
Desks, chrome steel
Desks, roll-top
Dining room sets
Dinettes
Display cases
Dressers
Dry sinks
Etageres, chrome steel
Etageres, plastic
File cabinets
Hampers
Hutches
Kitchen furniture
Lamps
Lamps, cypress knee
Lamps, insulator
Lamps, Tiffany style
Log holdres
Lowboys
Mirrors
Music benches
Music centers
Music centers, chrome steel
Music stands
Office centers, home
Pedestals, plastic
Phonograph record holders/
    browsers
Picture frames
Plastic furniture
Racks, archery gear
Racks, china/pewter
Racks, cosmetic
Racks, fishing gear
Racks, gun/rifle
Racks, magazine
Racks, spice

Racks, spoon/silverware
Racks, towel/tissue
Racks, trouser
Settees
Settles, fireside
Sewing centers
Shadow boxes
Shaker style furniture
Shoe bars
Speaker enclosures
Stands
Stools
Susans, stereo tape
Tables
Tables, card
Tables, cobblers bench
Tables, cocktail
Tables, cocktail, chrome steel
Tables, coffee
Tables, coffee, plastic
Tables, cribbage
Tables, cube, plastic
Tables, dining
Tables, display
Tables, dressing
Tables, double-X frame,
    plastic
Tables, drop leaf
Tables, end
Tables, end, chrome steel
Tables, nest of
Tables, night
Tables, occasional
Tables, trestle
Telephone centers/stands
Telephone centers/stands,
    plastic
Toilet paper dispensers
TV stands
Valets
Wardrobes
Waterbeds
Whatnot shelves
Wine racks, plastic
Wrought iron furniture, see
    METALWORKING projects
FURNITURE, children's
    American Plywood Association
    Better Homes and Gardens

Cohasset Colonials – by Hagerty
Craft Patterns Studio
Craftplans
Furniture Designs
U-Bild Enterprises
FUZZ boxes
Howard
Lafayette Radio Electronics
Technical Writers Group
GARAGE door openers, electric
Heath Company
GARAGES
L. M. Brunier & Associates,
Inc.
Craft Patterns Studio
Craftplans
Hammond Barns
International Mill & Timber Co.
Mechanix Illustrated
Minnesota Woodworkers
Supply Co.
National Plan Service
Pan Abode, Inc.
Popular Mechanics, Dept. CO
Standard Homes Co.
Vermont Log Buildings, Inc.
Western Wood Products Asso-
ciation
GARBAGE compactors
Heath Company
GARBAGE diverters
Little Jim Dandy Garbage
Diverter
GAS/smoke sensors (see also
Burglar/fire alarms)
Radio Shack
GASOLINE engines (see Engines,
gasoline)
GATEWAYS
Craft Patterns Studio
GAZEBOS
California Redwood Associa-
tion
Craft Patterns Studio
Sturdi-Built Mfg. Co.
Western Wood Products Asso-
ciation
GAZEBOS, geodesic domes
Redwood Domes

GEIGER counters
Howard
Henry Francis Parks Labora-
tory
GENERATORS, power (see Power
generators)
GEODESIC domes
Cathedralite Domes
Dome-Iciles
Geodesic Domes
Geodesic Structures
Popular Science Plans Division
Redwood Domes
Zomeworks Corp.
GLIDERS (see also Hang-gliders)
Duster Sailplane Kits
Explorer Aircraft Co.
Pacific Aircraft Co.
GLOVES (see Mitts, down)
GOLD/silver recovery units
Creative Products
GOLF clubs
Golf Day Products
GRANDFATHER clocks (see
Clocks, grandfather)
GREENHOUSES
Craft Patterns Studio
Greenhouse Specialties Co.
Herter's, Inc.
Lifelite, Inc.
Lord & Burnham
Mechanix Illustrated
National Greenhouse Co.
Peter Reimuller-Greenhouse-
man
Sturdi-Built Mfg. Co.
Texas Greenhouse Co., Inc.
Turner Greenhouses
GREENHOUSES, geodesic dome
Dome East
Janco Greenhouses
Redwood Domes
GRID-dip meters
Eico Electronic Instrument
Co., Inc.
Lafayette Radio Electronics
Trigger Electronics
GRINDERS, bench
Casting Specialties

GRINDERS, tool (see Tool grinders)
GRISTMILLS, lawn
　　Craft Patterns Studio
　　U-Bild Enterprises
GUITAR amplifiers (see Amplifiers, guitar)
GUITARS
　　Albert Constantine and Son, Inc.
　　Craftsman Wood Service Co.
　　The Guitar Center
　　Hughes Co.
　　International Violin Co.
GUN cabinets (see Cabinets, gun/rifle
GUN racks (see Racks, gun)
GYM'S, family
　　Popular Mechanics, Dept. CO
　　U-Bild Enterprises
HACKSAWS, power
　　Casting Specialties
HAILERS (see Foghorns/hailers)
HAM stations (see Station consoles, ham)
HAMMERED dulcimers
　　Hughes Co.
HAMPERS
　　U-Bild Enterprises
　　Yield House
HANG gliders
　　Bat-Glider Plans
　　Volmer Aircraft
HARMONIC distortion meters
　　Eico Electronic Instrument Co., Inc.
　　Heath Company
HARPS (see Irish harps)
HARPSICHORDS
　　Burton Harpsichords
　　Frank Hubbard Harpsichords, Inc.
　　Wm. P. Ratajak Harpsichords
　　William Post Ross-Harpsichord Maker
　　Schober Harpsichords, Inc.
　　The Williams Workshop
　　J. Witcher-Ancient Instruments

HEADBOARDS (see Beds/headboards)
HEADLIGHT dimmers/automatic
　　Technical Writers Group
HEADPHONES (see Earphones/headphones)
HEARING aids
　　Howard
HELICOPTERS
　　Bensen Aircraft Corp.
　　Compcop
HOBBY horses
　　Craft Patterns Studio
　　U-Bild Enterprises
HOLOGRAPHY
　　Technical Writers Group
HOME care/improvements (see under following subjects)
Add-a-room projects
Air conditioners, central
Air conditioners, mobile home
Attics
Awnings
Barns
Basement remodelling
Bell sensors, remote
Burglar/fire alarms, home or business
Cabanas
Cabinets, kitchen
Canopies, geodesic dome
Carports
Closets
Cupolas
Decks
Dens
Dormers
Elevators, home
Environments, geodesic dome
Fireplace mantels
Flooring, parquet
Garage door openers, electric
Garages
Garbage compactors
Garbage diverters
Gas/smoke sensors
Ironing centers
Kitchen islands
Kitchen remodelling

Laundry centers
Lean-to's
Lightning protectors
Microwave ovens
Mobile home beautification
Paneling wood
Porches
Room dividers
Sheds
Sheds, geodesic dome
Shelving
Shelving, chrome steel
Storage walls
Stairs, concrete
Swimming pools
Swimming pool filter systems
Vacuum cleaners, built-in
Valences
Ventilators, kitchen
Wall units
Water filters/purifiers/softeners
Water wells
Weathervanes
Windowboxes
Workshop centers
HOMES, vacation/leisure (see Vacation/leisure homes)
HOMES, year round (see Year round homes)
HORSE barns
Hammond Barns
HORSE corrals
Brinkman Mfg. & Fence Co., Inc.
Crest Kennel Co.
HOT-rod equipment
California Speed and Sport Shop
HOT-rod hardware
Cal Automotive, Inc.
Cal-Race Parts
Crower Cams & Equipment Co.
Don Garlit's Hi-Performance World, Inc.
Hank the Crank
Honest Charley, Inc.
IECO
Rayjay Industries, Inc.
Scat Enterprises

Speed Products Engineering (SPE)
J.C. Whitney & Co.
HOUSEBOATS
Arcmarine Corp.
David D. Beach, Naval Architect
John Brandlmayr, Ltd.
Champion Boats of California
Clark Craft Boat Co.
Glen L. Marine
Viktor Harasty
Huck Finn, Inc.
J.W. Lawson, Jr., Naval Architect
Nils Lucander
Luger Boat Kits
Mechanix Illustrated
George E. Meese
Popular Mechanics, Dept. CO
Samson Marine Design, Ltd.
Science & Mechanics Publishing Co.
Supercraft Products
U-Bild Enterprises
HOUSING (see under following subjects)
A-frames
Aircraft shelters, geodesic dome
Apartments/income producing units
Barn homes
Cabins/cottages
Cabins, log
Chalets
Geodesic domes
Mobile homes, see VEHICLES
Tipis
Vacation/leisure
Year round
Yurts
HOVERCRAFT
Curtis Dyna-Products Corp.
Hoversport, Inc.
Palmer Aerosystems
Universal Hovercraft
Venture Aero-Marine'

22

HUNTING knives (see Knives,
    hunting/bowie)
HURDY gurdys
    J. Witcher Ancient Instruments
HUTCHES
    Cohasset Colonials -by Hagerty
    Albert Constantine and Son,
        Inc.
    Craft Patterns Studio
    Furn-A-Kit, Inc.
    Furniture Designs
    Old South Pattern Co.
    Stanley Tools
    Yield House
HYDROFOILS
    Dak Hydrofoils
    Science & Mechanics Publish-
        ing Co.
HYDROPLANES
    Champion Boats of California
    DeSilva Boats
    Glen L. Marine
    Hal Kelly's Tested Plans
    Mechanix Illustrated
    George E. Meese
    Popular Mechanics, Dept. CO
    Science & Mechanics Publish-
        ing Co.
ICEBOATS
    Science & Mechanics Publish-
        ing Co.
    Taft Marine Corp.
ICE karts
    Science & Mechanics Publish-
        ing Co.
IGNITION analyzers
    Anderson Engineering
    Heath Company
IGNITION, capacitive discharge
    Anderson Engineering
    Beco, Inc.
    C-D Systems
    Delta Products, Inc.
    Eico Electronic Instrument
        Co., Inc.
    Howard
    McGee Radio Co.
    Radio Shack
    Trigger Electronics

IMPEDENCE bridges
    Heath Company
INBOARDS
    David D. Beach, Naval Archi-
        tect
    John Brandlmayr, Ltd.
    George Calkins
    Champion Boats of California
    Clark Craft Boat Co.
    DeSilva Boats
    Glen L. Marine
    Nils Lucander
    Luger Boat Kits
    George E. Meese
    A.D. Nelson
    Harold H. Payson
    Science & Mechanics Publish-
        ing Co.
    Texas Dory Boat Plans
    Alexander W. Vetter
INFRA-red detectors
    Edmund Scientific Co.
INSECT traps, electronic
    Creative Products
INTERCOMS
    Bigelow Electronics
    Digiac Corp.
    Heath Company
    Howard
    Lafayette Radio Electronics
    Radio Shack
INTERCOMS, cab-to-camper (see
    Cab-to-camper intercoms)
INTERMODULATION analyzers
    Heath Company
IRISH harps
    Hughes Co.
IRONING centers
    U-Bild Enterprises
JACKETS, down
    Carikit
    Frostline, Inc.
JAMMERS
    Howard
JAPANESE teahouses
    Craft Patterns Studio
    Popular Science Plans Division
JEEP/Scout, repowering
    Hoosier Machine Products Co.

JIG saw patterns
    Craft Patterns Studio
    Craftplans
    Mastercraft Plans
    Minnesota Woodworkers
        Supply Co.
JIGS (see Fishing lures/jigs/
    sinkers)
KARTS
    Braco Mfg. Co.
    Brown's Motorsports
    Gilliom Mfg. Co.
    K & P Mfg.
    Lees Cycle-City Ltd.
    Plans
    Schmieder Motors
    Science & Mechanics Publish-
        ing Co.
    Stanley W. Tull Co., Inc.
KAYAKS (see also Can-yaks)
    James Bliss & Co., Inc.
    Craft Patterns Studio
    Dedham Kayaks
    Folboat Corp.
    Viktor Harasty
    Mechanix Illustrated
    Outdoor Sports
    Quicksilver Boats
    Rogue Kayaks
    Science & Mechanics Publish-
        ing Co.
    Sportcraft Co.
    Trailcraft, Inc.
KENNELS/runs
    American Fence Co.
    Brinkman Mfg. & Fence Co.,
        Inc.
    Crest Kennel Co.
    Bob Long Kennel Runs
KEYERS, electronic
    Eico Electronic Instrument
        Co., Inc
    Heath Company
KITCHEN cabinets (see Cabinets,
    kitchen)
KITCHEN islands
    Better Homes and Gardens
    U-Bild Enterprises

KITCHEN furniture
    Better Homes and Gardens
KITCHEN remodelling
    Better Homes and Gardens
    Craft Patterns Studio
KITCHENS, camp
    Better Homes and Gardens
    U-Bild Enterprises
KITCHENS, children's
    U-Bild Enterprises
KITES
    Minnesota Woodworkers
        Supply Co.
KITES, man-carrying
    Popular Science Plans Division
KNIVES, hunting/bowie
    Golden Age Arms Co., Inc.
    Indian Ridge Traders
    Bob Schrimsher's Custom
        Knifemaker's Supply
    Van Sickle Cutlery Co.
LAMP posts
    Craft Patterns Studio
    U-Bild Enterprises
    Western Wood Products Asso-
        ciation
LAMPS
    Albert Constantine and Son,
        Inc.
    Craftplans
    Furniture Designs
    Minnesota Woodworkers
        Supply Co.
    Old South Pattern Co.
    Stanley Tools
    T.C. Industries
    U-Bild Enterprises
LAMPS, cypress knee
    Durel's
LAMPS, insulator
    Durel's
LAMPS, tiffany style
    Art Glass & Craft Studios
    Creative Corner
    Whittemore-Durgin Glass Co.
    Yield House
LANTERNS
    Held Products

LASERS
   Esco Products
   Jack Ford Science Projects
   Howard
   Metrologic Instruments, Inc.
   Plasma Systems
   Technical Writers Group
LATHES
   Gilliom Mfg. Co.
LATHES, metal
   Caldwell Industries
LATHES, wood
   Casting Specialties
LAUNDRY centers
   American Plywood Association
LAWN and garden (see under
     following subjects)
   Barbecue carts
   Barbecue dining sets
   Barbecue pits
   Christmas decorations
   Connestoga wagon settees
   Easter decorations
   Fences
   Fireplaces, outdoor
   Fountains
   Gateways
   Gazebos
   Greenhouses
   Greenhouses, geodesic dome
   Gristmills, lawn
   Japanese teahouses
   Lamp posts
   Lawn/patio furniture
   Markers/signs/figures
   Patio
   Pergolas
   Picnic tables/benches
   Planters
   Pools, garden
   Potting benches
   Push carts
   Settees, outdoor
   Sheds
   Sprinklers, underground
   Storage/tools houses
   Sun traps
   Swing, lawn
   Terraces

Trash bins
Tree Seats
Trellises
Workbenches
Wheelbarrow planters
Windmills, garden
Wishing wells, garden
LAWN/patio furniture
   American Plywood Association
   Better Homes and Gardens
   Albert Constantine and Son,
     Inc.
   Craft Patterns Studio
   Craftplans
   Mastercraft Plans
   Minnesota Woodworkers
     Supply Co.
   Science & Mechanics Publish-
     ing Co.
   U-Bild Enterprises
   Western Wood Products Asso-
     ciation
LAWN swings (see Swings, lawn)
LEAN-to's
   Vermont Log Buildings, Inc.
LIE detectors
   Howard
   Radio Shack
LIFTS, boat
   R.W. Nelson Structures, Inc.
   Reimann and Georger, Inc.
LIGHT detectors
   Edmund Scientific Co.
LIGHT/psychedelic shows
   Graymark Enterprises, Inc.
   Lafayette Radio Electronics
   Radio Shack
   Technical Writers Group
LIGHTNING protectors
   Robbins Lightning Protection
     Co.
LINE voltage monitors
   Heath Company
LINEAR amplifiers
   Heath Company
LOCOMOTIVES, midget (motorized)
   Caldwell Industries
LOG cabins (see Cabins, log)

LOG holdres
  Yield House
LOOMS
  Craftplans
  Minnesota Woodworkers
    Supply Co.
LOWBOYS
  Old South Pattern Co.
LUGGAGE carriers, car top
  Craft Patterns Studio
  Popular Mechanics, Dept. CO
LURES (see Fishing lures/jigs/
    sinkers)
LYRES, Ancient Greek
  Hughes Co.
MACHINIST'S chests
  Dandyplans
MAGAZINE racks (see Racks,
    magazine)
MANDOLIN'S
  The Guitar Center
MANTELS (see Fireplace mantels
MARINE engine conversions
  Clark Craft Boat Co.
  Federal Marine Motors Co.
  Lehman Mfg. Co., Inc.
  Luger Boat Kits
  Osco Motors
  Science & Mechanics Publish-
    ing Co.
  Stokes Marine Industries
MARINE engines, steam
  Reliable Industries, Inc.
  Semple Engine Co., Inc.
MARKERS/signs/figures
  Albert Constantine and Son,
    Inc.
  Craft Patterns Studio
  Craftplans
  Mastercraft Plans
  Minnesota Woodworkers
    Supply Co.
  U-Bild Enterprises
MARTIN houses
  Craft Patterns Studio
  Hammond Barns
  Mastercraft Plans
  U-Bild Enterprises
  Yield House

MEDICINE cabinets (see Cabinets,
    medicine)
MEGAPHONES
  Technical Writers Group
MERRY-go-rounds
  Minnesota Woodworkers
    Supply Co.
METAL assayers
  K/N Chemical & Supply Co.
METAL locators (see Treasure/
    metal locators)
METAL working (see under follow-
    ing subjects)
  Bells, brass
  Candelabras
  Candlesticks
  Christmas tree stand
  Compressors
  Door knockers
  Engines, gasoline
  Engines, jet
  Engines, motorcycle
  Engines, steam
  Fireplace sets
  Salt/pepper shakers, metal
  Telegraph keyer
  Trivets
  Wrought iron furniture/objects
METRONOMES
  Bigelow Electronics
  Electronic Aids
  Heath Company
  Henry Francis Parks Labora-
    tory
  Radio Shack
MICROPHONES, FM wireless
  Howard
  H.J. Knapp Co.
  Lafayette Radio Electronics
  Trigger Electronics
MICROWAVE ovens
  Heath Company
MIDGET autos (see Automobiles,
    midget (motorized))
MILLING machines
  Caldwell Industries
  Microm Co.
MILLING tables
  Caldwell Industries

MINI-bikes
  Brown's Motorsports
  Byco Distributing Co.
  Eastern Enterprises, Inc.
  Gilliom Mfg. Co.
  Heald, Inc.
  Heath Company
  K & P Mfg.
  Lees Cycle-City Ltd.
  Plans
  Sportstyl
  C.F. Struck Corp.
MINI-choppers
  Heald, Inc.
  Lees Cycle-City Ltd.
MINI-cycles
  Eastern Enterprises, Inc.
MIRRORS
  Cohasset Colonials -by Hagerty
  Craft Patterns Studio
  Furniture Designs
  Old South Pattern Co.
  Shaker Workshops
MISSILE trackers
  Howard
MITER clamps
  Germaco
MITTS, down
  Carikit
  Frostline, Inc.
MOBILE home beautification
  Viking Camper Supply, Inc.
  Western Wood Products Asso-
    ciation
MOBILE homes, conversion from
    buses
  Viking Camper Supply, Inc.
MOBILE homes, conversion from
    vans/trucks
  Viking Camper Supply, Inc.
MOBILES
  Minnesota Woodworkers
    Supply Co.
MODELMAKER'S press
  Casting Specialties
MOTOR/speed controllers
  Eico Electronic Instrument
    Co., Inc.
  Graymark Enterprises, Inc.

Howard
Lafayette Radio Electronics
Radio Shack
Trigger Electronics
MOTORCYCLES (see All terrain
    cycles (ATC's), Choppers,
    Engines, motorcycles,
    Mini-choppers, Mini-cycles,
    Sidecars, motorcycles,
    Trail bikes)
MOWERS, riding
  C.F. Struck Corp.
MULTIMETERS
  Bigelow Electronics
  Eico Electronic Instrument
    Co., Inc.
  Electronic Aids
  Heath Company
MULTIPLEX FM stereo adaptors
  Technical Writers Group
MULTI-signal tracers
  Eico Electronic Instrument
    Co., Inc.
  Trigger Electronics
MUSIC benches
  American Plywood Association
MUSIC centers
  Furn-A-Kit, Inc.
  Giles & Kendall
  Lafayette Radio Electronics
MUSIC centers, chrome steel
  Designer Kits, Inc.
  Yield House
MUSIC stands
  Craft Patterns Studio
MUSICAL instruments/equipment
    (see under following sub-
    jects)
  Amplifiers, guitar
  Attack delay units
  Balalaikas
  Bancimers (dulcimer fretted
    banjos)
  Banjos
  Bongos, electronic
  Cellos
  Clavichords
  Drums, electronic
  Dulcimers

Fuzz boxes
Guitars
Hammered dulcimers
Harpsichords
Hurdy gurdys
Irish harps
Lyres, ancient Greek
Mandolins
Metronomes
Organs
Ping pong effects (alternately
    route musical impulses)
Player piano electrifiers
Psaltries
Reed organ, electrifiers
Sitars
Sustain units (compensates
    delay of sound after
    instrument is struck)
Thumb pianos/West African
    instrument
Vibrato generators
Violins
Virginals
Waa-waa effects
NIGHT tables (see Tables, night)
NOISE pollution eliminators
    ("pink" noise)
    Paia Electronics, Inc.
OFFICE centers, home
    Craft Patterns Studio
    National Plan Service
    U-Bild Enterprises
OPTICAL tachometer (see Re-
    volution counters)
OPTICS/photography (see under
    following subjects)
    Black light
    Cameras obscura
    Color computers
    Color organs
    Contact printers
    Enlarger meters
    Enlargers
    Flash units, electrical
    Light/psychedelic show
    Microscopes
    Projectors, overhead
    Stroboscopes

Telescope mirror kits
Telescope mirror testers
Telescope mounts
Telescopes, reflector
Telescopes, refractor
Timers, photo
ORGAN, reed, electrifier (see
    Reed organ, electrifier)
ORGANS
    Artisan Organs
    Devtronix Organ Products
    Heath Company
    Schober Organ Corp.
ORGANS, color (see Color Organs)
OSCILLOSCOPE, dual trace
    switches)
    Hamlin Technical Products
OSCILLOSCOPES, triggersweeps
    Hamlin Technical Products
OSCILLOSCOPES/vectorscopes
    Eico Electronics Instrument
      Co., Inc.
    Heath Company
    Lafayette Radio Electronics
    McGee Radio Co.
    Trigger Electronics
OUTBOARDS
    American Plywood Association
    David D. Beach, Naval Archi-
      tect
    John Brandlmayr, Ltd.
    George Calkins
    Champion Boats of California
    Clark Craft Boat Co.
    DeSilva Boats
    Folboat
    Glen L. Marine
    Luger Boat Kits
    Mechanix Illustrated
    George E. Meese
    A.D. Nelson
    Harold H. Payson
    Science & Mechanics Publish-
      ing Co.
    T.L. Sinclair, Jr.
    Texas Dory Boat Plans
    Alexander W. Vetter
PA systems
    Heath Company

PADDLE-wheel boats
    Science & Mechanics Publish-
       ing Co.
    U-Bild Enterprises
PANELING, wood
    Western Wood Products Asso-
       ciation
PANTS, down
    Frostline, Inc.
PAPER punches
    Germaco
PARKAS
    Carikit
    Frostline, Inc.
PARQUET flooring (see Flooring,
    parquet)
PATIO furniture (see also Lawn/
    patio furniture)
    National Plan Service
PATIOS
    California Redwood Associa-
       tion
    Reinforced Plastics Div.,
       Reichhold Chemicals, Inc.
    Sakrete, Inc.
    Western Wood Products Asso-
       ciation
PEDESTALS, plastic
    Rohm and Haas Co.
PERGOLAS
    American Plywood Association
    Craft Patterns Studio
PETS (see under following subjects)
    Animal barns
    Bird houses
    Bird houses/feeders
    Dog houses
    Dog houses, automatic heated
    Dog kennels
    Horse barns
    Horse corrals
    Kennels/runs
    Martin houses
PHASE comparative analyzers
    Phase Corp.
PHONOGRAPH/radio combinations
    Digiac Corp.
    Heath Company

PHONOGRAPH record holders/
    browsers
    Bedford Lumber Co.
    Giles & Kendall
PHONOGRAPHS, portable
    Bigelow Electronics
    Electronic Aids
PHONOGRAPHS, stereo
    Heath Company
PHOTO timers (see Timers,
    photo)
PHOTOELECTRIC relays
    GC Electronics
    Howard
    Radio Shack
    Trigger Electronics
PICKUP covers
    Comstock Camper and Trailer
       Supply
    Glen L. Recreational Vehicles
    Luger Camper Kits
    Mechanix Illustrated
    Science & Mechanics Publish-
       ing Co.
    Trail-R-Club of America
    U-Bild Enterprises
    Viking Camper Supply, Inc.
PICNIC equipment
    American Plywood Association
PICNIC tables/benches
    Craft Patterns Studio
    National Plan Service
    U-Bild Enterprises
PICTURE frames
    Bedford Lumber Co.
    Western Wood Products Asso-
       ciation
PICTURE frames, plastic
    Rohm and Haas Co.
PING pong effects (alternately
    route musical impulses)
    Paia Electronics, Inc.
PING pong tables
    Craft Patterns Studio
    U-Bild Enterprises
PIPES, smoking
    Albert Constantine and Son,
       Inc.
    Yield House

PISTOLS, antique
  Connecticut Valley Arms Co.
  Dixie Gun Works
  E.M.F. Co., Inc.
  Fernwood Gun Supply
  Golden Age Arms Co., Inc.
  R.H. McCrory
PLANTERS
  Better Homes and Gardens
  California Redwood Association
  Craft Patterns Studio
  Craftplans
  Sakrete, Inc.
  U-Bild Enterprises
PLANTERS, wheelbarrow (see
    Wheelbarrow planters)
PLASTIC furniture
  Rohm and Haas Co.
PLAYER piano electrifiers
  Lee Music Mfg. Co.
PLAYGROUND equipment
  Better Homes and Gardens
  Craft Patterns Studio
  Dome East
PLAYGROUND equipment, geo-
    desic dome
  Dome East
  Zomeworks Corp.
PLAY houses
  American Plywood Association
  Better Homes and Gardens
  Craft Patterns Studio
  Hammond Barns
  National Plan Service
  U-Bild Enterprises
PLAYPENS
  Craft Patterns Studio
  U-Bild Enterprises
PLYAKS
  American Plywood Association
POLLUTION testers
  Edmund Scientific Testers
  Urban Systems
POLYGRAPHS (see Lie detectors)
PONCHOS
  Carikit
  Frostline, Inc.

PONTOON boats
  Glen L. Marine
  Herter's, Inc.
  Huck Finn, Inc.
  Rotocast Products, Inc.
  Science & Mechanics Publish-
    ing Co.
  Supercraft Products
POOL tables
  Craft Patterns Studio
  Mechanix Illustrated
  Popular Mechanics, Dept. CO
  Sportsman Mfg. Co.
POOLS (see Swimming pools,
    Wading pools)
POOLS, garden
  Sakrete, Inc.
PORCHES
  Craft Patterns Studio
PORTS, boat
  Supercraft Products
POTTER'S wheels
  Oak Hill Industries
POTTING benches
  Diko
  U-Bild Enterprises
"POTTY" rockers, colonial
  Old South Pattern Co.
POWER generators
  B-UR-O Company
POWER suppliers, AC-DC
  Bigelow Electronics
  Digiac Corp.
  Eico Electronic Instrument
    Co., Inc.
  Electronic Aids
  GC Electronics
  Graymark Enterprises, Inc.
  Heath Company
  Lafayette Radio Electronics
  Techni-kit
  Universal Electronics Co.
POWER suppliers, DC-AC
  Creative Products
  Henry Francis Parks Labora-
    tory
  Trigger Electronics

POWER suppliers, regulated/
   variable
   Bigelow Electronics
   Eico Electronic Instrument
      Co., Inc.
   Electronic Aids
   Graymark Enterprises, Inc.
   Heath Company
   Phase Corp.
   Techni-kit
   Trigger Electronics
   Universal Electronics Co.
PREGNANCY testers
   Edmund Scientific Testers
PRESS (see Modelmaker's
   press)
PROJECTORS, overhead
   Edmund Scientific Testers
PSALTRIES
   Here, Inc.
   The String Shop
PSYCHEDELIC lights (see Lights/
   psychedelic shows)
PUNCHES, paper, (see Paper
   punches)
PUPPET theatres
   Craft Patterns Studio
PUSH carts
   Garden Way Research
RACKS, archery/gear
   Bedford Lumber Co.
   Craft Patterns Studio
RACKS, china/pewter
   Science & Mechanics Publish-
      ing Co.
RACKS, cosmetic
   Yield House
RACKS, cue (see Cue racks)
RACKS, fishing gear
   Bedford Lumber Co.
   Minnesota Woodworker's
      Supply Co.
   Yield House
RACKS, gun/rifle
   Bedford Lumber Co.
   Craft Patterns Studio
   Craftplans
   Durel's
   Giles & Kendall

Minnesota Woodworkers
   Supply Co.
Old South Pattern Co.
U-Bild Enterprises
Yield House
RACKS, magazine
   Craft Patterns Studio
   Furniture Designs
   Minnesota Woodworkers
      Supply Co.
   U-Bild Enterprises
   Yield House
RACKS, magazine, plastic
   Rohm and Haas Co.
RACKS, spice
   Craft Patterns Studio
   Old South Pattern Co.
RAKCS, spoon/silverware
   Albert Constantine and Son,
      Inc.
   Craft Patterns Studio
   Old South Pattern Co.
   U-Bild Enterprises
   Yield House
RACKS, towel/tissue
   Yield House
RACKS, trouser
   Yield House
RADAR
   Technical Writers Group
RADAR detectors
   Radio Shack
RADIOS, aircraft monitor
   Eico Electronic Instrument
      Co., Inc
   Heath Company
   Howard
   Trigger Electronics
RADIOS, AM
   Bigelow Electronics
   Digiac Corp.
   Eico Electronic Instrument
      Co., Inc.
   Electronic Aids
   Graymark Enterprises, Inc.
   Heath Company
   Lafayette Radio Electronics
   McGee Radio Co.

Progressive Edu-Kits, Inc.
Radio Shack
RADIOS, FM
Heath Company
Howard
Progressive Edu-Kits, Inc.
Radio Shack
Trigger Electronics
RADIOS, portable
Bigelow Electronics
Electronic Aids
Heath Company
RADIOS, short wave
Digiac Corp.
Eico Electronic Instrument
Co., Inc.
Graymark Enterprises, Inc.
Heath Company
Radio Shack
RADIOS, sun powered
Graymark Enterprises, Inc.
Howard
RADIOS, transistor
Bigelow Electronics
Digiac Corp.
Electronic Aids
GC Electronics
Graymark Enterprises
RADIOS, weather/police
Heath Company
RAFTS
Huck Finn, Inc.
Glen L. Marine
Supercraft Products
RAILROAD engines, midget
(motorized)
Popular Mechanics, Dept. CO
RAMPS, boat
Arco Mfg. Co., Inc.
R-C bridges
Bigelow Electronics
Eico Electronic Instrument
Co., Inc.
McGee Radio Co.
R-C substitution boxes
Lafayette Radio Electronics
RECEIVERS, CB/SW
Heath Company
Howard

Lafayette Radio Electronics
RECEIVERS, ham
Heath Company
RECORD cabinets (see Cabinets,
phonograph record)
RECTIFIERS, selenium (see
Selenium rectifiers)
REED organ, electrifiers
Lee Music Mfg. Co.
REMOTE controls/switches
Heath Company
Paia Electronics, Inc.
REMOTE writers
Technical Writers Group
RESISTANCE substitution boxes
Bigelow Electronics
Eico Electronic Instrument
Co., Inc.
Graymark Enterprises, Inc.
Heath Company
Lafayette Radio Electronics
REVOLUTION counters (optical
tachometer)
Paia Electronics, Inc.
RF signal generators
Bigelow Electronics
Eico Electronic Instrument
Co., Inc.
Heath Company
Lafayette Radio Electronics
McGee Radio Co.
Radio Shack
Trigger Electronics
RIFLE cabinets (see Cabinets,
gun/rifle)
RIFLES, antique
Connecticut Valley Arms Co.
Dixie Gun Works
Finnysports
Golden Age Arms Co., Inc.
R.H. McCrory
Numrich Arms Corp.
ROADSTERS
Bird Automotive
Cal Automotive, Inc.
J.C. Whitney & Co.
ROCKING toys
American Plywood Association
Craft Patterns Studio

U-Bild Enterprises
Yield House
ROOM dividers
American Plywood Association
Better Homes and Gardens
Craft Patterns Studio
Furn-A-Kit, Inc.
Science & Mechanics Publishing Co.
U-Bild Enterprises
ROTATING speaker simulators
Paia Electronics, Inc.
ROWBOAT type (rowboats, prams, dinghies, etc.)
American Plywood Association
James Bliss & Co., Inc.
E.R. Butler & Sons
Clark Craft Boat Co.
Craft Patterns Studio
Glen L. Marine
Viktor Harasty
Mechanix Illustrated
George E. Meese
Minnesota Woodworkers Supply Co.
Harold H. Payson
Popular Science Plans Division
Quicksilver Boats
Rooster Boat Co.
Science & Mechanics Publishing Co.
Seafarer Fiberglass Yachts, Inc.
T.L. Sinclair, Jr.
Taft Marine Corp.
Texas Dory Boat Plans
U-Bild Enterprises
RUNABOUTS
American Plywood Association
David D. Beach, Naval Architect
John L. Brandlmayr, Ltd.
Champion Boats of California
Clark Craft Boat Co.
Craft Patterns Studio
DeSilva Boats
Fulboat Corp.
Glen L. Marine
Hal Kelly's Tested Plans

J.W. Lawson, Jr., Naval Architect
Luger Boat Kits
A.D. Nelson
Popular Mechanics, Dept. CO
Texas Dory Boat Plans
U-Bild Enterprises
RUNS/kennels (see Kennels/runs)
RUSH furniture (see Cane/rush furniture)
SAIL cars
Popular Science Plans Division
SAILING, cruising
American Plywood Association
Jay R. Benford & Associates, Inc.
John Brandlmayr, Ltd.
Clark Craft Boat Co.
Francis A. Dugan
Easterly Yachts
David Furnig-Boat Designs
Glen L. Marine
Viktor Harasty
International Amateur Boat Building Society
J.W. Lawson, Jr., Naval Architect
Nils Lucander
Luger Boat Kits
Mechanix Illustrated
George E. Meese
Metalmast Marine, Inc.
Edwin Monk & Son
A.D. Nelson
Ocean Shore Designs
Harold H. Payson
Romack Marine
Samson Marine Design, Ltd.
San Francisco Pelican Boats
Science & Mechanics Publishing Co.
Seafarer Fiberglass Yachts, Inc.
Seven Seas Press
Spencer Boats, Ltd.
Texas Dory Boat Plans
Yacht Constructors
SAILING, day sailers
American Plywood Association
James Bliss & Co., Inc.

John Brandlmayr, Ltd.
E. R. Butler & Sons
Clark Craft Boat Co.
Craft Patterns Studio
Dedham Kayaks
Francis A. Dugan
Folboat Corp.
David Furnie - Boat Designs
Glen L. Marine
Viktor Harasty
J.W. Lawson, Jr., Naval
   Architect
Nils Lucander
Mechanix Illustrated
George E. Meese
Edwin Monk & Son
Outdoor Sports
Harold H. Payson
Popular Mechanics, Dept. CO
Popular Science Plans Division
Quicksilver Boats
Rooster Boat Co.
San Francisco Pelican Boats
Science & Mechanics Publish-
   ing Co.
Seafarer Fiberglass Yachts,
   Inc.
Snug Harbor Boat Works
C. F. Struck Corp.
Taft Marine Corp.
Texas Dory Boat Plans
U-Bild Enterprises
Vanderstadt & McGruer, Ltd.
SAILS/sail gear
   Metalmast Marine, Inc.
   Ocean Engineering Products
     Co.
   Quicksilver Boats
   Sailrite Kits
   Taft Marine Corp.
SALT/pepper shakers, metal
   Germaco
SALT/pepper sets, wood
   Albert Constantine and Son,
     Inc.
   Shop Supply House
SAND boxes
   American Plywood Association
   Craft Patterns Studio

U-Bild Enterprises
Western Wood Products Asso-
   ciation
SANDERS, belt
   Germaco
   Gilliom Mfg. Co.
SANDERS, disk
   Germaco
   Gilliom Mfg. Co.
SAUCERS, underwater
   Michigan Water Specialties, Inc.
SAUNAS
   Mechanix Illustrated
SAWS, bench
   Gilliom Mfg. Co.
SAWS, circular
   Casting Specialties
SAWS, tilt Arbor
   Gilliom Mfg. Co.
SAWS, tilt table
   Gilliom Mfg. Co.
SCANDINAVIAN furniture (see
   Danish/Scandinavian furni-
   ture)
SCIENCE fair projects
   Edmund Scientific So.
   Eico Electronic Instrument
     Co., Inc.
   Jack Ford Science Projects
   Frazer & Associates
   GC Electronics
   K/N Chemical & Supply Co.
   Lafayette Radio Electronics
   Olson Electronics
   Henry Francis Parks Labora-
     tory
   RCA
   Radio Shack
   Sercolab
   Sheard Science Supplies, Inc.
   Technical Writers Group
   Urban Systems
SCIENCE toys
   Edmund Scientific Co.
   Radio Shack
SCUBA scooters
   Science & Mechanics Publish-
     ing Co.
SEATS, tree (see Tree seats)

SELENIUM rectifiers
  Science & Mechanics Publish-
    ing Co.
SEMICONDUCTOR curve tracers
  Lafayette Radio Electronics
  McGee Radio Co.
SETTEES
  Cohasset Colonials -by Hagerty
  Albert Constantine and Son,
    Inc.
  Craft Patterns Studio
  Furniture Designs
SETTEES, connestoga wagon (see
    Connestoga wagon settees)
SETTEES, outdoor
  Craft Patterns Studios
  U-Bild Enterprises
SETTLES, fireside
  Old South Pattern Co.
SEWING centers
  American Plywood Association
  Better Homes and Gardens
  Craft Patterns Studio
  National Plan Service
  Yield House
SEX determining kits
  Edmund Scientific Co.
SHADOW boxes
  Craft Patterns Studio
  Craftplans
  Minnesota Woodworkers
    Supply Co.
SHAKER style furniture
  Cohasset Colonials -by Hagerty
  Old South Pattern Co
  Shaker Workshops
SHAPERS
  Caldwell Industries
SHAPERS, spindle (see Spindle
    shapers)
SHEDS
  American Plywood Association
  Better Homes and Gardens
  Craft Patterns Studio
  Hammond Barns
  Mastercraft Plans
  Popular Mechanics, Dept. CO
SHEDS, geodesic dome
  Redwood Domes

SHELVES, corner (see Corner
    shelves)
SHELVES, whatnot (see Whatnot
    shelves)
SHELVING
  Better Homes and Gardens
  U-Bild Enterprises
  Western Wood Products Asso-
    ciation
SHELVING, chrome Steel
  Furn-A-Kit, Inc.
SHOE bars
  U-Bild Enterprises
SIDE-wheelers
  Reliable Industries, Inc.
SIDECARS, motorcycle
  Side Strider, Inc.
SIGNAL generators
  Bigelow Electronics
  Lafayette Radio Electronics
SIGNAL generators, RF (see RF
    signal generators)
SIGNAL probes/injectors
  Radio Shack
SIGNAL probes/tracers
  Bigelow Electronics
  Digiac Corp.
  Eico Electronic Instrument
    Co., Inc.
  Heath Company
  Lafayette Radio Electronics
  McGee Radio Co.
  Progressive Edu-Kits, Inc.
  Trigger Electronics
SINE/square generators
  Trigger Electronics
SINE/square wave generators
  Eico Electronic Instrument
    Co., Inc.
  Heath Company
  Lafayette Radio Electronics
SINKERS (see Fishing lures/jigs/
    sinkers)
SIRENS
  Heath Company
SITARS
  Hughes Co.

SLEEP inducers, electronic
  Henry Francis Parks Laboratory
SLEEPING bags
  Carikit
  Frostline, Inc.
SLOTLESS racing
  Heath Company
SMALL tools (hammers, screwdrivers, etc.)
  Casting Specialties
SMOKE sensors (see Gas/smoke sensors)
SNOWMOBILES
  Land-Grabber, Inc.
  Science & Mechanics Publishing Co.
  C. F. Struck Corp.
SNOWMOBILES, conversion to ATV's
  Herter's, Inc.
SOLAR furnaces
  Edmund Scientific Co.
SOLAR powered radios (see Radios, sun powered)
SOLDERING guns
  Bigelow Electronics
  Digiac Corp.
SOUND intensity meters
  Technical Writers Group
SOUND telescopes
  Howard
  Technical Writers Group
SOUND transmission over light beams
  Technical Writers Group
SPEAKER enclosures
  Craft Patterns Studio
  Furniture Designs
  Lafayette Radio Electronics
SPECTROSCOPES
  Jack Ford Science Projects
SPECTRUM analyzers, electronic
  Heath Company
SPICE cabinets (see Cabinets, spice)
SPICE racks (see Racks, spice)
SPINDLE shapers
  Gilliom Mfg. Co.

SPINNING wheels
  Albert Constantine and Son, Inc.
  Craftplans
  Haltec Corp.
  Minnesota Woodworkers Supply Co.
  Old South Pattern Co.
  Popular Mechanics, Dept. CO
  Selva Company
SPORTING equipment (see under following subjects)
  Arrows
  Bows
  Crossbows
  Cue racks
  Duck decoys
  Exercise machines
  Fish locators/spotters
  Fishing, plastic worms
  Fishing lures/jigs/sinkers
  Fishing rods
  Fly tying kits
  Golf clubs
  Gyms, family
  Kites, man-carrying
  Knives, hunting/bowie
  Ping Pong tables
  Pistols, antique
  Pool tables
  Rifles, antique
  Saucers, underwater
  Saunas
  Scuba scooters
  Surf boards, sailing
  Tackle boxes
  Taxidermy
  Water skis
SPRINKLERS, underground
  Rain Jet Corp.
STAIRS, concrete
  Science & Mechanics Publishing Co.
STANDS
  Old South Pattern Co.
STATION consoles, ham
  Heath Company
STEAMBOATS
  Mechanix Illustrated

Reliable Industries, Inc.
STEAM engines (see Engines, steam)
STEAM whistles, electronic
  Paia Electronics, Inc.
STEREO cabinets (see Cabinets, stereo/hi-fi
STEREO/hi-fi amplifiers
  Bigelow Electronics
  Carston Studios
  Digiac Corp.
  Dynaco, Inc.
  Eico Electronic Instrument
    Co., Inc.
  Harman/Kardon
  Heath Company
  Lafayette Radio Electronics
  McGee Radio Co.
  Radio Shack
  Trigger Electronics
STEREO/hi-fi, compact systems
  Heath Comapny
STEREO/hi-fi, preamplifiers
  Carston Studios
  Dynaco, Inc.
  Lafayette Radio Electronics
  McGee Radio Co.
  Trigger Electronics
STEREO/hi-fi, receivers
  Carston Studios
  Eico Electronic Instrument
    Co., Inc.
  Heath Company
  Lafayette Radio Electronics
  McGee Radio Co.
  Radio Shack
  Trigger Electronics
STEREO/hi-fi, speakers
  CTS of Paducah, Inc.
  Heath Company
  McGee Radio Co.
  Radio Shack
STEREO/hi-fi, tuners
  Dynaco, Inc.
  Eico Electronic Instrument
    Co., Inc.
  Heath Company
  Lafayette Radio Electronics
  McGee Radio Co.

Radio Shack
Trigger Electronics
STERN-wheelers
  John Brandlmayr, Ltd.
  Edwin Monk & Son
  Reliable Industries, Inc.
STOOLS
  Furniture Designs
  Old South Pattern Co.
  H. H. Perkins Co.
  Savin Handicrafts
  Shaker Workshops
  Stanley Tools
  Yield House
STORAGE benches (see Benches, storage)
STORAGE/tool houses
  American Plywood Association
  National Plan Service
  Western Wood Products Association
STORAGE walls
  Better Homes and Gardens
  Craft Patterns Studio
STORAGES, boat
  American Plywood Association
STROBOSCOPES
  Edmund Scientific Co.
  Eico Electronic Instrument
    Co., Inc.
  Graymark Enterprises, Inc.
  Howard
  Lafayette Radio Electronics
  Plasma Systems
  Radio Shack
  Science & Mechanics Publishing Co.
  Technical Writers Group
  Trigger Electronics
STUD locators, electronic
  Paia Electronics, Inc.
SUBMARINES
  Popular Mechanics, Dept. CO
SUBMARINES, historic (the "Monitor")
  Reliable Industries, Inc.

SUBSTITUTION boxes (see Re-
    sistance substitution boxes,
    Capacitor substitution box-
    es, Decade capacitance
    boxes, R-C substitution
    boxes)
SUNDIALS
    Craftplans
    Minnesota Woodworkers
        Supply Co.
SUN traps
    Western Wood Products Asso-
        ciation
SURFBOARDS
    Outdoor Sports
SURFBOARDS, sailing
    Mechanix Illustrated
    Taft Marine Corp.
SURVEILLANCE devices (see
    Espionage/surveillance
    devices)
SURVEYING transits
    G. DeVries
SUSANS, stereo tape
    Yield House
SUSTAIN units (compensates for
    delay of sound after instru-
    ment is struck)
    Paia Electronics, Inc.
SWEATERS, down
    Frostline, Inc.
SWEEP/marker generators
    Eico Electronic Instrument
        Co., Inc.
    McGee Radio Co.
SWIMMING pools (see also Wading
    pools)
    Cascade Industries Inc.
    Craft Patterns Studio
    U-Bild Enterprises
SWIMMING pool filter systems
    Poolcraft
SWINGS
    Better Homes and Gardens
    U-Bild Enterprises
SWINGS, lawn
    Craft Patterns Studio
    Mastercraft Plans
    U-Bild Enterprises

SWITCHES, electronic (see
    Electronic switches)
SWITCHES, voice operated (see
    Voice operated relays/
    switches)
SYNTHESIZERS, surf
    Paia Electronics, Inc.
SYNTHESIZERS, wind
    Paia Electronics, Inc.
SYNTHESIZERS, wind chimes
    Paia Electronics, Inc.
TABLES
    Cohasset Colonials -by Hagerty
    Albert Constantine and Son,
        Inc.
    U-Bild Enterprises
TABLES, card
    Albert Constantine and Son,
        Inc.
    Craft Patterns Studio
    Furniture Designs
    Minnesota Woodworkers
        Supply Co.
    U-Bild Enterprises
TABLES, cobbler's bench
    Craft Patterns Studio
    Old South Pattern Co.
    U-Bild Enterprises
TABLES, cocktail
    Bedford Lumber Co.
    Albert Constantine and Son,
        Inc.
    Craft Patterns Studio
    Craftplans
    Furniture Designs
    Giles & Kendall
    Minnesota Woodworkers
        Supply Co.
    Yield House
TABLES, cocktail, chrome steel
    Designer Kits, Inc.
TABLES, coffee
    Bedford Lumber Co.
    Craft Patterns Studio
    Design Craftsman
    Giles & Kendall
    Old South Pattern Co.
    Stanley Tools
    U-Bild Enterprises

Yield House
TABLES, coffee, plastic
    Rohm and Haas Co.
TABLES, cribbage
    Yield House
TABLES, cube, plastic
    Rohm and Haas Co.
TABLES, dining
    Cohasset Colonials -by Hagerty
    Craft Patterns Studio
    Design Craftsman
    Furniture Designs
    U-Bild Enterprises
    Yield House
TABLES, display
    Yield House
TABLES, dressing
    Better Homes and Gardens
    U-Bild Enterprises
TABLES, double-X frame, plastic
    Rohm and Haas Co.
TABLES, drop leaf
    Albert Constantine and Son,
      Inc.
    Craft Patterns Studio
    Furniture Designs
    Old South Pattern Co.
    Shaker Workshops
    Yield House
TABLES, end
    Bedford Lumber Co.
    Albert Constantine and Son,
      Inc.
    Craft Patterns Studio
    Craftplans
    Furniture Designs
    Giles & Kendall
    Stanley Tools
    U-Bild Enterprises
    Yield House
TABLES, end, chrome steel
    Designer Kits, Inc.
TABLES, nest of
    Furniture Designs
    Old South Pattern Co.
    U-Bild Enterprises
TABLES, night
    Bedford Lumber Co.
    Cohasset Colonials -by Hagerty

Craft Patterns Studio
Furniture Designs
TABLES, occasional
    Cohasset Colonials -by Hagerty
    U-Bild Enterprises
TABLES, trestle
    Albert Constantine and Son,
      Inc.
    Craft Patterns Studio
    Furniture Designs
    Old South Pattern Co.
    Shaker Workshops
    Stanley Tools
    Yield House
TACHOMETERS
    Digiac Corp.
    Graymark Enterprises, Inc.
    Heath Company
    Howard
    Radio Shack
TACHOMETERS & dwell angle
    meters
    Bigelow Electronics
TACKLE boxes
    U-Bild Enterprises
TANNING kits
    U-Tan Co.
TAXIDERMY
    Herter's, Inc.
    Mould-N-Mount, Inc.
    Taxidermy Supply Co.
    Van Dyke Supply Co.
TEAHOUSES (see Japanese tea-
    houses)
TELEGRAPH keyer
    Casting Specialties
TELEPHONE amplifiers
    Digiac Corp.
    Eico Electronic Instrument
      Co., Inc.
    Howard
    Radio Shack
TELEPHONE centers/stands
    American Plywood Association
    Bedford Lumber Co.
    U-Bild Enterprises
TELEPHONE centers/stands,
    plastic
    Craft Patterns Studio

Rohm and Haas Co.
Yield House
TELEPHONE transmitters, wire-
less
Howard
H.J. Knapp Co.
TELESCOPE mirror kits
Edmund Scientific Co.
Esco Products
Telescopics
University Optics, Inc.
TELESCOPE mirror testers
University Optics, Inc.
TELESCOPE mounts
Mechanix Illustrated
Science & Mechanics Publish-
ing Co.
TELESCOPES, reflector
Edmund Scientific Co.
Esco Products
Mechanix Illustrated
Telescopics
Uinversity Optics, Inc.
TELESCOPES, refractor
Edmund Scientific Co.
TELESCOPES, sound (see Sound
telescopes)
TENT campers
Luger Camper Kits
Science & Mechanics Publish-
ing Co.
TENTS
Carikit
Frostline, Inc.
TERRACES
National Plan Service
THUMB pianos (West African
instrument)
Here, Inc.
Hughes Co.
The String Shop
TIC-TAC-TOE machines
Technical Writers Group
TIME base generators
Phase Corp.
TIMING lights
Heath Company
Radio Shack

TIMERS, photo
Heath Company
TIPIS
Nomadics-Tipi Makers
TOILET paper dispensers
Old South Pattern Co.
TOOL cabinets
Craft Patterns Studio
TOOL caddies
Craft Patterns Studio
U-Bild Enterprises
TOOL chests
U-Bild Enterprises
TOOL grinders
Gilliom Mfg. Co.
TOOL sheds (see Storage/tool
houses)TOO
TOOL stands
Craft Patterns Studio
TOOLS (see under following sub-
jects)
Anvils
Bending brakes
Block planes
Drill presses
Grinders, bench
Hacksaws, power
Lathes
Lathes, metal
Lathes, wood
Milling clamps
Milling machines
Milling tables
Modelmaker's press
Paper punches
Saws, tilt arbor
Sanders, belt
Sanders, disk
Saws, bench
Saws, circular
Saws, tilt table
Shapers
Small tools (hammer, screw-
drivers, etc.)
Soldering guns
Spindle shapers
Stud locators
Tool grinder
Vises

TOW trailers
  Braco Mfg. Co.
TOY cars/trucks (see Cars/trucks, toy)
TOY chests
  American Plywood Association
  Better Homes and Gardens
  Craft Patterns Studio
  Furniture Designs
  Minnesota Woodworkers
    Supply Co.
  U-Bild Enterprises
  Western Wood Products Association
TOYS
  American Plywood Association
  Craft Patterns Studio
  Mastercraft Plans
  Minnesota Woodworkers
    Supply Co.
  Science & Mechanics Publishing Co.
  Stanley Tools
  U-Bild Enterprises
TOYS, educational (tell time, add, etc.)
  Craftplans
  Minnesota Woodworkers
    Supply Co.
TOYS, geodesic dome
  Dome East
TOYS, musical (using Swiss musical movements)
  Minnesota Woodworkers
    Supply Co.
TOYS, rocking (see Rocking toys)
TRACTORS, garden/suburban
  Braco Mfg. Co.
  Science & Mechanics Publishing Co.
  C.F. Struck Corp.
TRACTORS, steam (midget)
  Caldwell Industries
TRAIL bikes
  Heald, Inc.
  Heath Company
  C.F. Struck Corp.
TRAILERS
  Craft Patterns Studio

Glen L. Recreational Vehicles
Luger Camper Kits
Mechanix Illustrated
Science & Mechanics Publishing Co.
Trail-R-Club of America
U-Bild Enterprises
Viking Camper Supply, Inc.
J.C. Whitney & Co.
TRAILERS, boat
  Clark Craft Boat Co.
  Glen L. Marine
  Luger Boat Kits
  Science & Mechanics Publishing Co.
TRAILERS, for trail bikes, ATV's, Snowmobiles
  Heald, Inc.
TRAILERS, tow (see Tow trailers)
TRAINS/locomotive-play
  Better Homes and Gardens
TRANSCEIVERS, CB/ham/single-banders
  Eico Electronic Instrument Co., Inc.
  Heath Company
TRANSFORMER/yoke testers
  Eico Electronic Instrument Co., Inc.
  Lafayette Radio Electronics
TRANSISTOR-diode curve testers
  Eico Electronic Instrument Co., Inc.
TRANSISTOR testers
  Bigelow Electronics
  Eico Electronic Instrument Co., Inc.
  Heath Company
  Howard
  Lafayette Radio Electronics
  McGee Radio Co.
  Radio Shack
  Trigger Electronics
TRANSITS (see Surveying transits)
TRANSMITTERS, FM wireless
  GC Electronics
  Howard
  H.J. Knapp Co.

TRANSMITTERS, ham
  Heath Company
TRANSMITTERS, phone/CW
  Heath Company
  Progressive Edu-Kits, Inc.
TRAPS, insect, electronic (see
    Insect traps, electronic)
TRASH bins
  U-Bild Enterprises
TREASURE/metal locators
  Bigelow Electronics
  Digiac Corp
  Eico Electronic Instrument
    Co., Inc.
  Jack Ford Science Projects
  Heath Company
  Howard
  Lafayette Radio Electronics
  McGee Radio Co.
  Relco Industries
  Radio Shack
  Science & Mechanics Publish-
    ing Co.
  Technical Writers Group
TREE seats
  Craft Patterns Studio
  U-Bild Enterprises
TRELLISES
  Western Wood Products Asso-
    ciation
TRICYCLES
  U-Bild Enterprises
TRIGGERED pulse generators
  Phase Corp.
TRIKES
  Kel Manufacturing
TRIMARANS
  John Brandlmayr, Ltd.
  Jim Brown-Trimarans
  Canadian Multihull Services
  Norman A. Cross, Naval Archi-
    tect
  Tri-Star Trimarans
  Lauren Williams Sailing Tri-
    marans
TRIVETS
  Germaco
TRUCKS, off road
  Popular Mechanics, Dept. CO

TUBE testers
  Bigelow Electronics
  Eico Electronic Instrument
    Co., Inc.
  Heath Company
  Lafayette Radio Electronics
  McGee Radio Co.
  Radio Shack
  Trigger Electronics
TUNE-up meters
  Heath Company
TUNERS (see FM Tuners)
TV cabinets (see Cabinets, TV)
TV cameras
  ATV Research
  Technical Writers Group
TV commercial eliminators
  Henry Francis Parks Labora-
    tory
TV remote controls
  Technical Writers Group
TV sets, black & white
  Heath Company
TV sets, color
  Heath Company
TV stands
  Stanley Tools
  Yield House
TV stools
  Bedford Lumber Co.
TVM's
  Eico Electronic Instrument
    Co., Inc.
  McGee Radio Co.
TVOM's
  Eico Electronic Instrument
    Co., Inc.
  McGee Radio Co.
TV vector monitors
  Heath Company
ULTRASONIC cleaners
  Henry Francis Parks Labora-
    tory
UTILITY chests
  Dandyplans
  U-Bild Enterprises
UTILITY function oscillators
  Phase Corp.

VACATION/leisure homes
American Plywood Association
American Timber Homes, Inc.
Bellaire Log Cabin Mfg. Co.
Better Homes and Gardens
Bloch Brothers
L.M. Brunier & Associates,
   Inc.
Cedar Homes Mfg. Corp.
Craft Patterns Studio
Custom Builders Corp.
Fab-A-Log of Washington
Futuro Corp.
Garlinghouse Co., Inc.
Hammond Barns
Hexagon Housing Systems, Inc.
Home Building Plan Service
Home Planners, Inc.
International Homes of Cedar
Lindal Cedar Homes
Mechanix Illustrated
Mills Cabin Mills, Inc.
Modular Concepts, Inc.
National Log Construction of
   Montana
National Plan Service
Pan Abode, Inc.
Pease Co.
Pierson Homes Prefabricators
Popular Mechanics, Dept. CO
Popular Science Plans Division
Shelter-Kit, Inc.
Tension Structures, Inc.
U.S. Dept. of Agriculture
Vermont Log Buildings, Inc.
Western Wood Products Asso-
   ciation
Yankee Barns, Inc.
VACUUM cleaners, built-in
Tee-Jon Industries
VACUUM tube amplifiers
Dynaco, Inc.
VALENCES
Craft Patterns Studio
VALETS
Design Craftsman
Stanley Tools
U-Bild Enterprises
Yield House

VAN conversion to mobile home
Trail-R-Club of America
VEHICLES (see under following
   subjects)
Air boats
All terrain cycles (ATC's)
All terrain vehicles (ATV's)
Automobile, midget (motorized)
Baja bugs/buses
Bicycles, motorized
Bulldozers, garden/suburban
Campers
Choppers (motorcycles)
Dune buggies
Electric cars
Four-wheel drive conversion
   to tracked vehicles
Hot-rod equipment
Hot-rod hardware
Hovercraft
Ice karts
Karts
Locomotives, midget (motor-
   ized)
Mini-bikes
Mini-choppers
Mini-cycles
Mobile homes, conversion from
   buses
Mobile homes, conversion from
   vans/trucks
Mowers, riding
Pick-up covers
Railroad engines, midget
   (motorized)
Roadsters
Sail cars
Sidecars, motorcycle
Snowmobiles
Snowmobiles, conversion to
   ATV's
Snowmobiles, conversion to
   wheeled vehicle
Tow trailers
Tractors, garden/suburban
Tractors, steam
Trail bikes
Trailers

Trailers, for trail bikes, ATV's snowmobiles
Trikes
Trucks, off road
Van conversion to mobile home
VENEERING/wood inlay
  Albert Constantine and Son, Inc.
  Craftsman Wood Service Co.
  Homecraft Veneer
  Minnesota Woodworkers Supply Co.
VENTILATORS, kitchen
  Science & Mechanics Publishing Co.
VESTS, down
  Carikit
  Frostline, Inc.
VIBRATO generators
  H.J. Knapp Co.
  Henry Francis Parks Laboratory
  Technical Writers Group
VIOLINS
  Craftplans
  International Violin Co.
  Minnesota Woodworkers Supply Co.
VIRGINALS
  William Post Ross – Harpsichord Maker
VISES
  Casting Specialties
  Germaco
VOICE operated relays/switches
  Howard
  Lafayette Radio Electronics
  Henry Francis Parks Laboratory
  Trigger Electronics
VOLOMETERS
  Bigelow Electronics
VOLTAGE regulators
  Beco, Inc.
VOM's
  Bigelow Electronics
  Digiac Corp.
  Eico Electronic Instrument Co., Inc.

Graymark Enterprises, Inc.
Heath Company
Lafayette Radio Electronics
McGee Radio Co.
Radio Shack
Trigger Electronics
VTVM's
  Eico Electronic Instrument Co., Inc.
  Heath Company
  Lafayette Radio Electronics
  McGee Radio Co.
  Radio Shack
  Trigger Electronics
WAA-waa effects
  Paia Electronics, Inc.
WADING pools
  U-Bild Enterprises
WALKIE-talkies
  Digiac Corp.
Wall units
  Better Homes and Gardens
  Craft Patterns Studio
  Furn-A-Kit, Inc.
  U-Bild Enterprises
  Western Wood Products Association
WARDROBES
  Bedford Lumber Co.
  Better Homes and Gardens
WATER filters/purifiers/softeners
  J.T. McCarthy Co.
WATER skis
  Larand Enterprises
WATER wells
  Deeprock Mfg. Co.
WATERBEDS
  Florida Waterbed Corp.
  Innerspace Environments, Inc.
WATT inverters
  Eico Electronic Instrument Co., Inc.
WATTMETER/SWR bridges
  Heath Company
WEATHER centers (thermometers, barometers, etc.)
  Craft Patterns Studio
WEATHER stations
  Technical Writers Group

WEATHERVANES
  Craft Patterns Studio
  Craftplans
  Minnesota Woodworkers
    Supply Co.
  U-Bild Enterprises
WELLS (see Water wells)
WHATNOT shelves
  Albert Constantine and Son,
    Inc.
  Minnesota Woodworkers
    Supply Co.
  Science & Mechanics Publish-
    ing Co.
WHEELBARROW planters
  Craft Patterns Studio
  Mastercraft Plans
  U-Bild Enterprises
WINDMILLS, garden
  Craft Patterns Studio
  Craftplans
  Mastercraft Plans
  U-Bild Enterprises
WINDOW boxes
  U-Bild Enterprises
WINDSHIELD wiper controllers
  Henry Francis Parks Labora-
    tory
  Radio Shack
WINE racks, plastic
  Rohm and Haas Co.
WISHING wells, garden
  Craft Patterns Studio
  U-Bild Enterprises
WOOD inlay (see Veneering/wood
    inlay)
WOOD turning projects
  Western Wood Products Asso-
    ciation
WOODWORKING (see under follow-
    ing subjects)
  Alphabet patterns
  Browsing bins (display matted
    works)
  Cabinets, oversized (for artists,
    photographers)
  Drafting tables
  Display panels (art display)
  Jig saw patterns

Looms
Machinists chests
Pipes, smoking
Potter's wheels
Salt-pepper sets, wood
Spinning wheels
Tool cabinets
Tool caddies
Tool chests
Tool Stands
Utility chests
Veneering/wood inlay
Workbenches
Wood turning projects
WORKBENCHES
  Better Homes and Gardens
  Albert Constantine and Son,
    Inc.
  Craft Patterns Studio
  Craftplans
  Diko
  Gilliom Mfg. Co.
  Mechanix Illustrated
WORKBOATS/commercial boats
  Jay R. Benford & Associates,
    Inc.
  John Brandlmayr, Ltd.
  George E. Meese
  Edwin Monk & Son
  A.D. Nelson
  Reliable Industries, Inc.
  Romack Marine
  Samson Marine Design, Ltd.
WORKSHOP centers
  Better Homes and Gardens
  Craft Patterns Studio
  Mechanix Illustrated
  National Plan Service
  U-Bild Enterprises
WROUGHT iron furniture/objects
  Creative Educational Services,
    Inc.
X-ray fluoroscopes
  Creative Products
YEAR round homes
  American Timber Homes, Inc.
  Better Homes and Gardens
  L.M. Brunier & Associates,
    Inc.

Craft Patterns Studio
Custom Builders Corp.
Fab-A-Log of Washington
Futuro Corp.
Garlinghouse Co, Inc.
Hexagon Housing Systems, Inc.
Home Building Plan Service
Home Planners, Inc.
International Homes of Cedar
International Mill & Lumber Co.
Lindal Cedar Homes
National Plan Service
Standard Homes Co.
U.S. Dept. of Agriculture
Yankee Barns, Inc.
YURTS
Dawes Hill Community
The Yurt Foundation

COMPANY INDEX

AMERICAN FENCE CO.
8205 So. 71 Highway
Kansas City, Mo. 64132

PRODUCTS:

Kennels/runs

Pre-fabricated dog runs, kennels, and pens. Easy to assemble, to move or rearrange or add to. Units are self-supporting with no posts to set and no gates to hang. A variety of sizes are available or special sizes may be made to order.

Brochure and price lists free

AMERICAN MOTORSPORT MFG.
P. O. Box 268
Costa Mesa, Calif. 92627

PRODUCTS:

Choppers (motorcycle)

Kits and parts for motorcycle choppers. Features the "Climax" which combines the advantages of a sprung front end with the appeal of the rigid. Cycle accessories, too.

30 page color illustrated catalog $1.00

AMERICAN PLYWOOD ASSOCIATION
1119 A Street
Tacoma, Wash. 98401

PRODUCTS:

BOATS
Outboards
Plyaks
Rowboat type (rowboats, prams,
  dinghies, etc.)
Runabouts
Sailing, cruising
Sailing, day sailers

BOATING EQUIPMENT
Storages, boat

CAMPING
Campers, folding   Picnic equipment

CHILDREN'S THINGS
Bunk beds
Furniture, children's
Playhouses
Rocking toys
Sandboxes
Toy chests
Toys

FURNITURE
Bars
Beds/headboards
Cabinets
Cabinets, fishing gear
Cabinets, gun/rifle
Music benches
Sewing centers
Telephone centers/
  stands

HOME CARE/IMPROVEMENT
Carports
Closets
Laundry centers
Room dividers
Sheds

HOUSING
A-frames   Cabins/cottages   Vacation/ leisure homes

LAWN & GARDEN
Fences
Lawn/patio furniture
Pergolas
Storage/tool houses

PETS
Dog kennels

The American Plywood Association is a trade promotion
association for the softwood plywood industry in the
United States. It offers a wide variety of inexpensive

AMERICAN PLYWOOD ASSOCIATION, cont'd

plans for the do-it-yourselfer, ranging in price from 25¢ (the majority of plans) to $1.00.

The "Consumer Do-it-yourself Literature Index" lists available plans and is free

AMERICAN TIMBER HOMES, INC.
Escanaba, Mich. 49829

PRODUCTS:

A-frames	Vacation/leisure homes
Chalets	Year round homes

Complete kit packages for homes made of treated Northern White cedar requiring no paint or stain on exterior except for trim. Vacation and year round homes. Standard designs can be altered to suit individual needs and a custom plan service is available. Homes are modular, and one can start with a modest building and add on as his budget permits or as is needed. Homes range in size from 320 sq. ft. to 2,980 sq. ft. and prices start at $2,985.00.

Portfolio of designs $1.00

ANDERSON AIRCRAFT CORP.
41 Sunnyside Rd.
Mahwah, N. J. 07430

PRODUCTS:

Amphibians

Plans only for the Anderson Kingfisher, a sport amphibian. Tractor engine design makes for easier building and safety. Engine options 100 HP to 140 HP. Wing options, used Piper or homebuilt. Plywood and fiberglass construction.

Information packet $3.00

ANDERSON ENGINEERING
Epsom, N. H. 03239

PRODUCTS;

Ignition analyzers
Ignition, capacitive discharge

Kits and completed capacitive discharge ignition systems.
Also supplies parts and components for electronic ignition
systems.

Illustrated catalog 10¢

ARCMARINE CORP.
2370 North Flower St.
Santa Ana, Calif. 92706

PRODUCTS:

Houseboats

Convert your camper, trailer or pickup cover to a houseboat.
The foundation craft consists of two fiberglass hulls, 28 ft.
long, between which is a deck 12 ft. wide by 26 ft. long.
Simply anchor your trailer or any other structure on top
for an instant houseboat. At the stern of both hulls are engine wells and transoms for single or twin engines. Component parts with instructions for assembly.

Information packet free

ARCO MFG. CO., INC.
P. O. Box 817
1701   13th Ave. North
Grand Forks, N. D. 58201

PRODUCTS:

Ramps, boat

ARCO MFG. CO., INC. (Cont'd)

Kits and instructions for boat ramp kits for inboards and outboards. Two models: one for boats 1,000 lbs. to 1,800 lbs., another for boats 1,800 lbs. and over. Boat ramp kits are designed for one man installation and removal.

Information free

ART GLASS & CRAFT STUDIOS
401 Bloomfield Ave.
Verona, N. J. 07044

PRODUCTS:

Lamps, Tiffany style

All kits include stained glass cut to size, flux, solder, lead, light socket, 3 ft. chain, cord, hardware, instructions. Kits are from $19.50 to $40.00.

Illustrated color brochure free

ARTISAN ORGANS
128 E. Wheeler Ave.
Arcadia, Calif. 91006

PRODUCTS:

Organs

Kits, parts, components for the larger organ. Church and theatre sizes. Also makes completed organs. 167 page "Organ Builder's Manual", $5.00.

Literature and price lists free

ASPEN LURES
Box 2918
Aspen, Col. 81611

PRODUCTS;

Fishing lures/jigs/sinkers
Fishing rods

Lure kits and fishing rod kits. Also tools for making fishing
tackle. Line of fisherman's gear is constantly expanding.

10 page illustrated catalog free

ATV RESEARCH
13th & Broadway
Dakota City, Neb. 68731

PRODUCTS:

TV cameras

Solid state TV camera kits with 31 page step-by-step illus-
trated construction manual. Also parts for TV cameras,
TV cameras suitable for home, factory, school, stores.
Technical literature, plans, schematics for TV cameras.

18 page illustrated catalog free

BABYLON ELECTRONICS
P. O. Box J
Carmichael, Calif. 95608

PRODUCTS:

Digital displays

Digital display kits as well as all types of integrated circuit (IC) components.

Brochure free

MARION E. BAKER
912 Salem Dr.
Huron, O. 44839

PRODUCTS:

Airplanes

Plans only for a unique full Delta shape prop plane. Was the first prop Delta for its size licensed in the United States. Plans $75.00.

Brochure $3.00

BAT-GLIDER PLANS
P. O. Box 7115
Amarillo, Tex. 79109

PRODUCTS:

Hang gliders

Plans only for the Bat-Glider, a hang glider based on the simple form of the bat. It is a cross between a glider and a parachute with the most desirable points of each combined to give a glider that can be self-launched, glide at a reasonable speed and angle, and land easier than a parachute. Materials can be easily purchased locally. One can build this hang glider for under $20 even if he has to buy every part.

Illustrated brochure free

BAT–RE–BIKE CO.
P. O. Box 732
Cherry Hill, N. J. 08003

PRODUCTS:

Bicycles, motorized

BAT-RE-BIKE CO.   (Cont'd)

Using a Ford-type starter motor and an ordinary automobile battery, you can make your own pollutant-free battery powered bicycle. Plans and parts are available. This is not a toy and the bicycle is not recommended for street use. Any bicycle frame can be adapted.

Plans $2.00

DAVID D. BEACH, NAVAL ARCHITECT
400 East Randolph
Chicago, Ill. 60601

PRODUCTS:

| Cruisers | | Outboards |
| Houseboats | Inboards | Runabouts |

An established stock plan service for a wide range of plans for boat designs specifically suited for amateur builders, based on considerable experience with their problems and limitations of their abilities and equipment. Study plans also available. 16 ft. to 38 ft. Schools note: for vocational schools, will sell plans at cost, or even give them to the school if properly asked.

Descriptive sheets free. Enclose return stamped envelope, business size

BECO, INC.
P. O. Box 686
Salem, Va. 24153

PRODUCTS:

Ignition, capacitive discharge
Voltage regulators

Kits for 12-volt all silicon automotive voltage regulators. Integrated circuitry provides fast, accurate charging while

BECO, INC. (Cont'd)

temperature compensation insures accurate charge at any temperature. The regulator is adaptable to all 12-volt negative ground charging systems, whether using alternator or generator charging equipment. Options provide for lamp or ammeter charge indicators. Compared to completely assembled unit, which company also sells, save around 50% by building your own. Also offers kits for capacitive discharge ignition systems with a 3 year warranty. Models are 6 or 12 volts, negative or positive grounds. Savings over assembled models are 40 - 50%.

Literature free

BEDFORD LUMBER CO.
Box 65
Shelbyville, Tenn. 37160

PRODUCTS:

Beds/headboards
Bookcases
cabinets, gun/rifle
Cabinets, sewing
Cabinets, stereo/hi-fi
Cedar chests
Chest of drawers
Chests
Colonial style furniture
Desks
Phonograph record holders/browsers

Picture frames
Racks, archery/gear
Racks, fishing gear
Racks, gun/rifle
Tables, cocktail
Tables, coffee
Tables, end
Tables, night
Telephone centers/stands
TV stool
Wardrobes

Dozens of kits and plans for easily assembled knockdown furniture. Large line of aromatic red cedar chests and other cedar furniture. Other fine woods are also used in projects. Quality shop lumber, hardware, finishes. Special discounts for schools.

36 page color illustrated catalog 25¢

JOSEPH H. BELFORT
192 N. Clark St.
Chicago, Ill. 60601

PRODUCTS:

Formulas, chemical

Company specializes in chemical formulas for useful products, which can be manufactured for profit, if desired. Some examples: waterless hand cleaners, detergents, perfumes, hair color restorers, pest repellents, invisible inks, etc. Some formulas are original, others are actual analyses of popular brand products. Single formula $5.00, three for $10.00.

Catalog 25¢

BELLAIRE LOG CABIN MFG. CO.
P. O. Box 322
Bellaire, Mich. 49615

PRODUCTS:

Cabins/cottages   Chalets
Cabins, log   Vacation/leisure homes

18 models of log cabin kits made from White cedar logs. White cedar is the lightest in weight, highest in insulation value, and most durable in weather resistance of all the evergreens growing in the United States. It is the only wood in North America that is frost free, even at temperatures as low as 50 degrees below zero. All logs are split and air dried. All materials to the roof line are smooth-finished and and treated with repellent chemicals against rot, mold and termites. Engineering of the pre-cut materials is precise and accurate for easy assembly. No caulking between logs is required since the logs are splined. Blueprints are included in the cost of the kit.

18 page illustrated catalog with floor plans $1.00

JAY R. BENFORD & ASSOCIATES, INC.
1101 N. Northlake Way
Seattle, Wash. 98103

PRODUCTS:

Ferro-cement boats
Sailing, cruising
Workboats/commercial boats

50 stock plans for designs ranging from 17 ft. to 60 ft.
Stock plans include reasonable consultation throughout
construction. Study plans are available, as well as a
custom design service. Boats may be purchased in any
stage of construction. Materials, equipment and supplies may also be purchased through company at cost-
saving prices. Fiberglass hulls, mesh for ferro-cement
boats, and pipe frame kits are available as well. The
Company publishes two invaluable books: "Practical
Ferro-Cement Boatbuilding" ($10.00), and "Cruising
Boats/Sail & Power", 9th edition ($5.00), plus other
books for further reading.

31 page illustrated catalog of designs $1.00

BENSEN AIRCRAFT CORP.
Raleigh-Durham Airport
P. O. Box 2746
Raleigh, N. C. 27602

PRODUCTS:

Helicopters

Bensen Aircraft is the originator and first manufacturer
of do-it-yourself rotorcraft-type flying machines. Complete kits, partial kits, plans. Plans may be purchased
separately. In the past nineteen years since the company was founded, there has never been an in-flight
failure of any part made or sold by the company. All

BENSEN AIRCRAFT CORP. (Cont'd)

dealers are qualified training centers for gyrocopter pilots. List of dealers on request.

Illustrated catalog and price lists free

BETTER HOMES AND GARDENS
P. O. Box 374
Des Moines, Iowa   50302

PRODUCTS:

CAMPING
Kitchens, camp

CHILDREN'S THINGS

Bunk beds
Doll houses
Furniture, children's
Playground equipment

Playhouses
Swings
Toy chests
Trains/locomotives, play

FURNITURE

Bars
Bookcases
Bookshelves
Buffets
Cabinets
Cabinets, gun/rifle
Cabinets, stereo/hi-fi

Carts, hostess/tea
Desks
File cabinets
Kitchen furniture
Sewing centers
Tables, dressing
Wardrobes

HOME CARE/IMPROVEMENT

Add-a-room projects
Basement remodelling
Carports
Closets
Desks
Kitchen islands
Kitchen remodeling

Room dividers
Sheds
Shelving
Storage walls
Wall units
Workshop centers

HOUSING
Vacation/leisure homes

Year round homes

LAWN & GARDEN
Barbecue carts
Lawn/patio furniture

Planters
Workbenches

BETTER HOMES AND GARDENS (cont'd)

Plans only for over 200 project ideas. Emphasis is on projects for improving the comfort and living quality of your home surroundings. Plans are designed to guide the person with little experience to succeed in building these projects prepared by professional designers in conjunction with Better Homes and Gardens magazine. Plans are $2.00 each, 3 for $5.00. Also plans and blueprints for leisure and year round homes selected by the magazine.

Project Plans catalog, 50 pages, illustrated 50¢. Home Plans catalog $1.00

BIGELOW ELECTRONICS
P. O. Box 125
Bluffton, Ohio 45817

PRODUCTS:

Appliance testers
Battery testers
Capacitor substitution boxes
Code oscillators
Color organs
Earphones/headphones
Intercoms
Metronomes
Multimeters
Phonographs, portable
Power suppliers, AC—DC
Power suppliers, regulated/
    variable
Radios, AM
Radios, Portable

Radios, transistor
RC bridges
Resistance substitution boxes
RF signal generators
Signal generators
Signal probes/tracers
Soldering guns
Stereo/hi-fi, amplifiers
Tachometers and dwell angle
    meters
Transistor testers
Treasure/metal locators
Tube testers
Volometers
VOM's

Mail order distributor (established 1954) of inexpensive electronic kits manufactured by EMC Corp. and Kits Industries. Also supplies electronic small parts, hardware, cabinets made by companies such as Keystone, NT.T, LMB, Houle.

Flyer free; regular 122 page illustrated catalog, $1.00 deposit.

BINGHAM ARCHERY
Box 3013
Ogden, Utah 84403

PRODUCTS:

Arrows   Bows

Kits for making fully professional bows as well as arrows. Bow kits can be made from scratch or company will supply semi-finished bows which you then finish. Also offers laminating presses, laminating ovens, glues, a complete selection of archery tackle supplies and accessories. Instructional materials, including blueprints, are $2.50. These archery tackle kits are suitable for both school projects and individuals.

24 pages illustrated catalog 50¢

BIRD AUTOMOTIVE
P. O. Box 793
Fremont, Neb. 68025

PRODUCTS:

Roadsters

Complete kits or plans for two models of roadsters: Standard and Deluxe. Uses any popular Ford or Chevrolet V-8 engine. Fiberglass bodies with a choice of five metal-flake colors. Complete kit for the Standard roadster sells

for $249.95, Deluxe model for $399.95. 20 page illustrated plans $2.00.

Illustrated brochure $1.00

JAMES BLISS & CO. INC.
Route 128 (at Exit 61)
Dedham, Mass. 02026

PRODUCTS:

Canoes	Rowboat type (rowboats,
Fender Boards	prams, dinghies, etc.)
Kayaks	Sailing, day sailers

Offers some kits, but this is primarily a supermarket for
everything marine. Many thousands of items are stocked.
Order by mail or through their five stores — in Massachusetts (Dedham, Boston, Woburn, Seekonk) and Connecticut (Darien). Beautiful catalog makes shopping from it
fun.

260 page illustrated color catalog packed with marine
supplies of every kind, $1.00

BLOCH BROTHERS
3650 Dixie Highway
Drayton Plains, Mich. 48020

PRODUCTS:

Cabins/cottages	Cabins, Log	Vacation/leisure homes

Kits and plans for over 100 vacation/leisure homes in
conjunction with land development projects throughout

BLOCH BROTHERS (Cont'd)

the state of Michigan. Your home and land may be
bought together as a package.

48 page catalog of plans and land development projects,
in Michigan, free

BRACO MFG. CO.
P. O. Box 26186
Denver, Col. 80226

PRODUCTS:

Automobiles, midget (motorized)	Tow trailers
Karts	Tractors, garden/suburban

Kits, plans, parts. Plans may be purchased separately.
Build a two-passenger car from easily assembled kit. Also
available in kit form is a one-passenger car kit, tractor,
two-wheel tow trailer, four-wheel tow trailer, and a kart.
All parts in kits are machined and ready for assembly.
Also, design your own vehicles or equipment by purchasing the parts separately.

Illustrated catalog free

JOHN BRANDLMAYR, LTD.
1089 West Broadway
Vancouver, 9, B. C.
Canada

PRODUCTS:

Catamarans	Sailing, cruising
Cruisers	Sailing, day sailers
Houseboats	Stern-wheelers
Inboards	Trimarans
Outboards	Workboats/commercial boats
Runabouts	

JOHN BRANDLMAYR, LTD. (Cont'd)

Stock plans designed by John Brandlmayr. More than 100 plans available. Sailboats from 15 ft. to 53 ft., runabouts and cruisers from 14 ft. to 50 ft., commercial boats from 13 ft. to 130 ft. Boats in aluminum, fiberglass, plywood, steel. One of the largest collections of designs from an individual designer.

List of plans free

BREEZEY AIRCRAFT
8748 South 82nd Ct.
Hickory Hills, Ill. 60457

PRODUCTS:

Airplanes

Experimental pusher parasol type completely open cockpit airplane. Welded chrome molly tubing, fabric covered wings and tail surfaces. Plans only, $25.00.

Information and specifications $1.50

BRINKMAN MFG. & FENCE CO., INC.
Route 8, Huntoon & Auburn Rd.
Topeka, Kan. 66604

PRODUCTS:

Fences   Horse corrals   Kennels/run

Easily assembled dog kennels as well as enclosures for horses, sheep and other animals. Also manufactures assemble-yourself fencing. Products may be used for homes, kennels, rodeos, fairs, playgrounds, etc. Also manufactures completed horse or dog pick-up carriers, and fiberglass carriers for car-top transportation.

BRINKMAN MFG. & FENCE CO., INC. (cont'd)

Accessories of all kinds as well as custom designs for animal enclosures.

35 page illustrated catalog free

JIM BROWN—TRIMARANS
Swanton Rd.
Davenport, Calif. 95017

PRODUCTS:

Trimarans

Plans only for "Searunner" line of trimarans 25 ft., 31 ft., 37 ft., 40 ft. "Catalog" which sells for $4.00 is a 128-page manual for the trimaran enthusiast and would-be builder. A new book, "Searunner Construction", is a 320 page manual for cruising trimarans selling for $8.00. Like the catalog, only three times its size, it is profusely illustrated. These manuals are of interest not only to the trimaran enthusiast, but to anyone attracted to amateur boat building. Books are free with order of plans, or deductible from plans purchase. Plans for Searunner 25 — $100, Searunner 31 — $300, Searunner 37 — $400, Searunner 40 — $450.

Information free

BROWN'S MOTORSPORTS
19 Central St.
Worcester, Mass. 01608

PRODUCTS:

All terrain vehicles (ATV's)	Karts
Automobiles, midget (motorized)	Mini-bikes

Kits, parts, plans for making your own ATV, kart, midget

64

car or mini-bike. One of the largest stock of parts on the East Coast.

Plans book $1.00. Parts book, 29 pages illustrated $1.00

L. M. BRUNIER & ASSOCIATES, INC.
1304 S. W. Bertha Blvd.
Portland, Ore. 97219

PRODUCTS:

A-frames	Chalets
Apartments/income- producing units	Garages Vacation/leisure homes
Carports	Year round homes

Plans only and blueprints for these plans. Offers inexpensive plan books showing external pictures and floor plans from which blueprints may be selected. "350 New Homes-Custom Trend Homes" for $1.00; "250 One & Two Story Homes", with a vacation homes section for $1.50; "160 homes for Hillsides", for difficult sites, for $1.50; "148 Duplex Income Homes", for $1.50; finally, "135 Apartments", buildings of 3 through 33 units, for $2.00. All five plan books may be purchased for $6.00. Modifications, reversed plans, customized service are also available. One of the larger sources of plans and blueprints.

List of plans books free

B—UR—O COMPANY
34161B Coast Hwy.
Dana Point, Calif. 92629

PRODUCTS:

Alternator power source
Power generators

Plans only for adapting your car alternator to become an electric power source. It makes your car, truck or other vehicle a portable power source for operating electric drills, saws, sanders, chain saws, lights, etc. Plans are $5.00, and other parts required can be purchased at a hardware store for about $3.00. Also offers plans for making a portable electric power plant from junkyard alternator and used gas engine. These plans, $5.00.

Information free

BURTON HARPSICHORDS
917 "O" St.
P. O. Box 80222
Lincoln, Neb. 68501

PRODUCTS:

Harpsichords

Kits, plans, instructions. Kits come in two forms: BASIC and COMPLETE. The BASIC kit is for the person with a good knowledge of woodworking. The woods for the case must be selected and cut by the builder according to the detailed plans in the construction manuals. The COMPLETE kit includes everything needed (except for a few common tools and liquid finishing materials). All parts have been finished, including case parts. Four models in BASIC and COMPLETE forms available, ranging in price from $195 to $400 for the BASIC kit and $395 to $650 for the COMPLETE kit. Tone and appearance of the harpsichords have been favorably compared to professionally build instruments many times the cost.

20 page illustrated catalog free

BUSHBY AIRCRAFT CO.
848 Westwood Dr.
Glenwood, Ill. 60425

PRODUCTS:

Airplanes

Kits and plans for the Mustang II, a two-place airplane
designed for both sport and cross-country flying. "Deluxe", "Sport" and "Midget" models. All metal stressed
skin construction. Simplified construction techniques
are incorporated in the design. There are no jigs required, and no machining of parts.

Information packet $1.00

E. R. BUTLER & SONS
25 Mugford St.
P. O. Box 123
Marblehead, Mass. 01945

PRODUCTS:

Rowboat type (rowboats, prams, dinghies, etc.)
Sailing, day sailers

Kits with instructions for prams and day sailers. These
boats can be built by people with little or no experience.
Construction can be as short as two weekends with a
few evenings in between. You will need a space at least
11 ft. long by 7 in. wide, for the 8 ft. pram; two feet
longer for the 9 ft. 10 in., a one-car garage is a good
space. You can build it completely with hand tools
but an electric drill is a great timesaver.

Illustrated catalog free

BYCO DISTRIBUTING CO.
P. O. Box 6241
Omaha, Neb. 68106

PRODUCTS:

Mini-bikes

Kits and instructions for mini-bikes powered by 3½ H.P.
engine. All parts are enameled, except the bolts, bear-
ings or plated surfaces, so there is no need to paint it. Parts
and accessories may be purchased separately. Kits range
in price from $99.95 to $125.50.

Illustrated catalog and price lists 50¢

CAL AUTOMOTIVE, INC.
8044 Lankershim Blvd.
North Hollywood, Calif. 91605

PRODUCTS:

Hot rod hardware   Roadsters

Specializes in fiberglass auto bodies for roadsters of the
20's but also manufactures components for the hot rodder
and the customizer. Also, rigid special frames for motorcycles.

Illustrated catalog $1.00

CAL-RACE PARTS
Box 1251
Wilmington, Calif. 90744

PRODUCTS:

Hot rod hardware

CAL-RACE PARTS (Cont'd)

Offers engine rebuild kits, hi-compression kits, parts and quality components for the hot rodder and racer.

22 page illustrated catalog $1.50

CALDWELL INDUSTRIES
Box 170
Luling, Tex. 78648

PRODUCTS:
- CLOCKS
  - Synchronomes (master clocks) Wooden wheel
- METALWORKING
  - Engines, gasoline Engines, steam
- TOOLS
  - Drill presses Milling tables
  - Lathes, metal Shapers
  - Milling machines
- VEHICLES
  - Locomotives, midget (motorized)
  - Tractors, steam (midget)

Unusual kits and blueprints for the metalworking craftsman and do-it-yourselfer, imported from England. Most kits are in castings form and thus require machine tools and metalworking experience. A few only require assembling. Steam engines, steam tractors and lomomotives, gasoline engines, machine tools, etc. These are not toys or models, but they are small. The steam engine kits, for example, and there are 14 to select from, run from a fraction of a horsepower up to three horsepower. Projects are not of the run of the mill variety. They represent the finest in British engineering design. Also supplies completed British power tools for the discriminating hobbyist, clock kits, books for the home craftsman, important steam engines and other quality mechanical toys.

120 page illustrated catalog $2.00

CALIFORNIA CHOPPERS
730 N. Anaheim Blvd.
Anaheim, Calif. 92805 ·

PRODUCTS:

Choppers (motorcycle)

Everything you need to convert your present motorcycle
into a chopper. Quality custom accessories, too. Parts
and accessories are manufactured by other well-known companies as well as by the company itself. As new ideas
evolve into new and more unique custom hardware, sup-
plemental pages to the catalog will be sent without
charge.

46 page illustrated catalog free

CALIFORNIA REDWOOD ASSOCIATION
617 Montgomery St.
San Francisco, Calif. 94111

PRODUCTS:

Decks   Patios
              Gazebos
Fences   Planters

This is a trade association and as such does not have
house plans, do-it-yourself kits, or redwood lumber.
However, does publish an extensive collection of garden construction plans for redwood fences, benches,
decks, etc. Also has color "idea booklets".

Literature free

CALIFORNIA SPEED AND SPORT SHOP
298 Jersey Avenue
New Brunswick, N. J. 08901

PRODUCTS:

Hot rod equipment

CALIFORNIA SPEED & SPORT SHOP (Cont'd)

A one-stop store for hot rod and speed equipment of all types. Also carries equipment for karts, motorcycles, mini-bikes. One of the larger speed equipment retail outlets in the east.

Illustrated catalog $1.00

GEORGE CALKINS,
The Bartender
P. O. Box 607
Newport, Ore. 97365

PRODUCTS:

Cruisers   Inboards   Outboards

The Bartender combines the seaworthy characteristics of the dory and maneuverability of the planing hull, and gets its name from the purpose for which it was originally created — to navigate the rough bars off the Northwest coast of the United States. Plans only for five boats ranging from 19 ft. to 32 ft., plans from $30.00 to $150.00.

Illustrated catalog 50¢

CANADIAN MULTIHULL SERVICES
2 Thorncliffe Park Drive No. 47
Toronto 354
Ontario, Canada

PRODUCTS:

Catamarans   Trimarans

Study plans and plans for trimarans and catamarans from well-known designers including: Jim Brown, Norman Cross, Lock Crowther, Robert Harris, Hugo Myers, Jim Wharram. Also carries a line of books on multihull designs. Although essentially a design service, can also build hulls up to 55 ft., as well as supply parts and accessories at less cost than shown in regular catalogs.

Catalog — "50 Multihulls You Can Build" — $3.00. Price lists free

CARIKIT
P. O. Box 1153
Boulder, Col. 80302

PRODUCTS:

Boots, down	Ponchos
Jackets, down	Sleeping bags
Mitts, down	Tents
Parkas	Vests, down

Lightweight, durable, handcrafted outdoor gear made of superior materials is expensive. How to get top quality equipment with a limited budget? Buy the quality materials and supply the labor yourself. Complete kits with clear and detailed step-by-step instructions. Adults' as well as children's outdoor gear. Each kit piece is cut out, labeled and punched along hems, quilt lines and seams as a sewing guide. All hardware is included in the kits. Only a sewing machine and moderate experience are required. Prime Northern Goose Down is used. The down comes in pre-measured packets which are simply inserted into each channel of the parka, sleeping bag or other item.

14 page color illustrated catalog free

CARSTON STUDIOS
146 Old Brookfield Road N.
Danbury, Conn. 06810

PRODUCTS:

4-channel stereo amplifiers	Stereo/hi-fi, preamplifiers
Stereo/hi-fi, amplifiers	Stereo/hi-fi, receivers

A mail order discount house for electronic consumer products as well as for kits from such well-known manufacturers as Dynaco and EICO. Check their prices by mail, in person, or by phone.

Sales bulletins free

CARV—A—COY
P. O. Box 11
Lincoln, R. I. 02865

PRODUCTS:

Decoys, duck

Kits with plans or plans alone for making your own duck decoys. 15 models. No carving experience necessary. Glue together pre-cut shaped body sections. After gluing the sections together, you need only simple tools, such as a wood rasp, file and sandpaper to complete the body. Glue on the pre-carved head and you are ready for painting the decoy. If you prefer to make your decoys from "scratch", you can start with CARV—A—COY's full size, three view plan and make your own. To follow this method you should have either a jig saw, band saw, saber saw or coping saw available.

Brochure 25¢, refundable with purchase of kits or plans

CASCADE INDUSTRIES, INC.
Talmadge Rd.
Edison, N. J. 08817

PRODUCTS:

Swimming pools

Buster Crabbe swimming pool kits available from a network of local dealers. May be installed by owner — or by dealer's crew. Complete instructions and excavating diagrams. Pools come in rectangular and curved shapes. This firm invented the pre-fab technique of manufacturing in-ground swimming pools.

14 page color illustrated catalog 50¢

CASTING SPECIALTIES,
DIVISION OF C. F. STRUCK CORP.
Cedarburg, Wis. 53012

PRODUCTS:

METALWORKING

Candelabras	Christmas	Compressors
Candlesticks	tree stands	Telegraph keyer

TOOLS

Anvils	Modelmaker's press
Drill presses	Saws, circular
Grinders, bench	Small tools (hammers,
Hacksaws, power	screwdrivers, etc.)
Lathes, wood	Vises

Kits in semi-finished form for a variety of tools. All kits include necessary basic materials, castings, working drawings and step-by-step instructions. Skill requirements range from the machining of a simple screwdriver to the building of a heavy-duty air compressor. Most projects require power tools and some metal-working knowledge. Projects are ideals for school shop — and individuals, too. Also carries selected tools and supplies for the metalworking shop.

28 page illustrated catalog 50¢

CATHEDRALITE DOMES
P. O. Box B
Daly City, Calif. 94015

PRODUCTS:

Geodesic domes

Offers kits for two basic dome sizes: 26 ft. diameter with two openings, 485 sq. ft. floor area ($1,695); and 39 ft. diameter with five openings, 1100 sq. ft. floor space ($3,195). Domes may be clustered. The Mars dome, a 60 ft. dome with 2800 sq. ft. has been used for churches and nursery schools. Custom design service is available under the direction of a Registered Architect. Cathedralite Domes are approved by the International Conference of Building Officials, and carries Research Recommendation No. 2396.

Illustrated catalog free

C–D SYSTEMS
P. O. Box 484
Berkeley, Calif. 94701

PRODUCTS:

Ignition, capacitive discharge

Kit for a capacitive discharge ignition unit for cars and trucks. The circuit incorporates a variable spark length

as well as anti-theft switch. The Mach II kit sells for
$33.95, complete ready for installation, $49.95.

Illustrated brochure free

CEDAR HOMES MFG. CORP.
11654 Northeast 8th
Bellevue, Wash. 98005

PRODUCTS:

A-frames	Vacation/leisure homes
Chalets	Year round homes

Homes of Western Red Cedar. This wood contains a natural preservative oil which renders its heartwood highly resistant to decay and rot, and resists termites. Artificial
preservatives are unnecessary. When left in its unfinished
state, Western Red Cedar weathers to a soft driftwood
silver gray. 32 standard homes available either as complete working drawings with specs or as complete packaged pre-cut home ready for erection. Prices range from
$4,375.00 to $14,825.00, floor space from 480 sq. ft. to
2,525 sq. ft. Company distributes only to the eleven
western states, including Alaska and Hawaii.

General brochure free. Portfolio of designs $1.00

CHAMPION BOATS OF CALIFORNIA
13076 Saticoy St.
No. Hollywood, Calif. 91605

PRODUCTS:

Houseboats	Inboards	Outboards
Hydroplanes		Runabouts

11 models of sleek, fast racing boats. Your choice of plans
only, frame kits, or bare hulls. Also makes an all-fiberglass

CHAMPION BOATS OF CALIF. (Cont'd)

utility boat which will take on your camper or pickup cover to make an instant houseboat. Remove the camper or pickup cover and you have a utility boat for cruising, fishing, water skiing, etc. Install and remove with jacks. Takes about 20–30 minutes for transfer.

Information packet 50¢

CHARLIE F. & OTHERS
5657 Mill St.
Erie, Pa. 16509

PRODUCTS:

Display cases

Display and wall case kits for showing off your prize models or art objects, made of walnut. Kits are complete except for glass. Kits or plans alone.

Illustrated brochure free

CLARK CRAFT BOAT CO.
16 Aqua Lane
Tonowanda, N. Y. 14150

PRODUCTS:

Catamarans	Outboards
Cruisers	Rowboat type boats (row-
Ferro-cement boats	boats, prams, dinghies, etc.)
Houseboats	Runabouts
Hydroplanes	Sailing, cruising
Inboards	Sailing, day sailers
Marine engine conversions	Trailers, boat

200 designs in power and sail. Many sizes and types. You can select a boating project as a complete kit, as a frame

CLARK CRAFT BOAT CO. (Cont'd)

kit, as a hull kit, or as plans and patterns alone. Also carries a large line of marine hardware, supplies and accessories.

97 page illustrated portfolio of designs and catalog $1.00

COHASSET COLONIALS—BY HAGERTY
38 Parker Ave.
Cohasset, Mass. 02025

PRODUCTS:

Beds/headboards
Benches
Bookcases
Cane/rush furniture
Chairs
Chairs, ladder back
Chairs, rocking
Chests
Chest of drawers
Colonial style furniture
Cupboards

Desks
Furniture, children's
Hutches
Mirrors
Settees
Shaker style furniture
Tables
Tables, dining
Tables, night
Tables, occasional

Kits for furniture based on authentic 17th and 18th century colonial and Shaker models. Here is an opportunity to furnish your home with early American furniture you may have seen in museums and wished to own yourself. Kits are complete. Everything is accurately handcrafted and sanded ready for assembly. All necessary glue, screws, hardware, sandpaper, stain and assembly instructions are included. Also offers authentically modeled accessories such as candlesticks, ladles, lamps, and a selection of colonial style fabrics.

32 page color illustrated catalog 50¢

COMPCOP
Box 1267
Redwood City, Calif. 94064

PRODUCTS:

Helicopters

Portable one-man helicopter. Can be partially dis-
assembled and carried in trunk of car or easily carried,
ready to fly, in a pickup or boat trailer or towed on
its own wheels. Kits and plans. Plans may be purchased separately. Rotor diameter 12 ft., overall length
12 ft., overall height 5 ft. 8 in., gross weight 420 lbs.,
empty weight 135 lbs.

Information 10¢

COMSTOCK CAMPER AND TRAILER SUPPLY
Box 646
Parsons, Kansas 67357

PRODUCTS:

Campers   Pickup covers

Three models of pickup covers: 8 ft., 12½ ft., 14 ft. Blueprints and kits. Blueprints may be purchased separately, and
include material list and easy step-by-step assembling instructions. Also supplies interior and exterior accessories.

Literature 25¢

CONNECTICUT VALLEY ARMS CO.
Candlewood Hill Rd.
Higganum, Conn. 06441

PRODUCTS:

Pistols, antique   Rifles, antique

CONN. VALLEY ARMS CO. (Cont'd)

Percussion or flintlock muzzle loading pistol and rifle kits, with plans and instructions. Most of the difficult work has been done, so that a reasonably adept do-it-yourselfer can finish the kits with only simple tools. Either full kit or parts may be purchased separately. Company also sells completed muzzle loading and other historic arms as well as accessories.

Illustrated catalog $1.00

ALBERT CONSTANTINE AND SON, INC.
2050 Eastchester Road
Bronx, N. Y. 10461

PRODUCTS:

CLOCKS

Decor	Grandmother
Grandfather	Period

Wooden wheel

FURNITURE

Beds/headboards	Desks
Buffets	Hutches
Cabinets, collectors/curio	Lamps
Cabinets, gun/rifle	Racks, spoon/silverware
Cabinets, spice	Settees
Cane/rush furniture	Tables
Carts, hostess/tea	Tables, card
Chairs	Tables, cocktail
Chairs, captain's	Tables, drop leaf
Chairs, ladderback	Tables, end
Colonial style furniture	Tables, trestle
Cradles, colonial	Whatnot shelves

LAWN & GARDEN

Christmas decorations	Lawn/patio furniture

Markers/signs/figures

MUSICAL INSTRUMENTS

Dulcimers	Guitars

ALBERT CONSTANTINE & SON, INC. (Cont'd)

WOODWORKING

Alphabet patterns

Pipes, smoking

Salt/pepper sets, wood

Spinning wheels

Veneering/wood inlay

Workbenches

Complete kits with instructions for guitars, clocks, dulcimers, smoking pipes and a particularly large selection of wood inlay picture kits. Many projects are plans only, full-size. Where plans only, company will provide wood kits, although not pre-cut. An excellent source for veneers, fine woods, tools, finishes, hardware, upholstery supplies, books for woodworker or craftsman. Special school discounts available.

85 page color illustrated catalog and manual 50¢

W. M. COOKSON
James Wharram Designs
1553 Armacost
Los Angeles, Cal. 90025

PRODUCTS:

Catamarans

These catamaran designs represent modern adaptations of the ancient Polynesian sailing craft — the double canoe or the "Pahee" in which the Polynesians, for over 1,500 years discovered and colonized the vast reaches of the Pacific, a feat now recognized as one of the greatest seafaring exploits in the history of man. Designs have the aim to provide a safe, cheap-to-build, load carrying, shallow draft, fast catamaran, 8 designs, 16 ft. to 51 ft. Plans only $15 to $200.

Catalog and design portfolio $2.00

CRAFT PATTERNS STUDIO
Route 83 & North Avenue
Elmhurst, Ill. 60126

PRODUCTS:
BOATS
Kayaks	Runabouts
Rowboat type (rowboats, prams, dinghies, etc.)	Sailing, day sailers

CAMPING EQUIPMENT
Luggage carriers, car top

CHILDREN'S THINGS
Bunk beds	Play houses
Cars/trucks, toy	Play pens
Cradles	Playground equipment
Cradles, colonial	Puppet theatres
Cribs	Rocking toys
Doll houses	Sand boxes
Furniture, children's	Toy chests
Hobby horses	Toys

CLOCKS
Decor	Period
Grandfather	School
Grandmother	Weather centers (thermometers, barometers, etc.)

FURNITURE
Armoires	Chairs
Bars	Chairs, rocking
Beds/headboards	Chests
Benches	Colonial style furniture
Bookcases	Desks
Breakfast nooks	Dinettes
Breakfronts	Dressers
Buffets	Dry sinks
Cabinets	Hutches
Cabinets, collector's/curio	Mirrors
Cabinets, gun/rifle	Music stands
Cabinets, kitchen	Office centers, home
Cabinets, phonograph record	Planters
Cabinets, sewing	Racks, archery gear
Cabinets, spice	Racks, gun/rifle
Cabinets, stereo/hi-fi	Racks, magazine
Cabinets, TV	Racks, spice

Racks, spoon/silverware
Settees
Sewing centers
Shadow boxes
Speaker enclosures
Tables, card
Tables, cobbler's bench
Tables, cocktail

Tables, coffee
Tables, dining
Tables, drop leaf
Tables, end
Tables, night
Tables, trestle
Telephone centers/
  stands

HOUSING

Cabins/cottages   Vacation/leisure homes   Year round homes

HOME CARE/IMPROVEMENT

Add-a-room projects
Attics
Awnings
Basement remodeling
Cabinets, kitchen
Carports
Closets
Cupolas
Dens
Dormers
Fireplace mantels

Garages
Kitchen remodeling
Porches
Room dividers
Sheds
Storage walls
Swimming pools
Valences
Wall units
Weathervanes
Workshop centers

LAWN & GARDEN

Barbecue carts
Barbecue dining sets
Barbecue pits
Christmas decorations
Easter decorations
Fences
Fireplaces, outdoor
Gateways
Gazebos
Greenhouses
Grist mills, lawn
Japanese teahouses

Lamp posts
Lawn/patio furniture
Markers/signs/figures
Pergolas
Picnic tables/benches
Planters
Settees, outdoor
Swings, lawn
Tree seats
Wheelbarrow planters
Windmills, garden
Wishing wells, garden

PETS

Bird houses
Dog houses

Martin houses

SPORTING EQUIPMENT
- Arrows
- Bows
- Cue racks

- Ping pong tables
- Pool tables

VEHICLES
- Campers

- Trailers

WOODWORKING
- Jig saw patterns
- Tool cabinets
- Tools, caddies

- Tools, stands
- Workbenches

Plans and patterns only. Over 1,000 plans and patterns. Most plans sell for 65¢ each, and the others are also moderately priced. Packets of plans may be obtained for $2.50 each, for example: Windmill Packet, Boat Packet, Patio Furniture Packet, Home Cabinet Packet, etc. A clock book catalog is available for 25¢. Craft patterns are featured in newspapers throughout the country.

104 page illustrated catalog 50¢

CRAFTPLANS
8011 Lewis Rd.
Minneapolis, Minn. 55427

PRODUCTS:

CHILDREN'S THINGS
- Cars/trucks, play
- Doll furniture
- Doll houses
- Furniture, children's

- Toys, animated
- Toys, educational (tell time, add, etc.)
- Toys, musical (using Swiss musical movements)

CLOCKS
- Decor
- Grandfather
- Grandmother

- Period
- Wooden wheel

CRAFTPLANS (Cont'd)

FURNITURE
Cabinets, gun/rifle
Colonial style furniture
Desks
Lamps

Racks, gun/rifle
Shadow boxes
Tables, cocktail
Tables, end

HOME CARE/IMPROVEMENT
Garages

Weathervanes

LAWN & GARDEN
Christmas decorations
Fences
Fireplaces, outdoor
Lawn/patio furniture

Markers/signs/figures
Planters
Sundials
Windmills, garden

MUSICAL INSTRUMENTS/EQUIPMENT
Musical instruments

Violins

PETS
Birdhouses/feeders

SPORTING
Duck decoys

VEHICLES
Automobiles, midget (motorized)

WOODWORKING
Alphabet patterns
Jig saw patterns
Looms

Spinning wheels
Workbenches

Plans only for woodworking projects for fun and profit. Established in 1948 — over 1 million plans sold. Plans $1.00 to $2.00 which makes this an inexpensive plans source.

23 page illustrated catalog 25¢

CRAFT PRODUCTS CO.
Rte. 83 & North Ave.
Elmhurst, Ill. 60126

PRODUCTS:

CLOCKS
Decor

Grandfather

CRAFT PRODUCTS CO. (Cont'd)

CLOCKS (Cont'd)
- Grandmother
- Period
- School
- Weather instruments (thermometers, barometers, etc.)
- Wooden wheel

More than 25 plans for historic and contemporary clocks. Kits available for several. Parts, movements, woods for clockmaking. Plans are under $1.00.

67 page illustrated catalog "Clocks and Clockmaking" 25¢

CRAFTSMAN WOOD SERVICE CO.
2727 So. Mary St.
Chicago, Ill. 60608

PRODUCTS:

CLOCKS
- Grandfather

MUSICAL INSTRUMENTS
- Dulcimers
- Guitars

WOODWORKING
- Veneering/wood inlay

While company offers kits, basically a source of supplies for the woodworker. Catalog has over 2,000 items including: hardwoods, veneers, inlays, pre-cut veneer picture kits, lamp supplies, cabinet hardware, upholstery supplies, shop and hand tools, power tools, musical instruments and hardwood legs. Offers an impressive selection of wood inlays and veneers including wood inlay picture kits.

145 color illustrated catalog 50¢

CREATIVE CORNER
910 No. Marshfield Ave.
Chicago, Ill. 60622

PRODUCTS:

Lamps, Tiffany style

16 Tiffany style lamp kits. Authentic leaded stained glass. Special school discounts.

Literature free

CREATIVE EDUCATIONAL SERVICES, INC.
Box 663
West Caldwell, N. J. 07006

PRODUCTS:

Wrought iron furniture/objects

Company manufactures a simple tool set for making wrought iron furniture and objects for the student, hobbyist, or small business. Tool set is fastened to any work table with simple clamps. No heat, electricity, and very little space is required. Accessories and steel strips are available. 40 attractive and practical designs come along free with each tool set. Special provision for schools.

Brochure and information free

CREATIVE PRODUCTS
1551 East Loop 820
Fort Worth, Tex. 76112

PRODUCTS:

Alternator power source
Burglar/fire alarms, home or business

CREATIVE PRODUCTS (Cont'd)

Coin cleaners
Formulas, chemical
Gold/silver recovery units
Insect traps, electronic
Power suppliers, DC—AC
X—ray fluoroscopes

Plans only. Every plan also includes a Construction Manual. Construction manual contains: general description, theory of operation, construction, operation, schematic, parts list, list of illustrations. Projects are designed for simplicity and are fully tested.

14 page illustrated catalog free

CREST KENNEL CO.
2200 South Valentia St.
Denver, Colo. 80231

PRODUCTS:

Dog houses   Horse corrals   Kennels/runs

A complete line of easy-to-assemble kennels and runs for dogs, cats, and other animals, too. Modular, can add on. Also, four sizes of dog houses made of redwood for easy assembly. Horse corrals are new to the line of products. These corrals are built from 1—5/8 in. or 1—7/8 in. O. D. galvanized tubing. Easy to set up and portable. Choice of heights and lengths. All kits come with instructions.

15 page illustrated catalog free

NORMAN A. CROSS, NAVAL ARCHITECT
4326 Ashton
San Diego, Calif. 92110

PRODUCTS:

Trimarans

Plans only for trimarans, 24 ft. to 50 ft., 13 designs available. Plans cost from $60 to $600, study plans from $3.00 to $5.00. Portfolio of designs $2.00. Trimarans are growing more popular each year. They are easy to build, and there is no heavy ballast. The boats designed by Mr. Cross have won many races and have an excellent reputation.

Illustrated catalog free

CROSSBOWMAN
P. O. Box 723
Manteca, Calif. 95336

PRODUCTS:

Crossbows

Kits with plans for making the "Jayhawk Crossbow". In kit form costs $12.99, completed $22.95. Company stocks other crossbows completed and crossbow supplies.

10 page illustrated catalog 25¢

CROWER CAMS & EQUIPMENT CO.
3333 Main St.
Chula Vista, Calif. 92011

PRODUCTS:

Engine stands   Hot rod hardware

Precision, quality cam kits with a full line of custom valve train components. Also a new Cylinder Head Modification Department, Fuel Injection Department, Crowerglide Clutch Department and complete Research and Development Department. In addition provides an engine stand kit, the "Husky Boy" with a universal adapter. No additional adapters are necessary. Holds all automobile engines,

CROWER CAMS & EQUIPMENT CO. (Cont'd)

cylinder heads, automatic transmissions. The fully adjustable arms fit any bolt pattern.

112 page illustrated, information packed catalog $1.00

CTS OF PADUCAH, INC.
1565 North 8th St.
Paducah, Ky. 42001

PRODUCTS:

Stereo/hi-fi, speakers

Company manufactures loudspeakers and crossover components for hi-fidelity stereo speaker systems. Because the quality of sound reproduction is determined by internal dimensions, the shape of the cabinet, and the effectiveness of the air seal, the company's engineers provide plans for building speaker cabinets or enclosures for those who wish to build their own speaker systems or upgrade existing systems.

Illustrated brochure free

CURTIS DYNA–PRODUCTS CORP.
Box 297
Westfield, Ind. 46074

PRODUCTS:

Hovercraft

Hovercraft (air cushion vehicle) capable of traveling at high speeds over land and water. Kits and plans. Open or closed (all weather) cockpit designs.

Photos, specs, prices, $1.00

CUSTOM BUILDERS CORP.
3739 S. Lindbergh
St. Louis, Mo. 63127

PRODUCTS:

A-frames

Apartments/income pro-
    ducing units

Cabins/cottages

Cabins, log

Chalets

Vacation/leisure homes

Year round homes

Pre-cut package which you can assemble yourself, or the company will build it for you. Catalog of over 1,000 plans. The builder may incorporate his own ideas into any standard design, or create a completely new home from the very beginning. Company will build to any size and to any stage of construction. Mass purchasing, pre-design, pre-engineering, pre-cutting . . . . . and no middle man cuts costs down.

52 page illustrated catalog with floor plans for 55 houses $1.00

CUSTOM CYCLE DELIGHT, INC.
8846 Alondra Blvd.
Bellflower, Calif. 90706

PRODUCTS:

Choppers (motorcycle)

Parts for making your own choppers. Also carries custom parts and accessories for choppers and for all other bikes. A source too for obsolete and hard-to-find parts for Harley Davidson 1936 and later. 200 page catalog lists thousands of items.

200 page illustrated catalog $2.00

ANTON CVJETKOVIC
P. O. Box 323
Newbury Park, Calif. 91320

PRODUCTS:

Airplanes

Plans only for three airplanes. The CA—61 "Mini-Ace"
can be built as a side-by-side two seater with any Continental engine between 65 and 85 H. P. Alternatively, the
single seater can be fitted with a modified VW engine.
The CA—65 is a further development of the CA—61. It has
retractable landing gear and dual controls. Both the CA—61
and the CA—65 are plywood construction. The CA—65A
has the same configuration as the CA—65 but is all metal.

Information packet $3.00

DAK HYDROFOILS
P. O. Box 71
Sausalito, Calif. 94965

PRODUCTS:

Hydrofoils

Kits with plans for adding hydrofoils to catamarans. These
hydrofoils are made of aluminum. This is the first company in the field of hydrofoils for sailing boats.

Information free

DANDYPLANS
Box 14915
Phoenix, Ariz. 85063

PRODUCTS:

Drafting tables   Machinist's chests   Utility chests

DANDYPLANS (Cont'd)

Plans only. Easy to read tested plans.

8 page illustrated catalog 30¢

LEEON DAVIS
3501 Baumann Ave.
Midland, Texas 79701

PRODUCTS:

Airplanes

The DA—2A was designed for the home builder who wants
a practical airplane. Plans only. All metal, two place side-
by-side, tri-gear, enclosed cabin, light weight, useful load
of 500 pounds, stick control and no flaps for simplicity.

Catalog $2.00

ROY DAVIS RESEARCH LABORATORIES, see
JACK FORD SCIENCE PROJECTS

DAWES HILL COMMUNITY
Box 53
W. Danby, N. Y. 14896

PRODUCTS:

Yurts

Plans and instructions for making yurts (also known as the
Ger or Jur). Manual for making yurts is titled "Home's
Where Yurt", and is mostly by Jim Steinman. Quoting:
"We have found that costs of yurts can vary from 50 cents,
using all scrap materials and natural resources as we did
for our chicken house yurt, up to $600.00 and more, using
the solid board technique. Most of our yurts at Dawes Hill

DAWES HILL COMMUNITY (Cont'd)

have cost in the neighborhood of $100.00 to $200.00. As a matter of interest, local zoning laws have been a thing of concern. We have thus far avoided condemnation by calling our yurts "tent frames", which by definition makes them legal. Check your town zoning laws, but as a rule the town won't know what to do about something like a yurt, so you'll have nothing to worry about if you just go ahead and build it."

9 page illustrated plans and manual, suggested contribution $1.00

H. DE COVNICK & SON, INC.
P. O. Box 68
Alamo, Calif. 94507

PRODUCTS:

CLOCKS

Grandfather	School
Grandmother	Weather instruments (thermom-
Period	eters, barometers, etc.)

Semi-assembled case kits (over 60% assembled) with instructions for completion. Requires a minimum of woodworking experience and only normal hand tools. A large selection of imported movements, dials. Blueprints, plans or templates may be purchased separately. Company also sells finished clocks.

36 page illustrated catalog 50¢

DECOYS UNLIMITED
Box 69
Clinton, Ia. 52732

PRODUCTS:

Decoys, duck

DECOYS UNLIMITED (Cont'd)

Provides a system for the home manufacture of plastic decoys using a mold. The plastic used in the decoys is an expandable polystyrene which is far superior to the styrofoam used by commercial decoy makers. Because the system uses molds, the more decoys you make, the cheaper the unit cost. Suitable for individuals, clubs, or the small business.

Illustrated brochure free

DEDHAM KAYAKS
P. O. Box 207
West Lynn, Mass. 01905

PRODUCTS:

> Kayaks
> Sailing, day sailers

Kits for kayaks. Four models, 9 ft. to 15 ft. Ready-cut parts, easy to assemble. Can be built in one day. Kits also include a built-in mast step, so that if you wish, your kayak may be sailed with the addition of a sailing rig. Prices range from $39.95 to $59.95 for complete kits.

Illustrated catalog free

DEEPROCK MFG. CO.
P. O. Box 870
Opelika, Ala. 36801

PRODUCTS:

> Formulas, chemical
> Water wells

Drilling for water on suburban, rural or vacation sites is an expensive and risky proposition if you hire a contractor

DEEPROCK MFG. CO. (cont'd)

to drill for so much per foot. A dry hole can cost thousands of dollars. With a do-it-yourself drilling machine, you can drill your own water for only a few cents per foot. Company sells complete well drilling outfit called the "HYDRA-DRILL". One man, portable. Drills to 200 ft. with speeds to 40 ft. per hour. Cost $345.00. Also carries well drilling accessories.

Company in addition, is a source of chemical formulas, for example: silvering glass, invisible inks, furniture polish, photographs on cloth, silver cleaners, rush inhibitors, etc. These products sell for 10 to 50 times the cost of materials. You can save money by making them for your own use from simple materials easily available, or package and sell the products for profit. Formulas $1.00 each, 3 for $2.00, 10 for $5.00, all 20 formulas for $6.00 postpaid.

Information free

DELTA PRODUCTS, INC.
P. O. Box 1147
Grand Junction, Col. 81501

PRODUCTS:

Ignition, capacitive discharge

Kits with instructions for capacitive discharge electronic ignition systems. Capacitive discharge increases performance and eliminates many tune-up problems. Save by doing it yourself. For example, the Mark Ten model costs $44.95 assembled and $29.95 for the kit. Oldest and largest manufacturer of capacitive discharge ignition systems.

Brochure free

DESIGN CRAFTSMAN
P. O. Box 226
Lumberton, N. C. 28358

PRODUCTS:

> Desks, roll top
> Tables, coffee
> Tables, dining
> Valets

Plans only. Plans include instructions and materials list.
Four projects available: lazy susan dining table, game and
coffee table, roll-top desk, clothes valet.

Brochure 25¢

DESIGNER KITS, INC.
39—06 Crescent St.
Long Island City, N. Y. 11101

PRODUCTS:

Beds/headboards, chrome steel	Desks, chrome steel
Carts, hostess/tea, chrome steel	Etageres, chrome steel
Chairs, chrome steel	Music centers, chrome steel
Chrome steel furniture	Tables, cocktail, chrome steel
Couches, chrome steel	Tables, end, chrome steel

Company specializes in kits for making chrome steel furniture. Tubes, fittings, glass, and accessories are pre-cut
and pre-finished. No experience or special tools are required. This is a job of assembly, not of construction.
Simply use a mallet to tap the fittings into the open-ended
tubing. No bolts, nuts, screws, nor adhesives are required.
Follow the simple diagrams which show you exactly where
each fitting and tube goes, or you use your imagination to
create your own furniture units. By building your own
chrome steel furniture you can save 50% or more compared
to the retail price of similar furniture.

25 page illustrated catalog free

DE SILVA BOATS
P. O. Box 394
Sebastopol, Calif. 95472

PRODUCTS:

Hydroplanes   Outboards
Inboards   Runabouts

Plans only for powerboat racing boats. These boats have set
records in every category of powerboat racing since 1931.
In addition to plans, everything in supplies, racing hardware
and accessories is available to build and equip a high performance boat.

Catalog $1.00

G. DE VRIES
P. O. Box 413
Altadena, Calif. 91001

PRODUCTS:

Surveying transits

Transit level kit with surveying instructions, $5.00. Transit
is easy to use and measures vertical and horizontal angles
to 30 minutes. Use your camera tripod or tripod kit supplied by company for $10.00.

Information on request

DEVTRONIX ORGAN PRODUCTS
5872 Amapola Drive
San Jose, Calif. 95129

PRODUCTS:

Organs

DEVTRONICS ORGAN PRODUCTS (Cont'd)

Kits and components for making any size organ, from the largest to the smallest.

Illustrated 12 page catalog and price lists 25¢

DIGIAC CORP.
1261 South Boyle Ave.
Los Angeles, Calif. 90023

PRODUCTS:

Electronics

Appliance testers	Radios, transistor
Battery chargers	Signal probes/tracers
Battery chargers, automotive	Soldering guns
Broadcasters, neighborhood	Stereo/hi-fi, amplifiers
Color organs	Tachometers
Intercoms	Telephone amplifiers
Phonograph/radio combinations	Treasure/metal locators
Power suppliers, AC–DC	VOM's
Radios, AM	Walkie talkies
Radios, short wave	

Kits with instructions for 35 electronics projects. Products are oriented towards the school market. Therefore, when one completes the kit, one not only has a useful item but has gained educationally, too. Special discounts for schools (and others) ordering 5 or more of one kit.

Illustrated brochure free

DIKO
P. O. Box 91
Rowayton, Conn. 06853

PRODUCTS:

Potting benches	Workbenches

DIKO (Cont'd)

Plans for five different wood workbenches: (1) a heavy duty wall mounted bench; (2) a heavy duty free-standing bench; (3) a wall mounted bench without legs for easy cleaning underneath; (4) a lightweight wall unit suitable for potting; (5) a collapsible unit. Plans $1.50 each.

No catalog, just plans

DIXIE GUN WORKS
Union City, Tenn. 38261

PRODUCTS:

Pistols, antique   Rifles, antique

Kits for making historic revolvers and rifles, flintlock, muzzleloading, percussion. Also offers supplies, tools, parts, books for the arms buff. Their catalog is handsome, well laid out, highly illustrated. Because of the vast amount of information the catalog contains, it is an indispensable reference work for anyone interested in the lore and in the facts about antique firearms and accessories. Over 6,000 items are listed. At a price of $2.00 ("or send $3.00 if you like"), the catalog is a bargain. It is remarkably well done — a real labor of love.

362 page illustrated catalog $2.00

DOME EAST
325 Duffy Ave.
Hicksville, N. Y. 11801

PRODUCTS:

Beds, geodesic dome

Environments, geodesic dome

Greenhouses, geodesic dome

Playground equipment, geodesic dome

Playhouses, geodesic dome

Toys, geodesic dome

DOME EAST (Cont'd)

Kits using the geodesic dome principle from toys to greenhouses. LUVDOMES are small geodesic dome environments with a variety of uses as a sleepdome, pleasuredome,
encounterdome, playdome, readingdome, and so on, for
adults and children. LUVDOME replaces a whole house of
massive, "single-use" furniture. Can be set up anywhere
in a half an hour. Price is $249.95. GREENDOME is a
geodesic dome greenhouse, 14 ft. in diameter, 10 ft. high,
at $995.00. Greenhouse accessories are also available.

Illustrated literature free

DOME-ICILES
105 Marlborough St.
Boston, Mass. 02116

PRODUCTS:

Geodesic domes

Complete kits with instructions for geodesic domes 24 ft.
through 39 ft. in diameter, or completed domes with completely furnished interior. Company will also construct
domes on special order. The company offers a package
that includes an easily erected kit, land, and a means of
making a living in several rural locations. So, in effect,
a person can own his own house for as little as $8,000,
and by being a representative of Dome-Iciles and a representative of Shaklee products (a completely biodegrad-
able line of cleansers), a harmonious and creative life-style
is available to anyone who wants it.

Brochure and price lists free

DOWN EAST DORIES, see HAROLD H. PAYSON

DRYAD PRESS
6247 Eagle Rd.
Indianapolis, Ind. 46278

PRODUCTS:

Browsing bins (display matted works)
Cabinets, oversized (for artists, photographers)
Display panels (art display, bulletin board, etc.)

Plans only. Browsing bins, oversized cabinets, display panels, suitable for art or photographic materials.

Information free

FRANCIS A. DUGAN
Small Yacht Designs
One Country Club Rd.
Bellport, N. Y. 11713

PRODUCTS:

Sailing, cruising   Sailing, day sailers

10 sailboat designs, plans only, 18 ft. to 35 ft. Designed for the amateur builder. All plywood construction. Woods are readily available at your local lumber yards. Study plans, too.

Listing and description of designs 24¢, in stamps.

THE DULCIMER SHOPPE
P. O. Box 110
Mountain View, Ark. 72560

PRODUCTS:

Dulcimers

102

THE DULCIMER SHOPPE (Cont'd)

Kit dulcimer: all walnut, with laminated top and back, parts are pre-cut and sides are bent. Easy-to-follow instructions make assembly simple. Everything you need is included except glue, finish, and a few hours of loving labor. Kit is $31.95 plus postage and handling, while same instrument completed costs $68.00. Sells other finished folk instruments: guitar, banjo, Ozark mouth bow, zither, concertina, musical saw, calliope whistles, trombone flute, kazoo, recorders. Also books, records, accessories for folk instruments.

Brochure free

DUREL'S
Box 223
Covington, La. 70433

PRODUCTS:

> Lamps, cypress knee
> Lamps, insulator
> Racks, gun/rifle

Unusual lamp kits made from unusual objects. Cypress knees are growths taken from Bayou swamps. When used in a kit, they make a lamp a thing of beauty. Also a Cypress knee rack for guns or rifles. Another striking lamp kit is made from old power poles, including the original crosstie, base and insulator.

Illustrated catalog free

DUSTER SAILPLANE KITS
P. O. Box 1261
San Pedro, Calif. 90732

PRODUCTS:

> Gliders

Complete kits for making the BJ—1B"DUSTER", a small 13 meter (42 ft. 8 in.) all-wood sailplane, designed specifically for the home builder. It uses ribs sawn from 1/4 in. ply, and fuselage bulkheads of 3/4 in. ply. It goes together quickly, and is really a delight to fly. The 7 ft. center section stays on the fuselage, so no component is over 18 ft. long. It is built on a simple table made from a board 2 in. x 12 in. x 18 ft. long. It can be constructed and stored in an ordinary garage, can be transported by trailer on highways, and assembled, ready to fly, in a few minutes without tools, stands, racks or other special equipment.

Illustrated brochure free

DYNACO, INC.
3060 Jefferson St.
Philadelphia, Pa. 19121

PRODUCTS:

FM Tuners	Stereo/hi-fi, preamplifiers
4-channel stereo adapters	Stereo/hi-fi, tuners
Stereo/hi-fi, amplifiers	Vacuum tube amplifiers

Kits are supplied with full instructions and include all parts. All Dynaco kits are supplied with pre-assembled and pre-tested printed circuit modules. Quality instruments for the audio perfectionist. Save by building your own. For example, the FM tuner   FM-5 sells for $249.95 assembled, $149.95 as a kit; or the 4-channel stereo adapter sells for $29.95 assembled, $19.95 as a kit. Company does not sell kits directly. Prospective builders of Dynaco kits should go to their local dealer first. If you do not know which dealer carries kits, write to Dynaco and they will furnish name and address of dealer.

Information free

EASTERLY YACHTS
Div., Scheyd-Brennan, Inc.
1729 Lake Ave., Box 9104
Metairie, La. 70005

PRODUCTS:

Sailing, cruising

Complete kit for cruising racing sloop, the "Easterly 30".
Fiberglass one-piece hull, sleeps five, 30 ft. Basic hull and
deck package $4,250.00. The "Easterly 36" with a length
of 36 ft., costs $7,500.00 for the basic fiberglass hull and
deck. All other parts available for both boats.

Literature free

EASTERN ENTERPRISES, INC.
509 West Washington Blvd.
Los Angeles, Calif. 90015

PRODUCTS:

Mini-bikes   Mini-cycles

Complete kits for mini-bikes and mini-cycles. Kits may be
purchased with or without engines. Three models are
available. Kits from $104 to $169, including engine, and
from $47 to $99 for frameless engine.

Illustrated catalog 25¢

LEONARD R. EAVES
3818 N. W. 36th St.
Oklahoma City, Okla. 73112

PRODUCTS:

Airplanes

LEONARD R. EAVES (Cont'd)

The "Cougar 1" is a high wing monoplane seating two people side by side. The Cougar was designed by Robert Nesmith of Houston, Texas. Folding wings are all wood with 1/16th inch mahogany, 3 ply wood covering. Fuselage is tubular steel. Wingspan 20 ft. 3½ in., length 18 ft. 6 in., height 5 ft. 8 in., weight 700 lbs. dry, 1400 gross. Plans only, at $20.00.

Illustrated brochure 25¢

EDMUND SCIENTIFIC CO.
100 Edscorp Bldg.
Barrington, N. J. 08007

PRODUCTS:

EXPERIMENTAL/SCIENTIFIC

- Atomic energy laboratory
- Battery chargers
- Black light
- Burglar/fire alarms, home or business
- Cameras obscura
- Collimeters
- Color organs
- Computers
- Drug and narcotic identification kits
- Enlargers
- ESP tests
- Fiber optics
- Infra-red detectors
- Light detectors

- Light/psychedelic shows
- Microscopes
- Pollution testers
- Pregnancy testers
- Projectors, overhead
- Science fair projects
- Science toys
- Sex determining kits
- Solar furnaces
- Stroboscopes
- Telescope mirror kits
- Telescopes, reflector
- Telescopes, refractor
- Transistor clock

A mail order supply house for the experimenter, gadgeteer, hobbyist, student. Catalog is packed with over 4,000 items and new ones being added all the time. Simple and inexpensive devices to highly sophisticated equipment. Chemistry, physics, geology, optics, general laboratory supplies, etc.

EDMUND SCIENTIFIC CO. (Cont'd)

Books, tools, hobby supplies. A one-stop supermarket for most everything scientific.

147 color illustrated catalog free

EICO ELECTRONIC INSTRUMENT CO., INC.
283 Malta Street
Brooklyn, N. Y. 11207

PRODUCTS:

Appliance testers
Audio generators
Battery chargers
Battery testers
Bongos, electronic
Burglar/fire alarms, home
    or business
Capacitor substitution boxes
Capacitor testers
Code oscillators
Color bar generators
Color organs
CRT testers
Decade capacitance boxes
Decade resistance boxes
Engine analyzers
Faradohm bridges/analyzers
4-channel stereo adaptors
Grid-dip meters
Harmonic distortion meters
Ignition, capacitive discharge
Keyers, electronic
Motor/speed controllers
Multimeters
Multi-signal tracers
Oscilloscopes/vectorscopes
Power suppliers, AC–DC
Power suppliers, regulated/variable

Radios, aircraft monitor
Radios, AM
Radios, short wave
R–C bridges
Resistance substitution
    boxes
RF signal generators
Science fair projects
Signal probes/tracers
Sine/square wave generators
Stereo/hi-fi, amplifiers
Stereo/hi-fi, receivers
Stereo/hi-fi, tuners
Stroboscopes
Sweep/marker generators
Telephone amplifiers
Transceivers, CB/ham/
    single banders
Transformer/yoke testers
Transistor-diode curve tracers
Transistor testers
Treasure/metal locators
Tube testers
TVM's
TVOM's
VOM's
VTVM's
Watt inverters

EICO ELECTRONIC INSTRUMENT CO., INC. (Cont'd)

Kits with instructions for electronic projects sold only through EICO dealers and distributors of which there are 2,500 from coast-to-coast. There are also 200 authorized service stations to provide the same quality technical service and replacement parts you get from the factory. Largest manufacturer of electronics kits marketed through dealers and distributors in the world.

31 page illustrated catalog free

ELECTRONIC AIDS
2175 Greenspring Drive
Timonium, Md. 21093

PRODUCTS:

Amplifiers, mono	Power suppliers, AC–DC
Code oscillators	Power suppliers, regulated/
Metronomes	variable
Multimeters	Radios, AM
Phonographs, portable	Radios, portable
	Radios, transistor

Some 20 electronic kits with instructions of varying complexity, but all basically easy to construct. No kit should take longer than five hours to complete. All that is needed is a soldering iron. Kits are inexpensive, from $5.25 to $29.95, and are suitable for the school, hobbyist, or professional.

Illustrated brochure free

E. M. F. CO., INC.
P. O. Box 1248
Studio City, Calif. 91604

PRODUCTS:

Pistols, antique

E.M.F. CO., INC. (Cont'd)

Kit with instructions for a muzzle loading Kentucky percussion pistol, .41 caliber. Company sells, finished, modern and historically important firearms for gun collectors, plus matching accessories.

30 page illustrated catalog $1.00

EMG ENGINEERING CO.
18518 S. Broadway
Gardena, Calif. 90248

PRODUCTS:

Engines, jet

Kits with plans or plans alone for jet engine with 15–18 lbs. of thrust operated on liquid propane. Can be used to power go-karts, "Flying Platform", small helicopters. Weighs 5 pounds.

Information free

ENVIRONMENTAL PRODUCTS (EPD)
Box 1014
Glenwood Springs, Col. 81601

PRODUCTS:

Crystal frequency time standards
Digital displays
Frequency counters

Offers a unique line of MOD-kits. These kits perform relatively sophisticated tasks and yet can be easily assembled. Once a kit is assembled, only solderless jumpers are used to connect it to other kits. Also carries quality parts and components.

48 page illustrated catalog with application notes, free if bulk mailed, 25¢ for 1st class mailing

ESCO PRODUCTS
171 Oak Ridge Rd.
Oak Ridge, N. J. 07438

PRODUCTS:

> Lasers
> Telescope mirror kits
> Telescopes, reflector

Kits for making Newtonian reflector telescopes, 3 in. to
8 in. mirrors, 39 in. to 90 in. focal length. Mirror kits also
available from 3 in. to 8 in. Telescope parts and accessories. Can also furnish a kit containing all the finished
optical components necessary for building a CO_2 laser.

11 page illustrated catalog free

EXPERIMENTAL AIRCRAFT ASSOCIATION, INC.
P. O. Box 229
Hales Corners, Wisc. 53130

PRODUCTS:

> Airplanes
> Airplanes, antique
> Airplanes, biplanes

The aim of the Experimental Aircraft Association (EAA) is
to advance the cause of homebuilt aircraft. While the association does not have a catalog as such, it does offer plans
which are advertised in its monthly magazine, Sport Aviation. The association offers plans for a biplane, P-2, a fully
aerobatic single-place biplane. Spruce wings, steel tube
fuselage, detailed shop drawings, plus full size rib and jig
drawing. ($27.00 to EAA members, $37.50 non-members,
includes one year's membership to EAA). Also, plans for
an antique homebuilt, the Heath Parasol. Single seat,
powered by VW to 65 Continental. (Plans $23.00 to EAA
members and $32.00 to non-members, includes one year's
EAA membership). The EAA is also now offering a new
Arco-Sport plane at $50.00 for the plans and an informa-
tion packet for $4.00, postage paid.

EXPLORER AIRCRAFT CO.
5315 Palo Verde Drive
Edwards, Calif. 93523

PRODUCTS:

Amphibians   Gliders

Plans only for the Aqua-Glider which combines sport flying with water sports and has the additional appeal of its
antique appearance. The design, although of wood and
fabric structure, is strictly modern. Easy to build and
safe to fly. Technically the Aqua-Glider is a boat towed fly-
ing-boat(seaplane) glider. By FAA regulations (FAR Part
101) it can be operated with no restrictions as long as it is
flown below 150 feet under tow at least five miles from
airport control zones. This means that it is not necessary
to have it FAA certified nor is it necessary to have a pilot's
license to fly it. However, the Explorer PG-1 may be FAA
certified as an amateur built aircraft if the builder so de-
sires. Plans are $20.00. Cost of materials is around $300.00.

Illustrated catalog free

EXTENDED DIGITAL CONCEPTS
Box 9161
Berkeley, Calif. 94709

PRODUCTS:

Brainwave machines

Studies have shown that Zen meditators are able to produce
strong alpha brain rhythms continuously and at will.   Sub-
jectively, the alpha state is associated with mental alertness,
calmness and serenity. Offers a kit, an EEG monitor, with
which to delve into psycho-electronic biofeedback technology. Easy to construct, sells for $59.00.

Literature free

FAB-A-LOG OF WASHINGTON
14000 Interurban Ave.
Tukwila, (Seattle) Wash. 98618

PRODUCTS:

Cabins, log	Vacation/leisure homes
Chalets	Year Round Homes

Offers 20 standard home models and custom designs. Knotty, rustic, whole Lodge-pole logs are handpeeled with draw knives, knotched with precision and assembled like Lincoln logs for a rigid structure. The logs are numbered and color-coded for easy assembly. Kits and plans. Larger designs for institutional or commercial use are also available.

Information packet $2.00

FEDERAL MARINE MOTORS CO.
P. O. Box 56
Orland Park, Ill. 60462

PRODUCTS:

Marine engine conversions

Kits with instructions for converting your automobile engine into a marine engine. Also carries marine transmissions, flexible couplings, propulsion drives for inboards and outboards, marine instruments and controls.

11 page illustrated catalog free

FERNWOOD GUN SUPPLY
1725 Springbrook Rd.
Walnut Creek, Calif. 94596

PRODUCTS:

Pistols, antique

112

FERNWOOD GUN SUPPLY (Cont'd)

Three kits are presently offered: a 44 cal. derringer, a 36 cal. pistol, and a four barrel derringer. All are percussion. The finished pistols are smart looking and good shooters. Kits come with step-by-step instructions for assembly and working drawings. No special tools or skills required.

Brochure free

W. J. FIKE
P. O. Box 683
Anchorage, Alas. 99510

PRODUCTS:

Airplanes

Plans only for "Model E", low aspect ratio, cantilever closed land, high wing monoplane. The one piece wing is quickly and easily removable for highway towing and storage. It can easily operate off a 500-foot strip at sea level if the approaches are good. Span 29 ft. 1 in., length 18 ft. 8 in., height 5 ft. 5 in., wing chord 5 ft. Full plans set $35.00.

Information packet $2.00

FINNYSPORTS
2910 Glanzman Rd.
Toledo, Ohio 43614

PRODUCTS:

Arrows	Fishing rods
Fishing lures/jigs/sinkers	Rifles, antique

A one-stop department store by mail for fishing, hunting,

camping needs. Thousands of items are stocked. Name
it — and they probably have it.

Tremendous 292 page illustrated catalog free

FIRESIDE ANGLER, INC.
Box 823
Melville, N. Y. 11746

PRODUCTS:

> Fishing lures/jigs/sinkers
> Fishing rods
> Flytying kits

This company originated the one fly Pattern Kit. It is
designed to teach the novice flytyer to tie one pattern
only, but correctly. Each kit contains all the materials
necessary for the particular fly, a complete set of instructions, and a professionally tied fly to compare efforts
with. Company also offers tool kits, all necessary supplies for fishing sports, and books for the angler.

84 page illustrated catalog free

FLIGHT DYNAMICS, INC.
P. O. Box 5070
Raleigh, N. C. 27607

PRODUCTS:

> Amphibians

Plans only for an amphibian designed for the amateur, the
Flightsail VII. Takes anywhere from 85 to 125 H. P. engines. Airframe is constructed of bolted aluminum stif-
fened with styrofoam and covered with epoxy fiberglass.

The "stage" process of building allows you to fly the first

114

summer. Simply build the open framework, flexible wing design as Stage I. You can go to work next winter and install an engine, get the necessary licenses, and fly in Stage II. From then on you can add items as you desire to get to Stage III and then go anywhere in your amphibian.

Information packet $3.00

FLORIDA WATERBED CORP.
148 No. Brevard Ave.
Cocoa Beach, Fla. 32931

PRODUCTS:

Water beds

Water bed kits. Also sells water couches, water chairs, and water and air cushions, although not in kit form.

Brochure free

FOLBOAT CORP.
Stark Industrial Park
P. O. Box 7097
Charleston, S. C. 29405

PRODUCTS:

Canoes	Runabouts
Kayaks	Sailing, day
Outboards	sailers

Kits with step-by-step instructions for the smaller boat. Kits may be purchased as either a "Prefab" kit or a "Basic" kit. The Prefab kit requires no skill to assemble. Single piece frames simply interlock with prefab sections, are fastened with provided screws and glued. Factory finished hull and deck fabrics are vinyl coated in glossy

FOLBOAT CORP. (Cont'd)

colors of your choice. Nothing else to buy. "Basic" kit
has all frames, bow, stern, glue, etc., with full size patterns and instructions. You buy the plywood sections as
listed in the plans. Also manufactures completed boats.
Books, accessories are also available. Special school,
youth groups, institutions discount.

49 page color illustrated catalog with informative articles
on water — camping life, free

JACK FORD SCIENCE PROJECTS
P. O. Drawer 5750
Jacksonville, Fla. 32207

PRODUCTS:

Lasers	Spectroscopes
Science fair projects	Treasure/metal locators

Plans only for science projects. Also offers science courses
and brochures on science topics.

36 page catalog 50¢

FRAZER & ASSOCIATES
3809 Surfwood Rd.
Malibu, Calif. 90265

PRODUCTS:

Science fair projects

Inexpensive kits by RCA, Motorola. IC experiments, FET
experiments, etched circuit kits, etc. For the experimenter, hobbyist, science fair project. Also carries electronics
books.

Literature free

FROSTLINE, INC.
P. O. Box 2190
Boulder, Col. 80302

PRODUCTS:

Backpacks	Ponchos
Boots, down	Sleeping bags
Jackets, down	Sweaters, down
Mitts, down	Tents
Pants, down	Vests, down
Parkas	

Camping equipment of good quality is expensive. Save more than 50% by making your own. Kits are pre-cut, pre-labeled, with step-by-step instructions. Everything you need is included. Sizes for children and adults. Only best quality materials are used. All kits that require down installation come with down packets. Each packet is pre-weighed and packed to fit every individual compartment of your kit. To use, simply insert the packet into the proper compartment, and by pushing turn the packet inside out. When you withdraw the packet, the down is neatly inside.

31 page color illustrated catalog free

FURN-A-KIT, INC.
140 East Union Ave.
East Rutherford, N. J. 07073

PRODUCTS:

Bars	Dining room sets
Bookcases	Etagieres, chrome steel
Cabinets	Hutches
Cabinets, stereo/hi-fi	Music centers
Chairs	Room dividers
Chrome steel furniture	Shelving, chrome steel
Danish/Scandinavian furniture	Wall units

The Furn-A-Kit system is unusual. The company offers modular components from which you select components

FURN-A-KIT, INC. (Cont'd)

to suit your needs and tastes. Since all the components
are pre-fabricated, pre-assembled, pre-finished, and all the
necessary hardware is provided, you need only a screwdriver and a few knocks with a rubber mallet to complete
any project. Easy, step-by-step instructions. Comtempo-
rary, Mediterranean, and Provincial styles in oak, walnut,
or chrome steel. The collection of wall units is particularly large.

Illustrated 56 page catalog $1.00

DAVID FURNIE – BOAT DESIGNS
658 Francis Rd.
Richmond, B. C. Canada

PRODUCTS:

Sailing, cruising	Sailing, day sailers

12 sailing boat designs as kits or plans ranging from 17 ft.
6 in. to 48 ft. Full-size patterns, available for all vessels
under 30 ft. in length, are made to order. Prices are
quoted on application. Also offers wood kits, in any
stage of construction desired, for some boats: the 29 ft.
and 30 ft. sloop and the 36 ft. ketch or sloop. These kits
are made by NorlandBBoats, 2984 Norland Ave., Burnaby 2,
B. C., Canada, for which David Furnie acts as agent.

Information free. (A future catalog is being prepared to
cost $1.50. At publication time the catalog had not been
completed.)

FURNITURE DESIGNS
1425 Sherman Avenue
Evanston, Ill. 60201

PRODUCTS:

Bars	Bookcases
Beds/headboards	Buffets
Benches	Cabinets, collectors/curio

118

FURNITURE DESIGNS (Cont'd)

Desks
Desks, rolltop
Dressers
Cabinets, gun/rifle
Cabinets, stereo/hi-fi
Cane/rush furniture
Carts, hostess/tea
Chairs, captains'
Chairs, rocking
Chest of drawers
Chest on chests
Colonial style furniture
Corner shelves
Cradles, Colonial
Credenzas
Cribs
Cupboards
Danish/Scandinavian furniture

Dry sinks
Furniture, children's
Hutches
Lamps
Mirrors
Racks, magazine
Settees
Speaker enclosures
Stools
Tables, card
Tables, cocktail
Tables, dining
Tables, drop leaf
Tables, end
Tables, nest of
Tables, night
Tables, trestle
Toy chests

Full size plans. Professionally drawn plans include a complete list of materials, show and suggest proper joints, and by an "exploded" perspective sketch show how all parts are assembled. Over 135 plans in early American, Danish, juvenile, English oak, Spanish, French Provincial, Mediterranean. Educational discounts for designs in classroom use.

Illustrated 30 page catalog $1.00, refundable with first order.

FUTURO CORP.
1900 Rittenhouse Square
Philadelphia, Pa. 19103

PRODUCTS:

Vacation/leisure homes   Year round homes

Striking modernistic designs. The Futuro II, one of the

119

FUTURO CORP. (Cont'd)

larger models, looks very much like a flying saucer. Designs are of Finnish origin, in a variety of colors. Shells are of reinforced fiberglass. Units come with various options, including a sauna. Units come as knocked down kits and are ready for easy assembly at a site of your choice. Configurations of units may be used for nursery schools, motels, offices, etc.

Illustrated brochure free

GARDEN WAY RESEARCH
Charlotte, Vt. 05445

PRODUCTS:

Push carts

A large capacity, easy to handle two wheeled lawn and garden utility cart. The large diameter wheels allow the user to carry large loads with ease. The kits are easy to assemble, and come with all the metal parts, wheels and hardware along with illustrated assembly instructions. A kit buyer, by supplying his own plywood can save from $15 – $30 depending upon the size desired.

Illustrated catalog free

GARLINGHOUSE CO., INC.
2320 Kansas
P. O. Box 299
Topeka, Kan. 66601

PRODUCTS:

Apartments/income producing units	Chalets
Cabins/cottages	Vacation/leisure homes
Cabins, log	Year round homes

GARLINGHOUSE CO., INC. (Cont'd)

Plans only for houses in many styles and sizes. Plans are designed for conventional construction, which enables a "do-it-yourself" family to build a home any place in the country. The collection of plans is published in magazine format with pictures of finished homes and floor plans. There are 16 such magazines, most with more than 100 plans in each. All told the collection amounts to over 1,000 designs. Most of the plan collections sell for $1.00 each, complete collection of 16 books is $10.00. Write to company for list of plan books.

Information free

DON GARLIT'S HI-PERFORMANCE WORLD, INC.
3420 West Main St.
Tampa, Fla. 33607

PRODUCTS:

Hot rod hardware

Carries hot rod hardware kits from major manufacturers such as Crower Cams, Cyclone headers, Doug Thorley headers, Edelbrock manifolds, EELCO products, Holley Carburetors, Kustom products, Mickey Thompson products, etc. A mail order supermarket for the hot rod do-it-yourselfer.

50 page catalog $1.00

GASTON WOOD FINISHES
3630 E. 10th St.
Bloomington, Ind. 47401

PRODUCTS:

Clocks, decor

GASTON WOOD FINISH (Cont'd)

Offers refinishing materials of all kinds as well as furniture hardware. Clock kits and parts.

32 page illustrated catalog 50¢

GC ELECTRONICS
Div., Hydrometals, Inc.
400 South Wyman St.
Rockford, Ill. 61101

PRODUCTS:

Code oscillators   Radios, transistor
Photoelectric relays   Science fair projects
Power suppliers, AC–DC   Transmitters, FM wireless

Company's catalog is unusual in that not only does it offer hundreds of electronic parts and accessories but also contains plans for easy-to-build electronic projects. Catalog includes practical do-it-yourself information, charts, formulas, tables, even a handy ohms calculator as well as a wall chart of electronic symbols. More than a catalog of electronic parts, the catalog is a valuable handbook or guide for the electronic hobbyist and experimenter.

48 page illustrated catalog 50¢

GEMACO
P. O. Box 295
Garden Grove, Calif. 92642

PRODUCTS:

Metalworking

Bells, brass   Fireplace sets
Candelabras   Salt/pepper sets,
Candlesticks   metal
Door knockers   Trivets

122

GEMACO (Cont'd)

Tools

Block planes	Sanders, belt
Miter clamps	Sanders, disc
Paper punches	Vises

Company supplies castings, drawings and unusual hardware only, unless otherwise specified. While the company specializes in castings for the school shop and craft classes, the home craftsman would find the projects equally interesting. Also carries a full line of foundry supplies and equipment.

14 page illustrated catalog free

GENE'S TACKLE SHOP
Box 7701
Rochester, N. Y. 14622

PRODUCTS:

Flytying Kits

Everything necessary for flytying kits: tools, materials, hooks, leaders, etc. Also books for the angler.

16 page illustrated catalog including a "Beginners Flytying Guide" 15¢

GEODESIC DOMES
10290 Davison Rd.
Davison, Mich. 48423

PRODUCTS:

A-frames
Aircraft shelters, geodesic dome
Canopies, geodesic dome
Geodesic domes

GEODESIC DOMES (Cont'd)

Offers a variety of applications of the geodesic dome
principle in many sizes and types, from beach canopies
to dome aircraft shelters. Also inexpensive A-frames
using triangular cells. Geodesic domes for church structures, businesses, schools and nurseries, etc. Domes have
been approved by the International Congress of Building
Officials and the Southern Building Code Congress. Kits,
plans, instructions.

18 page illustrated catalog free

GEODESIC STRUCTURES, INC.
P. O. Box 176
Hightstown, N. J. 08520

PRODUCTS:

Geodesic domes

Complete kits for fashioning geodesic domes for residen-
tial, vacation, institutional, industrial use. 26 ft. to 59 ft.
diameter, 485 sq. ft. to 2,800 sq. ft. Price range from
$1,995 to $12,950. Model D-39, 39 ft. diameter, can be
constructed ready for occupancy for under $12 a square
foot, and can be set up by four men in two days. Smaller
models can be constructed in less time. Domes may be
clustered. Options available.

Illustrated catalog free

GILES & KENDALL
P. O. Box 188
Huntsville, Alabama 35804

PRODUCTS:

Bookcases
Cabinets, Hi-Fi/stereo

Cedar chests
Music centers

GILES & KENDALL (Cont'd)

Phonograph record
  holders/browsers
Racks, gun/rifle

Tables, cocktail
Tables, coffee
Tables, end

Ready-to-assemble furniture kits with plans and instructions made from aromatic Tennessee red cedar. Large line of cedar chests of various sizes and styles. Other projects made of cedar include bookcases, gun racks, tables, etc. Hardware, quality finishing materials, lumber. For schools, for shop, for home craftsman.

12 page color illustrated catalog 25¢

GILLIOM MFG. CO.
1109 N. 2nd Street
St. Charles, Mo. 63301

PRODUCTS:

Tools

Drill presses
Lathes
Sanders, belt
Sanders, disc
Saws, bench

Saws, tilt arbor
Saws, tilt table
Spindle shapers
Tool grinders
Workbenches

Vehicles

Automobiles, midget
  (motorized)

Karts
Mini-bikes

Full sized plans and kits for making machine tools yourself at considerable savings. Also home workshop parts, tools and accessories. Kits as well as plans to make mini-bikes from old 26-inch bicycle frame. Also, motorized midget automobile suitable for children, kit or plan.

Illustrated catalog 25¢

GLEN L MARINE
9152 Rosecrans
Bellflower, Calif. 90706

PRODUCTS:

Can-Yaks (combination canoe and kayak)	Pontoon boats
	Rafts
Catamarans	Rowboat type (rowboats, prams, dinghies, etc.)
Cruisers	
Houseboats	Runabouts
Hydroplanes	Sailing, cruising
Inboards	Sailing, day sailers
Outboards	Trailers, boat

Over 100 different designs for boats from 8 ft. to 49 ft. for construction by the amateur builder. Boats are plywood, although fiberglass covering kits are available. Plans, full size patterns, frame kits. Plans may be purchased separately, and price applied to purchase of kits. Plans only for boat trailer kits, in six sizes, to fit boats from 13' 6" to 25'. Also offers accessories, fastening kits, sail kits, fiberglass covering kits, boat building books.

96 page profusely illustrated boat catalog, "Plans-Patterns-Frame Kits", $1.00. "Marine Hardware" catalog, especially for boats designed by Glen L Marine, 69 pages illustrated, $1.00. "Boatbuilding Supplies" brochure, free.

GLEN L RECREATIONAL VEHICLES
9152 Rosecrans
Bellflower, Calif. 90706

PRODUCTS:

Campers	Pick-up covers	Trailers

15 models of recreational vehicle kits including campers, pick-up covers, trailers. Plans, patterns, instructional manuals, conponent kits, appliances, accessory kits. Plans and patterns may be purchased separately. Building your own unit saves labor costs, dealer markups, interest on financing,

126

and other service costs. Some save up to 50% and most save 1/3 by building it yourself.

23 page illustrated catalog free

GOLDEN AGE ARMS CO., INC.
Box 82
Worthington, O. 43085

PRODUCTS:

Knives, hunting/Bowie   Pistols, antique   Rifles, antique

Kits for antique rifles and pistols, percussion, flintlock. Also hunting knives kits. Parts, books, tools, accessories — everything for the historic arms hobbyist.

124 page illustrated catalog $1.00

GOLF DAY PRODUCTS
Box 305
Lake Forest, Ill. 60045

PRODUCTS:

Golf clubs

Kits, instructions, parts for making your own golf clubs or repairing them. A great project for those who like to tinker with clubs, or for winter when Northern golfers are shut in for several months, and of course a good way to beat the high cost of golf.

15 page "Golf Club Repair Manual" and catalog, illustrated, $1.00

GRAYMARK ENTERPRISES, INC.
P. O. Box 686
Farmingdale, N. J. 07727

PRODUCTS:

Electronics

Battery chargers
Burglar/fire alarms, home or
  business
Code oscillators
Motor/speed controllers
Power suppliers, AC—DC
Power suppliers, regulated/
  variable

Radios, AM
Radios, short wave
Radios, sun powered
Radios, transistor
Resistance substitution
  boxes
Tachometers
VOM's

Optics/photography

Black light
Color organs

Light/psychedelic shows
Stroboscopes

Some 30 electronics projects for the hobbyist and for the school from simple to advanced. Kits with instructions. Good selection of light shows for the home. Also electronic components and parts. Special provisions for schools.

55 page color illustrated catalog 25¢

GREENHOUSE SPECIALTIES CO.
9849 Kimker Lane
St. Louis, Mo. 63127

PRODUCTS:

Greenhouses

Plans for an inexpensive 14 ft. x 14 ft. greenhouse. Company supplies fiberglass panels and greenhouse accessories but not the frame. The frame materials, wood, can be readily purchased at your local lumberyard. You can thus save on freight, pre-cutting, handling, etc. Fiberglass paneling used is called "Crystal-Clear". It is specifically designed for greenhouses — not for carports, patios, fencing, and the like. It is guaranteed for 20 years and gives 95% light transmission which is as much, or more, than glass.

Price list with plans for greenhouse $1.00, deducted from any order

JOHN W. GREGA
355 Grand Blvd.
Bedford, O. 44146

PRODUCTS:

Airplanes

Plans only for the Gn-I Aircamper, a modernized version of the 1933 Pietenpol Aircamper, 65 to 85 H. P., 2-place Parasol, all wood and fabric construction. Rib drawing and major fittings full size. Plans set $25.00.

Inboard profile and photos $1.00

THE GUITAR CENTER
P. O. Box 15444
Tulsa, Okla. 74115

PRODUCTS:

Banjos   Guitars   Mandolins

Company does not sell kits for making guitars, banjos or mandolins, but it does sell all the materials and supplies needed for making them, as well as books on how to make these instruments. Many of the books are step-by-step illustrated guides on construction. The books together with

THE GUITAR CENTER (Cont'd)

the materials and supplies will allow you to construct your own fine instruments.

15 page illustrated catalog 25¢

HALTEC CORP.
32123 Winona Rd.
Winona, Ohio 44493

PRODUCTS:

Spinning wheels

Authentic reproduction of early American spinning wheel. Not only a beautiful decorator item, but an actual working wheel that can be used for spinning either wool or flax. Kit easy to assemble without special tools.

Brochure free

HAMLIN TECHNICAL PRODUCTS
1720 Kimberly Dr.
Sunnyvale, Calif. 94087

PRODUCTS:

Oscilloscope, dual trace switches
Oscilloscope, triggersweeps

Partial kits for improving the performance of oscilloscopes. The triggersweep gets rid of oscilloscope sync problems, enables you to look at all wave forms instantly and to have the sweep accuracy of expensive lab scopes. The dual trace switch kit allows you to see two wave forms simultaneous-ly — observe their phase relationship and differences. Both are partial kits. Company supplies only the difficult ingre-dients. To build these kits requires at least an electronic

HAMLIN TECHNICAL PRODUCTS (Cont'd)

technician or amateur radio background. The triggersweep
kit is $19.95, the dual trace switch $10.00.

Literature free for qualified inquiries

HAMMOND BARNS
Box 39027
Indianapolis, Ind. 46239

PRODUCTS:

CHILDREN'S THINGS

          Playhouses

HOME CARE/IMPROVEMENT

    Barns   Garages   Sheds

HOUSING

        Vacation/leisure homes

PETS

    Animal barns   Horse barns
    Doghouses   Martin houses

Plans only for making authentically styled barns ranging in
size from martin houses to full size barns suitable for a va-
cation/leisure home. Barns can be used for a variety of
purposes as children's playhouses, tool or utility sheds,
garages, etc.

Literature free

HANK THE CRANK
7253 Lankershim Blvd.
North Hollywood, Calif. 91605

PRODUCTS:

        Hot rod hardware

Kits for racing components, competition tested. One of

the largest manufacturers of custom crankshaft assemblies. Has gained a reputation nationally through articles about products in major hot rod, drag, and racing magazines.

Illustrated catalog with specs and prices, $2.00

VICTOR HARASTY
22 Second Ave.
Port Jefferson, N. Y. 11777

PRODUCTS:

Cruisers
Houseboats
Kayaks

Rowboat type (rowboats, prams, dinghies, etc.)
Sailing, cruising
Sailing, day sailers

46 plans only for boats from 7 ft. to 46 ft., sail and power. Amateur oriented designs easy to build. Plans are exceptional for their clarity.

Portfolio of designs, includes free dinghy plans $3.00

HARMON/KARDON
55 Ames Court
Plainview, L. I., N. Y. 11803

PRODUCTS:

Stereo/hi-fi, amplifiers

The Citation Twelve is a 120-watt solid state stereophonic amplifier of professional quality in kit form. The company has this to say about its product, and we quote because it sheds interesting light on the problems inherent in designing kits vs. manufactured products: "The process

132

of designing a kit is far more difficult than producing a complete manufactured product. In the factory, the engineer can control his design from inception until the final packaging. The kit builder has only his tools, his ingenuity and little, if any, test equipment. Therefore, the complex process of in-plant production and control which guarantees the fine finished product must somehow be inherent in the kit design. Even a novice who has never built a kit can complete the Citation Twelve without experiencing difficulty. Keynote in the amplifier's design is its total lack of complexity". Retail price of kit is $225.00.

Illustrated brochure free

HEALD, INC.
P. O. Box 1148
Benton Harbor, Mich. 49022

PRODUCTS:

All terrain cycles (ATC's)	Trail bikes
Mini-bikes	Trailers, for trail bikes,
Mini-choppers	ATV's, snowmobiles

19 models of mini-bikes and trail bikes as kits with step-by-step instructions for assembling. Top quality components and extra heavy construction to allow for any kind of rugged off-road and all-weather use. Bikes have wide tires, automatic shifting torque sensing transmissions, heavy No. 40 motorcycle chain. Also offers a trailer kit for hauling trail bikes, ATV's, snowmobiles, etc. Kits range in price from $169.95 to $349.95. Also stocks a complete line of accessories for bikes.

Illustrated brochure and price lists free

HEATH COMPANY
Benton Harbor, Mich. 49022

PRODUCTS:

AUTOMOTIVE EQUIPMENT

Battery chargers, automotive
Cab-to-camper intercoms
Ignition analyzers

Tachometers
Timing lights
Tune-up meters

BOATING

Depth sounders
Foghorns/hailers

Fuel vapor de-
detectors

CHILDREN'S THINGS

Slotless racing

ELECTRONICS

Amplifiers, 4-channel
Amplifiers, ham
Amplifiers, mono
Audio generators
Battery chargers
Calculators, electronic
Capacitor testers
Capacitor substitution boxes
Code oscillators
CW rigs
Decade capacitance boxes
Decade resistance boxes
4-channel stereo adaptors
4-channel stereo amplifiers
8-track players/recorders
FM stereo generators
Frequency meters
Harmonic distortion meters
Impedance bridges
Intercoms
Intermodulation analyzers
Keyers, electronic
Line voltage monitors
Linear amplifiers
Multimeters
PA systems

Phonograph/radio combinations
Phonographs, stereo
Power suppliers, AC—DC
Power suppliers, regulated/
variable
Radios, aircraft monitors
Radios, AM
Radios, FM
Radios, portable
Radios, short wave
Radios, weather/police
Receivers, CB/SW
Receivers, ham
Remote controls/ switches
Resistance substitution boxes
RF signal generators
Signal, probes/tracers
Sine-square wave generators
Sirens
Spectrum analyzers,
electronic
Station consoles, ham
Stereo/hi-fi, amplifiers
Stereo/hi-fi, compact
systems
Stereo/hi-fi, receivers

134

HEATH CO. (cont'd)

ELECTRONICS (Cont'd)

Stereo/hi-fi, speakers
Stereo/hi-fi, tuners
Transceivers, CB/ham/
   single-banders
Transistor testers
Transmitters, ham
Transmitters, phone/CW

Tube testers
TV sets, black & white
TV sets, color
TV vecotor monitors
VOM's
VTVM's
Wattmeter/SWR bridges

EXPERIMENTAL/SCIENTIFIC

Chart recorders
Frequency counters

Oscilloscopes/vectorscopes
Treasure/metal locators

HOME CARE/IMPROVEMENT

Burglar/fire alarms, home
   or business
Garage door openers, electric

Garbage compactors
Microwave ovens

MUSICAL INSTRUMENTS

Amplifiers, guitar
Distortion boosters

Metronomes
Organs

OPTICS/PHOTOGRAPHY

Color computers

Timers, photo

SPORTING EQUIPMENT

Fish locators/spotters

VEHICLES

Mini-bikes

Trail bikes

World's largest manufacturer and supplier of electronic (and other) kits. Over 350 "HEATHKIT" kits, from amplifiers to vectorscopes, with plans and instructions. 90 day guarantee on parts, and service if you get into trouble, either through the factory or through the chain of Heathkit Electronic Centers throughout the U. S. Heathkit manuals which accompany kits may be purchased separately. Line of kits available from the company is constantly changing and expanding. Consult latest catalog.

80 page color illustrated catalog free

HELD PRODUCTS
9 Lakeview Drive
Farmington, Conn. 06032

PRODUCTS:

Bird houses   Clocks, wooden wheel   Lanterns

Kits with instructions for wooden wheel clocks based on
authentic 14th and 15th century models. Kits contain all
necessary materials, pre-machined parts and explicit assembly instructions. No special skills or tools are required.
Also offers a kit for a medieval lantern, a bird house, and
a model Dutch windmill.

Color illustrated catalog free

HERE, INC.
410 Cedar Ave.
Minneapolis, Minn. 55404

PRODUCTS:

MUSICAL INSTRUMENTS
Bancimers (dulcimer fretted   Psalteries
     banjos)   Thumb pianos (West
Banjos   African instruments)

Kits with instructions for building folk instruments. No
special tools or skills are required. Can save half the cost
by building your own. Also supplies books on building
and playing folk instruments. Special discounts for
schools.

Illustrated catalog free

HERTER'S, INC.
Waseca, Minn. 56093

PRODUCTS:

Arrows   Fishing lures/jigs/sinkers
Clocks, wooden wheel   Fishing rods

Flytying kits	Snowmobiles, conver-
Greenhouses	sion to ATV's
Pontoons	Taxidermy

The subtitle of Herter's catalog reads: The Authentic
World Source for Fishermen, Hunters, Guides, Gunsmiths,
Law Enforcement Officers, Tackle Makers, Forest Rangers,
Commercial Fishermen, Trappers, Explorers, Precious
Gems for Investors, Couturier Textiles and Yarns., and this
is no exaggerated claim. Encyclopedic catalog of thousands
of items, over 650 pages, defies comparison with any similar catalog. Founded in 1893, this is a sportsman's department store by mail.

650 page illustrated catalog $1.00, refundable on first order.
Seasonal catalog free.

HEXAGON HOUSING SYSTEMS, INC.
905 N. Flood St.
Norman, Okla. 73069

PRODUCTS:

Apartments/income producing	Vacation/leisure homes
units	Year round homes
Cabins/cottages	

Hexagonal shaped houses (made up of six equilateral tri-
angles for strength) as nearly as possible completely manufactured and pre-finished in the factory for construction
by the do-it-yourselfer without special tools or skills.
These units have been used for cabins, motels, schools,
offices. 15 designs from 700 sq. ft. to 5,200 sq. ft. The
designs are flexible and allow for options.

Information packet $1.00

E. HILLE – THE ANGLER'S SUPPLY HOUSE
815 Railway Street
P. O. Box 269
Williamsport, Pa. 17701

PRODUCTS:

Fishing lures/jigs/sinkers
Fishing rods

Flytying kits

A well-stocked supply house for all fishermen's needs.
Especially strong in rod making kits.

100 page illustrated catalog free

HOME BUILDING PLAN SERVICE
2235 N. E. Sandy Blvd.
Portland, Ore. 97232

PRODUCTS:

A-frames
Apartment/income producing
units

Cabins/cottages
Vacation/leisure homes
Year round homes

Plans only. Firm has been designing homes for 27 years.
These plans are offered in inexpensive magazine format,
$1.00 to $2.50. Hundreds of plans to select from. Also
sells books for the do-it-yourself homebuilder.

Literature list free

HOME PLANNERS, INC.
16310 Grand River Ave.
Detroit, Mich. 48227

PRODUCTS:

A-frames
Cabins/cottages
Chalets

Vacation/leisure homes
Year round homes

138

HOME PLANNERS, INC. (Cont'd)

Over 950 designs created by Richard B. Pollman. Plans are available in magazine format: "215 - 2 & 1½ story homes"; "160 - one-story homes" (all over 2,000 sq. ft.); "250 - one-story homes" (all under 2,000 sq. ft.); "165 multi-level homes" (split-levels, hillsides, bi-levels); "183 - vacation homes". These sell for $2.00 each, or all five for $6.95 (over 950 designs, 2,500 illustrations, many in color, 800 pages.) Blueprints for each design may be purchased. One of the larger sources of home plans.

Catalog: "84 Home Designs – For Traditional and Contemporary Tastes". $1.25

HOMECRAFT VENEER
P. O. Box 3
Latrobe, Pa. 15650

PRODUCTS:
Veneering/wood inlay

No kits as such but tools and supplies for veneering, laminating, and marquetry. Over 80 different wood veneers to choose from.

Catalog which includes veneering instructions, 25¢

HONEST CHARLEY, INC.
P. O. Box 8535
Chattanooga, Tenn. 37421

PRODUCTS:
Hot rod hardware

Company is not a kit company, but rather because it stocks and sells thousands of hot rod, racing, and automotive items

139

HONEST CHARLEY, INC. (Cont'd)

(150 different product lines), many items are in kit form. Company calls itself "The Racing World's Supermarket". One can order through the catalog or at the 18 stores company now has (and adding new ones all the time).

141 page illustrated catalog 50¢

HOOSIER MACHINE PRODUCTS CO.
314 S. E. Sixth St.
Pendleton, Ore. 97801

PRODUCTS:

Jeep/Scout, repowering

Kits and plans for power and transmission conversions for Jeeps and Scouts. Why repower? Despite the best of materials, sound engineering and quality craftsmanship in manufacture, Jeep and Kaiser engines lack the torque and ability to stand up to the needs of continuous heavy driving. Company also manufactures and sells transmission conversion kits, Chevy V/8 front motor mounts and rear axle conversion kits.

Illustrated catalog and price lists free

HOUSE OF CLERMONT
525 Skyview Drive
Nashville, Tenn. 37206

PRODUCTS:

Clocks, Decor

Kits for two wall clocks. Also clock parts.

Brochure 10¢

HOVERSPORT, INC.
313 Balsam St.
Palm Beach Gardens, Fla. 33403

PRODUCTS:

Hovercraft

Offers three models of kits or completed hovercraft. Most popular and advanced model is the HS–IB, the "Sting-Ray", a single place, all fiberglass saucer-shaped craft with over-all dimensions of 8 ft. by 2½ ft. The side panels of the craft are removable and thus the craft is transportable by car. Can be assembled in as little as six hours. Plans may be purchased separately. Also offers parts and accessories for hovercraft.

Information packet $2.00, refundable with next order.

HOWARD
P. O. Box 35271
Detroit, Mich. 48235

PRODUCTS:

Burglar alarms, automobile
Ignition, capacitive discharge
Tachometers

ELECTRONICS

Espionage/surveillance devices	Receivers, CB/SW
Intercoms	Sound telescopes
Jammers	Telephone amplifiers
Microphones, FM wireless	Telephone transmitters, wireless
Motor/speed controllers	Transistor checkers
Radios, aircraft monitor	Transmitters, FM wireless
Radios, FM	Voice operated relays/ switches
Radios, sun powered	

EXPERIMENTAL/SCIENTIFIC

ESP tests	Lie detectors
Geiger counters	Missile trackers
Hearing aids	Photoelectric relays
Lasers	Treasure/metal locators

HOME CARE/IMPROVEMENT
Burglar/fire alarms, home or business

MUSICAL INSTRUMENTS
Fuzz boxes

OPTICS/PHOTOGRAPHY
Color organs   Stroboscopes
Enlarger meters

SPORTING EQUIPMENT
Fish locators/spotters

Plans only for a collection of over 50 electronic and scientific projects. Construction plans are designed for low cost and easy assembly. The plans include parts lists, circuit diagrams and instructions. All components are available at most electronics parts stores. Projects are 'solid state' for trouble-free and reliable operation.

Catalog 25¢

H. P. K. MODELS
P. O. Box 34, Centuck Station
Yonkers, N. Y. 10710

PRODUCTS:

Engines, steam

Kits for unusual imported English steam engines in castings form. These engines are small but not models. They require metalworking tools to complete. Kits include drawings. Some engines just need assembling and are suitable for those without tools or metalworking experience.

28 page illustrated catalog $1.00

FRANK HUBBARD HARPSICHORDS, INC.
185-A Lyman St.
Waltham, Mass. 02154

PRODUCTS:

Harpsichords

Kits for 18th century harpsichords. No detail of the original which has any relation to the production of the tone or the feel of the action has been sacrificed. Two kit versions are available, one of which makes a single-manual and the other a double-manual harpsichord. Either version can be purchased in any of several stages of completion: (1) BASIC KIT; (2) BASIC KIT plus case parts; (3) BASIC KIT plus assembled case; (4) BASIC KIT plus assembled case and all parts. The BASIC KIT requires some woodworking competence, the more completed versions, of course, require less. The more parts completed by the company does increase the cost, but this system of choices allows the builder to determine how much time and effort he wishes to put into the project in relation to his skill.

Illustrated catalog and price lists free

HUCK FINN, INC.
8333 Sunset Rd. N. E.
Minneapolis, Minn. 55432

PRODUCTS:

Docks/piers	Pontoon boats
Houseboats	Rafts

Pontoon boat kits with full instructions from 17 ft. to 42 ft. Modular pontoon sections simply bolt together for easy construction. Pontoon boat kits are complete except for wood decking materials. These are standard items in any lumber store. Pontoons can also be used for rafts and piers.

Illustrated brochure free

HUGHES CO.
8665 West 13th Ave.
Denver, Col. 80215

PRODUCTS:

Balalaikas	Irish harps
Dulcimers	Lyres, ancient Greek
Guitars	Sitars
Hammered dulcimers	Thumb pianos (West African instruments)

Kits for making your own folk musical instruments, and save considerable money thereby. Thus a completed balalaika costing $37.00 (model B32M3) can be bought in kit form for $8.85, or a dulcimer completed (model M37M4) costing $29.95 can be bought in kit form for $11.95. Savings for other instruments and models are comparable. Instruments can be made by the amateur without special tools or skills. The assembly time varies from 4 to 5 hours for a small dulcimer to 40 or 50 hours for a guitar. Special school discounts for lots of 3 or more.

Illustrated catalog free

IECO
2314 Pico Blvd.
Santa Monica, Calif. 90405

PRODUCTS:

Dune buggies   Hot rod hardware

Quality chassis, engine, accessory specialties and parts for the high performance enthusiast: VW, Corvair, and dune buggy. Company is now working on a high performance program for Chevrolet's Vega.

34 page illustrated VW catalog and 26 page Corvair catalog $1.00 — refundable with first order.

IMAGINEERING ASSOCIATES, INC.
Box 3132
San Francisco, Calif. 94119

PRODUCTS:

4-wheel drive conversion to tracked vehicles

Kit with instructions for adding tracks to your 4-wheel drive
vehicle. The Caterpillar-type treads adapt to any 4-wheel
drive and are mounted on to regular wheel housings. The
tracks allow you to go over any kind of terrain whether it
be snow, sand or mud exactly like an all-terrain vehicle.
The conversion is simple, and you can replace the tracks
with wheels just as easily.

Illustrated brochure free

INDIAN RIDGE TRADERS
P. O. Box X-50
Ferndale, Mich. 48220

PRODUCTS:

Knives, hunting/Bowie

All necessary parts for making your own hunting, historic
and other knives. Company avoids complete kits because
they tend to lock the user into a single way of doing things
and there is no one best way to make a knife. They prefer
to offer parts and to give the maker individual advice on
his problems by mail.

12 page illustrated catalog with discussion of knife lore free

INFORMER ALARM SUPPLIES CO.
10 Cherry Hill Rd.
Baltimore, Md. 21225

PRODUCTS:

Burglar alarms, automobile
Burglar/fire alarms, home or business

INFORMER ALARM SUPPLIES CO. (Cont'd)

Kits for all types of burglar and fire alarms. The average home or commercial installation can be done in one short weekend, following the easy instructions provided, and with only the most basic tools. Since all professional alarm systems are battery operated with a very low current drain, there is no high voltage wiring necessary, and therefore no need for permits or danger of shocks or other hazards.

19 page illustrated catalog free

INNERSPACE ENVIRONMENTS, INC.
310 Sutter St.
San Francisco, Calif. 94108

PRODUCTS:

Waterbeds

Kits for making waterbeds. Come in two sizes: king (72 by 84 in.) and queen (60 by 80 in.), and sell for around $149.00. For information on local outlets write to company.

Brochure free

INTERNATIONAL AMATEUR BOAT BUILDING SOCIETY
3183 Merrill
Royal Oak, Mich. 48072

PRODUCTS:

Cruisers   Sailing, cruising

The Society offers plans. It does not have a catalog as such but shows the boats for which it has plans in the Society's official magazine, "Amateur Boat Building". The magazine

reports on designs, building methods, activities, plus boat
building news of interest to the amateur boat builder.
"Amateur Boat Building" is published bi-monthly and the
subscription costs $6.00 per year which includes the cost of
membership in the Society. If you are sold on the idea of
amateur boat building, this is the organization and the magazine to look into.

INTERNATIONAL CATAMARANS
P. O. Box 160
Highland, Mich. 48031

PRODUCTS:

Catamarans

The build-it-yourselfer can construct a 45 ft. catamaran for
one-quarter of what it costs to buy a factory-built one. Offers completed fiberglass hull, and plans for completing boat
using readily available marine plywood and other lumber.
45 ft. catamaran for cruising, racing, or houseboat.

Illustrated information packet $1.00

INTERNATIONAL HOMES OF CEDAR
P. O. Box 3074
Seattle, Wash. 98114

PRODUCTS:

Cabins/cottages	Vacation/leisure homes
Chalets	Year round homes

Packaged, precision pre-cut cedar homes. Your plan or
theirs, for any climate. Exterior designs vary from chalet to
ultra-modern and ranch style to colonial. Costs of package
vary depending on material and design. Costs are $6.90 per

square foot using roof trusses in the house or building with plasterboard ceilings throughout. With open beam ceilings using 2 in. T & G decking for ceiling, the costs are about 80¢ more per square foot. Laminated wood walls used provide excellent insulation against heat or cold. They are sounder and stronger than solid wood of the same size and grade.

Catalog with sample floor plans and price lists free

INTERNATIONAL MILL AND TIMBER CO.
Bay City, Mich. 48706

PRODUCTS:

Garages   Year round homes

Kits and plans for building your own year round home, under the brand name of "Sterling Homes". Over 50 designs to select from. These homes range for a basic shell from $4,068.00 to $8,160.00. Freight charges are prepaid to most stations east of the Mississippi River and north of the southern boundary line of Tennessee and North Carolina, excepting the states of Wisconsin, Illinois, Kentucky, and Tennessee. Complete set of plans are $30.00, placed to your credit if you later order a home. Garage kits with instructions, also.

43 page color illustrated catalog with floor plans 25¢

INTERNATIONAL VIOLIN CO.
414 East Baltimore St.
Baltimore, Md. 21202

PRODUCTS:

Cellos   Guitars   Violins

INTERNATIONAL VIOLIN CO. (Cont'd)

Kits with instructions for making quality stringed instruments. Also woods, tools, accessories for making or repairing violins, violas, cellos, basses, guitars.

Catalog free

JANCO GREENHOUSES
J. A. Nearing Co., Inc.
10788 Tucker St.
Beltsville, Md. 20705

PRODUCTS:

Greenhouses

Aluminum greenhouses with double-strength glass. Each part, including glass, is pre-cut to size, marked and identified to correspond with a set of blueprints for each particular model. Instructions detail each step for easy assembly. Three types of greenhouses are offered: (1) Free standing — an independently erected structure, set apart from other buildings; (2) Even-Span — basically like a free-standing model (with a center ridge line) but one gable end is eliminated and attached to your home; (3) Lean-To — can be fitted into a narrow space against your house or will fit into an "L" shaped corner. Models range in size from a 6 ft. by 11 ft. hobby lean-to to full commercial sizes. Prepaid delivery. Accessories for heating, cooling, ventilation, water control, etc.

39 page color illustrated catalog free

JAVELIN AIRCRAFT CO., INC.
9175 East Douglas
Wichita, Kan. 67207

PRODUCTS:

Airplanes, biplane

JAVELIN AIRCRAFT CO., INC. (Cont'd)

A side-by-side two-place biplane, the WICHAWK. It has structural geometry similar to the Stearman Biplane and some of its aerodynamic features. The airplane is smaller and quicker on the controls than store-bought airplanes, but not so touchy as to cause trouble for a new pilot. It is a strong airplane, about 20% stronger than a Stearman, 12 G's positive and 6 negative. Designed to meet all F. A. A. requirements, it could easily be a Certified airplane. The WICHAWK drawing file of 50 drawings sells for $125.00.

Information packet $3.00

JHS ENTERPRISES
Box 81
Point Clear, Ala. 36564

PRODUCTS:

Clocks, cuckoo

Hand-painted 10 in. cuckoo clock kit for $16.95. Easy to assemble and educational. Also sells completed cuckoo and other West German clocks.

Illustrated catalog 25¢ refundable with first order.

J. P. F.
1844 Woodlawn, N. W.
Canton, Ohio 44708

PRODUCTS:

Elevators, home

Plans only for a home elevator which the do-it-yourself-er, with some basic knowledge of the use of tools and

with the ability to read prints, can build. The cost of
having someone else construct your home elevator is high.
Save up to 70% by doing it yourself. Instructions and
blueprints $5.00.

No catalog, only blueprints

JURCA PLANS
581 Helen St.
Mt. Morris, Mich. 48458

PRODUCTS:

      Airplanes   Airplanes, antique

Plans only for replica fighters: MJ2 Tempete; MJ5 Sirocco; MJ6 Twin; MJ7 2/3 P 51; MJ77 3/4 P 51; MJ8 FW190
3/4; MJ 3/4 ME109; MJ10 3/4 Spit; MJ 12 3/4 P 40.
Only the MJ 2–5–7 are presently flying – others soon.
These are replica fighters and must be respected in this
manner and flown as designed. All aircraft except Twin
are stressed for aerobatics.

Document sheets for each design $2.00

K/N CHEMICAL & SUPPLY CO.
P. O. Box 748
San Bernardino, Calif. 92402

PRODUCTS:

      Metal assayers   Science fair projects

Offers a field laboratory kit for testing the presence of gold,
silver, mercury, lead, or platinum. Also carries a full line of
laboratory ware and chemicals for the experimenter or the
scientist.

28 page illustrated catalog 50¢, refundable with first order

K & P MFG.
330 South Irwindale Ave.
Azusa, Calif. 91702

PRODUCTS:

Dune buggies Karts Mini-bikes

Oldest and largest kart manufacturer in the United States.
Also builds a line of dune bugs and mini-bikes. Kit or completed. Plans are available on the "HumBug" kart, the
"DuneBug", and the "Flea" mini-bike. Parts, accessories,
related items.

Information packet with plans and price lists $1.00

K & S AIRCRAFT SUPPLY
4623 Fortune Rd. S. E.
Calgary, 23, Alberta
Western Canada

PRODUCTS:

Airplanes Airplanes, biplane

Plans, parts, components for two airplanes: the CAVALIER
and the JUNGSTER. The JUNGSTER 1 is a small, all-wood
construction biplane, aimed primarily for aerobatics and general sport flying. The JUNGSTER 1 closely resembles the
8/10 scale Bucker Jungmeister. The JUNGSTER 11 airplane
is an outgrowth of the earlier JUNGSTER 1 biplane. It was
designed to retain the pleasure of flying an open cockpit
sports airplane and yet provide more speed for cross-country
flying. The airplane is stressed for aerobatics and performs
aerobatic maneuvers well. The SA102 – 102 POINT 5 CAV-
ALIER: is an all-wood two-place side-by-side aircraft offering simple, economical, appealing lines and high performance
with a variety of optional engines for more power.

Information packet for either plane $3.00 each, general cata-
log $1.00

KEL MANUFACTURING
2131 South Dupont Drive
Anaheim, Calif. 92806

PRODUCTS:

Trikes

Trike kit powered by VW engine. No welding, just bolts on
to your VW or Porsche engine and transaxle. Body is hand-
laid fiberglass and comes complete with upholstered seat.
The body comes in standard Yellow. Trike is safe because
it is visible in traffic. One of the major causes of accidents
is auto drivers do not see or recognize oncoming motorcycles. From front, side and rear the trike is a machine that
commands respect. Safe also by design, as the rider is pro-
tected from rear end, side and head-on collision by engine,
wheels and front end. Complete kit, $795.

Illustrated catalog free

HAL KELLY'S TESTED PLANS
P. O. Box 1767
Fort Pierce, Fla. 33450

PRODUCTS:

Hydroplanes   Runabouts

Plans only for hydroplanes and runabouts. 9 models to select from. Plans with full-size rib drawings from $5.00 to
$12.00. Each plan includes photographs of the boat being
built and in action. The drawings are simple and all com-
plicated naval architect terms are omitted. These boats
have won over 500 trophies in the U. S. A. and abroad.

15 page illustrated catalog 35¢, stamps or coins

LANDIS G. KETNER
P. O. Box 762
Vero Beach, Fla. 32960

PRODUCTS:

Airplanes

Plans only for a Formula One class racer sportplane, the
"Shoestring". The original aircraft has won first place in
the National Championship Formula 1 races, Reno, Nevada,
for the last five years. The wings are of wood construction,
built as one unit, and fabric covered. The fuselage frame
is welded tubular steel structure. Span 19 ft., length 17.65
ft., height 56 in., wing area 66 sq. ft., empty weight 525 lbs.

Information packet $3.00

KING RESEARCH LABS, INC.
801 S. 11th Ave.
Maywood, Ill. 60153

PRODUCTS:

Burglar alarms, automobile
Burglar/fire alarms, home or business

Kits with instructions for newly developed burglar alarms
featuring the use of sensitive transducers. These transducers (in place of unsightly tapes) pick up unusual sounds
and thus give early warning of unwanted intruders.

Information packet $1.00

KITTRIDGE BOW HUT
P. O. Box 598
Mammoth Lakes, Calif. 93546

PRODUCTS:

Arrows   Bows

154

KITTRIDGE BOW HUT (Cont'd)

Bow and arrow kits, and a supermarket for archery tackle
of all types. Company in addition offers camping and
hunting equipment, tools for making and repairing archery
tackle, books on hunting and archery. Catalog is called
"Archer's Bible", and contains excellent articles on how to
select your bow, how to select arrows, hunting with bow
and arrow, etc.

192 page illustrated catalog and "Archier's Bible" 25¢

H. J. KNAPP CO.
3174 8th Avenue S. W.
Largo, Florida 33540

PRODUCTS:

Amplifiers, guitar	Telephone transmitters, wireless
Code oscillators	Transmitters, FM wireless
Microphones, FM wireless	Vibrato generators

Offers modules which in conjunction with equipment you
already have at hand make for interesting and useful electronic projects. Primary advantage is cheapness. For $2.95
you can build a wireless code oscillator which allows you to
broadcast into any AM radio. You only need a telegraph
key, a 9-volt battery, and of course an AM radio. Also for
$2.95, you can have a module which will allow you to
broadcast directly without wires into your AM radio. All
you need is a one-megohm potentiometer, a nine-volt transistor battery, a few feet of any kind of wire as an antenna,
and of course a phonograph and an AM radio. Company
stocks electronic parts for these and other projects.

20 page illustrated catalog free

THE LACEY M–10 CO.
Box 7165
Burbank, Calif. 91505

PRODUCTS:

Airplanes

Plans only for the M–10, a two-place airplane small enough to be towed behind a car and stored in a 24-foot garage. Plans, 8 sheets 18 x 24 in. blue lines on white paper, $8.00 postpaid.

Illustrated brochure 10¢

LAFAYETTE RADIO ELECTRONICS
111 Jericho Turnpike
Syosset, L. I., N. Y. 11791

PRODUCTS:

AUTOMOTIVE EQUIPMENT

Burglar alarms, automobile
Engine analyzers

ELECTRONICS

Appliance testers
Audio generators
Battery testers
Bird call imitators
Broadcasters, neighborhood
Capacitor substitution boxes
Capacitor testers
Circuit testers
Code oscillators
Color bar generators
CRT testers
4-channel stereo adapters
Grid-dip meters
Intercoms
Microphones, FM wireless
Motor/speed controllers
Power suppliers AC–DC

Power suppliers, regulated/
 variable
Radios, AM
R–C substitution boxes
Receivers, CB/SW
Resistance substitution boxes
RF signal generators
Semiconductor curve tracers
Signal generators
Signal probes/tracers
Sine/square wave signal
 generators
Stereo/hi-fi, amplifiers
Stereo/hi-fi, preamplifiers
Stereo/hi-fi, receivers
Stereo/hi-fi, tuners
Transformers/yoke testers

LAFAYETTE RADIO ELECTRONICS (cont'd)

ELECTRONICS (Cont'd)
- Transistor testers
- Tube testers
- VOM's
- VTVM's

EXPERIMENTAL/SCIENTIFIC
- Computers
- Fiber optics
- Oscilloscopes/ vectorscopes
- Science fair projects
- Treasure/metal locators
- Voice operated relays/ switches

FURNITURE
- Music centers
- Speaker enclosures

HOME CARE/IMPROVEMENT
- Burglar/fire alarms, home or business

MUSICAL INSTRUMENTS
- Bongos, electronic

EQUIPMENT
- Fuzz boxes

OPTICS/PHOTOGRAPHY
- Black light
- Color organs
- Light psychedelic shows
- Stroboscopes

Kits for electronics projects. Also electronic parts, tools, books. Consumer electronic products of a wide variety such as stereo equipment, radios, tape recorders, ham equipment, and so on. May order through the company's 53 stores across the U. S. or by mail through the catalog.

135 page illustrated catalog free

LANCER ENGINEERING
P. O. Box 544
Pekin, Ill. 61554

PRODUCTS:

Engines, gasoline   Engines, steam

Build your own small gas or steam engines from .25 HP to 3 HP. A wide selection is available including 9 gas and 3

LANCER ENGINEERING (Cont'd)

steam engine designs. Single to eight cylinders, air cooled and water cooled, in both 4 and 2 cycle designs. The basic engine kits are not ready to assemble or ready to run but are casting kits which must be finished on a home-shop lathe. Plans may be purchased separately.

50 page illustrated catalog $1.25

LAND–GRABBER, INC.
P. O. Box 346
Windom, Minn. 56101

PRODUCTS:

Snowmobiles, conversion to wheeled vehicles

Offers a kit to convert a snowmobile to a year-round wheeled vehicle. Unit fits any snowmobile and is completely adjustable. Easily installed. Speeds of up to 70 miles an hour on an 18 H. P. engine may be obtained. Choice of wheel sizes.

Brochure free

LARAND ENTERPRISES
P. O. Box 34
Harbor City, Calif. 90710

PRODUCTS:

Water skis

Each ski is individually hand crafted to suit the requirements of each customer. All models are pressure laminated from 7 to 15 pieces of select ash using waterproof, epoxy type glue. Bindings are made from 3/16 in. thick, black neoprene rubber. All skis may be purchased in kit form. Kits are completely shaped blanks. All required materials are included. Also custom water skis and complete line of water ski accessories.

Illustrated brochure free

J. W. LAWSON, JR., NAVAL ARCHITECT
13205 Ovalstone Lane
Bowie, Md. 20715

PRODUCTS:

Houseboats	Sailing, cruising
Runabouts	Sailing, day sailers

Plans for day sailers, overnight cruising sloops, sport runabouts, express runabouts, cruising yawls, houseboats, motor yachts. Boats range from 17 to 64 ft. in length. Plans are available "as is" or with professional consultation at extra cost. Plans from $30 to $250, with consultation service from $80 to $450.

29 page illustrated catalog, including valuable information on "Steps to Boat Ownership", $2.00

LEE MUSIC MFG. CO.
525 Venezia Ave.
Venice, Calif. 90291

PRODUCTS:

Player piano electrifiers
Reed organ electrifiers

Kits for electrifying player pianos and reed organs so that playing is effortless. These electric silent suction units work at the flick of a switch and can be installed in 15 minutes. Especially good for the elderly or handicapped.

LEE MUSIC MFG. CO.   (Cont'd)

While company does not stock parts for player pianos or reed organs, it does offer a free list on request of sources for parts and supplies.

Brochure free

LEES CYCLE–CITY LTD.
746 S. W. Marine Dr.
Vancouver 14, B. C. Canada

PRODUCTS:

Karts   Mini-bikes   Mini-choppers

Complete kits and plans. Plans may be purchased separately. Plans for mini-bike and kart $1.00 each; plans for mini-chopper $1.50. Kits have thick wall tubing frames, internal brakes, 420 drive chain, clutch, fenders — as standard features.

Catalog 50¢

LEHMAN MFG. CO., INC.
800 E. Elizabeth Ave.
Linden, N. J. 07036

PRODUCTS:

Marine engine conversions

ECON-O-POWER is the trade name for marine engine conversion equipment manufactured by Lehman Mfg. Co., Inc. This equipment can be purchased through boatyards and marine supply houses or directly from the company. A full line of marine engine conversion kits with full instructions, gasoline and diesel. All engine transmission parts as well as

LEHMAN MFG. CO., INC. (Cont'd)

accessories are available. Oldest company in field, since 1932.

66 page illustrated catalog with complete technical data and a how-to guide 50¢

LIFELITE, INC.
1025 Shary Circle
Concord, Calif. 94520

PRODUCTS:

Greenhouses

Attractive small, wood greenhouses. Two plans: Plan "A", complete except for shelving and is "ready-to-erect"; Plan "B", offered to those who have a moderately equipped home workshop and enjoy working with wood. Following plans and directions, will give the same results as Plan "A" with considerable saving in cost. Plan "A" sells for $487.00, plan "B" $369.00. Greenhouse is hexagonal shaped, wood with metal fasteners, fiberglass panels. Also cooling, heating, benches and other accessories for the greenhouse.

Literature free

LINDAL CEDAR HOMES
10411 Empire Way S.
Seattle, Wash. 98178

PRODUCTS:

A-frames	Vacation/leisure homes
Cabins	Year round homes

Kits and plans for more than 70 designs of kiln dried Canadian cedar. Homes for beach or mountain or year round use. Cedar resists decay and insect or vermin attack, is an

161

LINDAL CEDAR HOMES (Cont'd)

excellent insulator, and it blends perfectly with any environment. All parts are pre-cut and numbered, making assembly quick and easy. Company tailors shipping costs to meet competition anywhere. Plans package consists of complete construction plans, fully illustrated erection manual, and number-coded parts list. Plans package is $35.00, with price applicable to purchase price. Cedar buildings may also be used for churches and clubhouses.

36 page full-color plan book $1.00

LITTLE JIM DANDY GARBAGE DIVERTER
9 Brighton Ave.
Box 447
Bolinas, Calif. 94924

PRODUCTS:

Garbage diverters

Plans only. It diverts ground-up vegetable matter from one's kitchen sink to the garden for easy composting. Ecology begins at home. Plans $1.00

No catalog

E. LITTNER
P. O. Box 272
St. Laurent
Montreal 379 (Quebec) Canada

PRODUCTS:

Airplanes

Plans and kits for the "Zenith", a two seater, all metal plane, designed by C. Heintz. Plans only for designs by Claude Piel: "Cougar" — a single seater, racing airplane,

all wood construction ($75 for plans); "Diamant" —3—4
seater, all wood airplane ($100, plans); "Tourbillon" —
single seater, fully aerobatic airplane, all wood construction ($60, plans); "Beryl" — fully aerobatic tandem
seater ($80, plans); "Super-Emeraude" — side by side
2-seater, all wood construction ($60, plans); "Edelweiss"
— side by side 2-seater equipped with a retractable tricycle landing gear, aluminum alloy of the semi-monocoque
structure ($125, plans.)

Information package for each plane $2.00

BOB LONG KENNEL RUNS
Route 3 North
Gambrills, Md. 21504

PRODUCTS:

Kennels/runs

Wide range of kennel runs. Modular design allows freedom
to meet individual requirements. Free standing, no concrete footings required. Portable. Takes 15 minutes to
set up or take down.

Illustrated 16 page catalog free

LORD & BURNHAM
2 Main St.
Irvington, N. Y. 10533

PRODUCTS:

Greenhouses

Aluminum greenhouses in many sizes, widths, styles. Prepaid delivery. Two major lines: the ORLYT and the
SUNLYT, in free-standing, attached, or lean-to models.

LORD & BURNHAM (Cont'd)

Also, SOLAR 500, the least expensive and easiest to assemble. All you do is open the numbered cartons, connect the factory-assembled, factory glazed panels together. One size nut and bolt is used throughout, so a screwdriver and wrench are the only tools needed. On-site installation is less than a day's work for a couple of good do-it-yourselfers. Also a full line of heating, cooling and other greenhouse accessories. Free, informative booklets available, examples: "Typical Wiring/Plumbing Layouts", "Potting Shed Plans", "Your New Greenhouse", etc.

31 page color illustrated catalog free

NILS LUCANDER
P. O. Box 3184
Brownsville, Texas 78520

PRODUCTS:

Cruisers	Sailing, cruising
Houseboats	Sailing, day sailers
Inboards	

Plans only for a collection of some 40 designs, from 15 ft. to over 65 ft. Plywood, ferro-cement, fiberglass, steel, aluminum. Study plans are available.

1973 illustrated catalog $3.00

LUGER BOAT KITS
Luger Industries, Inc.
3800 West Highway 13
Burnsville, Minn. 55378

PRODUCTS:

Cruisers	Inboards
Houseboats	Marine engine conversions

164

LUGER BOAT KITS (Cont'd)

Outboards   Sailing, day sailers
Runabouts   Trailers, boat
Sailing, cruising

Fiberglass boat kits from 14 ft. to 32 ft. Save at least half
by building your own boat. Step-by-step instructions have
been carefully planned to make the job of completion easy
for those with no experience. All parts are pre-finished,
and everything needed down to the smallest screw is provided, so that all you do is assemble. Boats have been
thoroughly pre-tested and thousands are in use. Economy
kits are also available. These kits are less costly than the
standard kits because some deluxe features of the standard
kits have been redesigned or eliminated. Bare hull kits are
also available. Carries boat accessories, boat trailers, marine
engines, marine conversion kits, etc.

80 page color illustrated catalog free

LUGER CAMPER KITS
Luger Industries, Inc.
3800 West Highway 13
Burnsville, Minn. 55378

PRODUCTS:

Campers   Tent campers
Pickup covers   Trailers

Kits with easy-to-follow instructions for making your own
campers, pickup covers, trailers, or tent campers and save
up to 50% over the cost of factory finished products. All
parts have been pre-finished and everything is included.
Construction is only a matter of assembly. The products
have been thoroughly pre-tested under all kinds of operating conditions. Although the kits are complete, modifications according to personal tastes can be made.

28 page color illustrated catalog free

LURE–CRAFT MFG. CO.
3422 Valleyview Dr.
Bloomington, Ind. 47401

PRODUCTS:

Fishing lures/jigs/sinkers
Fishing, plastic worms

Kits for making plastic worms. Fishermen can make their
own plastic worms for profit or for their own personal use
at a fraction of the price they would pay retail. Company
makes and stocks over 200 different molds and plastic
supplies. Also carries fishing lures, hooks, fishing necessi-
ties.

28 page illustrated catalog with instructions on plastic
worm-making   free

MASON & SULLIVAN
39 Blossom Ave.
Osterville, Mass. 02655

PRODUCTS:

Clocks, Decor	Clocks, School
Clocks, Grandfather	Clocks, Weather instruments
Clocks, Grandmother	(thermometer, barometers,
Clocks, Period	etc.)

Complete kits with plans for 16 clocks, weight-powered,
battery-powered and electric. Mouldings are furnished
about an inch longer than you actually require. Does not
pre-cut parts to exact size because all lumber, even when
thoroughly cured, has a tendency to expand and contract
slightly with changes in humidity. You get a perfect fit
by mitering the parts yourself according to the dimensions
given in the plans. Plans and blueprints may be purchased
separately. Also offers parts, cases, movements, chimes.

23 page illustrated catalog 25¢

MASTERCRAFT PLANS
7041 N. Olcott Ave.
Chicago, Ill. 60631

PRODUCTS:

LAWN & GARDEN
Christmas decorations	Swings, lawn
Lawn/patio furniture	Toys
Markers/signs/figures	Wheelbarrow planters
Sheds	Windmills, garden

PETS
Bird houses   Martin houses

WOODWORKING
Jigsaw patterns

Full size patterns only. Craft projects come in packets by subject, $1.50 per packet. No individual patterns. Projects suited for individual home craftsman, elementary shop students, Boy Scout groups.

Literature, stamped self-addressed envelope

J. T. McCARTHY CO.
P. O. Box 7012
Milwaukee, Wis. 53213

PRODUCTS:

Water filters/purifiers/softeners

Save on the high cost of labor and increasing freight rates on water softeners and filters by assembling them yourself. Nearly 50% savings can be achieved.

Catalog $2.00 refundable on first order.

McGEE RADIO CO.
1901–07 McGee St.
Kansas City, Mo. 64108

PRODUCTS:

AUTOMOTIVE EQUIPMENT
Burglar alarms, automobile
Ignition, capacitive discharge

ELECTRONICS

Battery chargers

Capacitor testers

Circuit testers

Color bar generators

Radios, AM

RC bridges

RF signal generators

Semiconductor curve tracers

Signal/probes/tracers

Sine square wave generators

Stereo/hi-fi, amplifiers

Stereo/hi-fi, preamplifiers

Stereo/hi-fi, receivers

Stereo/hi-fi, speaker systems

Stereo/hi-fi, tuners

Sweep/marker generators

Transistor testers

Tube testers

TVM's

TVOM's

VTVOM's

VOM's

EXPERIMENTAL/SCIENTIFIC

Oscilloscopes/vectorscopes   Treasure/metal locators

HOME CARE/IMPROVEMENT
Burglar/fire alarms, home or business

Offers electronic kits manufactured by leading companies
such as Eico and Dynaco. Also carries electronic parts,
tools, TV's, stereo equipment, radios for auto and home,
surplus parts, and an especially broad range of speakers and
speaker parts.

176 page illustrated catalog free

R. H. McCRORY
P. O. Box 13
Bellmore, N. Y. 11710

PRODUCTS:

Pistols, antique   Rifles, antique

R. H. McCRORY (Cont'd)

Plans, books and manuals on how to construct muzzle loading pistols and rifles. Company is devoted solely to muzzle loading do-it-yourself publications.

Brochure free

MECHANIX ILLUSTRATED
Plans Service
Fawcett Building
Greenwich, Conn. 06830

PRODUCTS:

BOATS

Canoes	Outboards
Catamarans	Rowboat type boats (rowboats,
Cruisers	prams, dinghies, etc.)
Houseboats	Sailing, cruising
Hydroplanes	Sailing, day sailers
Kayaks	Steamboats

FURNITURE

Colonial style furniture	Desks
Commodes	Desks, rolltop

HOME CARE/HOME IMPROVEMENT

Garages	Workshop centers

HOUSING

Cabins/cottages	Vacation/leisure homes

LAWN & GARDEN

Greenhouses

METALWORKING PROJECTS

Engines, gasoline

OPTICS/PHOTOGRAPHY

Contact printers	Telescope mounts
Enlargers	Telescopes, reflectors
Slide printers	

SPORTING EQUIPMENT

Pool tables	Saunas	Surf boards, sailing

MECHANIX ILLUSTRATED (Cont'd)

VEHICLES

All terrain vehicles (ATV's)	Campers
Automobiles, antique	Pickup covers
Automobiles, midget (motorized)	Trailers

WOODWORKING

Workbenches

117 plans. Wide range including boats, models, telescopes, photo equipment, workbenches, general projects, furniture, auto projects, etc. Plans only.

44 page illustrated catalog includes a wealth of information on basic shop facts $1.00

GEORGE E. MEESE
194 Acton Rd.
Annapolis, Md. 21403

PRODUCTS:

Cruisers	Rowboat type (rowboats, prams,
Houseboats	dinghies)
Hydroplanes	Sailing, cruising
Inboards	Sailing, day sailers
Outboards	Workboats, commercial boats

Plans only for 30 boats ranging from a 7 ft. 6 in. pram dinghy to a 34 ft. cruiser, designed for the amateur builder. Plans range in price from $6.50 to $60.00. Plans for tugs, barges, fishing vessels and other commercial boats also available. Building plans are large scale drawings prepared by naval architects and marine engineers.

31 page illustrated catalog of boat designs $1.00

METALMAST MARINE, INC.
55 Providence St.
Putnam, Conn. 06260

PRODUCTS:

Sailing, cruising   Sails/sail gear

Company has two divisions — (1) The spar shop, (2) the boat shop. Both divisions offer kits. The spar shop carries masts, booms, rigging for all size boats, 22 — 50 ft. Supplies aluminum extrusions (either anodized or mill finish) or complete masts or components for you to assemble. The boat shop offers cruising sailboats designed by Bill Tripp.

Illustrated catalog free

METROLOGIC INSTRUMENTS, INC.
143 Harding Ave.
Bellmawr, N. J. 08030

PRODUCTS:

Lasers

A leading, reputable manufacturer of well designed and engineered laser equipment. Offers five laser kits ranging in price from $83.00 to $122.00. Products meet and exceed all government specifications and standards. Also supplies parts and accessories for laser.

Illustrated catalog free

MEYER AIRCRAFT
5706 Abby Drive
Corpus Christie, Texas 78413

PRODUCTS:

Airplanes, biplane

MEYER AIRCRAFT (Cont'd)

The Meyer "Little Toot" is a single seat sport biplane. Fully aerobatic. Aircraft stressed for 10 G's plus. 180 to 200 H. P. recommended for aerobatics. Plans only. Costs of plans $75.00.

Information packet $2.00

MICHIGAN WATER SPECIALTIES, INC.
P. O. Box 397
Union Lake, Mich. 48085

PRODUCTS:

Saucers, underwater

Underwater saucer is towed behind a surface power vehicle or large sailboat and wearing only a face mask or full scuba gear, you effortlessly maneuver down and up, back and forth. The angle of the plane as you move through the water determines the speed of ascent and descent. You control this angle. Kit and instructions, $15.95 – $17.95.

Literature free

MICROM CO.
P. O. Box 2313
Santa Ana, Calif. 92707

PRODUCTS:

Milling machines

Build your own horizontal milling machine. Castings, parts. Castings can be bought either in rough or semi-finished form. Blueprints are $2.50, detailed machining instructions $3.00. Also sells completed machine.

Brochure free

172

MICRO–Z ELECTRONICS SYSTEMS
Box 2426
Rolling Hills, Calif. 90274

PRODUCTS:

Frequency meters, digital

Digital meter kits for CB, service shop, hams. AM or SSB transmitters to 35 MHz. 100 H-z readout with NIXIE tubes. Fully guaranteed for one year. All parts, including printed circuit board and detailed instructions. Kit sells for $134.50, assembled $164.50.

Brochure free

MIDLAND TACKLE CO.
66 Route 17
Sloatsburg, N. Y. 10974

PRODUCTS:

Fishing lures/jigs/sinkers   Fishing rods

Materials and equipment for molding sinkers and jigs, lure parts, rod building, etc. A fisherman's store by mail. Both salt and fresh water fishing tackle.

44 page illustrated catalog free

MILLER HAVENS ENTERPRISES
2944 Randolph Ave.
Costa Mesa, Calif. 92626

PRODUCTS:

Baja Bugs/buses

With the Baja Bug kit you can convert your family VW

beetle or VW bus into an off-road runabout or dune buggy.
Complete kits with parts, accessories and instructions.

31 page illustrated catalog and informational booklet 25¢

MILLS CABIN MILLS, INC.
M-75, P. O. Box 156
Boyne City, Mich. 49712

PRODUCTS:

A-frames	Chalets
Cabins, log	Vacation/leisure homes

Pre-cut parts for vacation homes for easy erection. Over
20 designs to choose from, or you supply your own custom
design.

Illustrated catalog and information packet $1.00

MINNESOTA WOODWORKERS SUPPLY CO.
925 Winnetka Ave. North
Minneapolis, Minn. 55427

PRODUCTS:

BOATS
Rowboat-type boats (rowboats, prams, dinghies, etc.)

CHILDREN'S THINGS

Cribs	Toy chests
Doll furniture	Toys
Doll houses	Toys, educational (tell
Kites	time, add, etc.)
Merry-go-rounds	Toys, musical (using Swiss
Mobiles	musical movements)

CLOCKS

Decor	Period
Grandfather	Wooden wheel

MINNESOTA WOODWORKERS SUPPLY CO.
(cont'd)

FURNITURE
- Bars
- Cabinets, collectors/curio
- Cabinets, fishing gear
- Cabinets, gun/rifle
- Cabinets, sewing
- Chairs
- Cobblers benches
- Desks
- Lamps
- Racks, fishing gear
- Racks, gun/rifle
- Racks, magazine
- Shadow boxes
- Tables, card
- Tables, cocktail
- Whatnot shelves

HOME CARE/IMPROVEMENT
- Garages
- Weathervanes

LAWN & GARDEN
- Christmas decorations
- Lawn/patio furniture
- Markers/signs/figures
- Sundials

MUSICAL INSTRUMENTS
- Violins

PETS
- Bird houses/feeders

SPORTING EQUIPMENT
- Duck decoys

VEHICLES
- Automobiles, Midget (motorized)

WOODWORKING
- Alphabet patterns
- Jigsaw patterns
- Looms
- Spinning wheels
- Veneering/wood inlay

Complete woodworkers catalog. Dozens of plans, most full-size. Company also offers furniture hardware (many hard-to-get items), veneers, moldings, tools, upholstery supplies, lamp parts, etc. Some kits, mostly plans for the hobbyist, craftsman, school, shop.

92 page illustrated catalog 50¢

MODULAR CONCEPTS, INC.
P. O. Box 70
100 Ontario St.
East Rochester, N. Y. 14445

PRODUCTS:

A-frames
Apartments/income-producing
   units

Cabins/cottages
Chalets
Vacation/leisure homes

Instead of constructing buildings piece by piece, whole wall
sections, interior partitions, and even roof sections are modu-
larized. It is easier and quicker to assemble such a structure
from large modules than to have to measure, mark, cut, raise
in position, nail and hammer piece by piece, hour after hour.
In most cases a modular home can be put up in 48 hours.
Pre-engineering insures uniformity and reliability. Kits with
plans for simple assembly. 35 models to choose from, 480
sq. ft. to 1,872 sq. ft., prices from $4,656 to $19,819.
Many options. Also custom designs for homes and businesses.

Portfolio of designs and a "Home Planning Kit", $2.00

MONG SPORT
1128 Irwin Drive
Hurst, Tex. 76053

PRODUCTS:

Airplanes, biplane

Plans only for a small biplane: span 16 ft. 10 in., length
14 ft. 1 in., wing area 80 sq. ft., empty weight 550 lbs.
Single lift strut rather than flying wires. Fuselage and tail
group, welded steel tubing. Wings, spruce spars and plywood ribs, all fabric covered. Cost of construction —
$1,000 to $2,000 depending on engines used and other
salvage items. Plans set $39.00.

Information packet $1.00

176

EDWIN MONK & SON
610 National Bldg.
Seattle, Wash. 98104

PRODUCTS:

Cruisers

Stern wheelers

Sailing, cruising

Workboats/commercial

Sailing, day sailers

boats

Over 150 designs, plans only, for pleasure and workboats.
Stock plans, and also patterns or templates are carried for
about 20 of the designs selected as suitable for the amateur
boat builder. These patterns or templates are made by E. H.
Thorsen & Son, a reliable firm experienced in boat building
and patterns. They are on heavy paper and are accompanied
by a set of instructions as to their use. The purchase of a
plan entitles one to free consultation on problems of construction right up to completion of the boat.

75 page illustrated portfolio of designs and catalog $3.00

MONNET EXPERIMENTAL AIRCRAFT
410 Adams
Elgin, Ill. 60120

PRODUCTS:

Airplanes

Partial kits, components, and plans for the "Sonerai". The
"Sonerai" is a mid-wing, sport plane, racer designed to meet
all Professional Race Pilots Association requirements for
Formula Vee Racing. It uses a 1600 cc VW engine. The
wing is all aluminum and is composed of two panels that
fold along the side of the fuselage enabling the plane to be
towed tail first on its own gear.

Literature free

MONTESSA MOTORS, INC.
3657 Beverly Blvd.
Los Angeles, Calif. 90004

PRODUCTS:

    Engines, gasoline   Engines, motorcycle

A kit with instructions for assembling a two-stroke 50cc
motorcycle engine. Price of kit is $125.00. Can be used
for a wide variety of recreational uses such as go-karts,
small boats, powering tools, etc. Easy to assemble and
comes with carrying case. Also useful for schools and mechanical classes featuring two-stroke engines. Imported
from Spain.

Brochure free

MOONEY MITE AIRCRAFT
Box 3999 Dept. XM
Charlottesville, Va. 22903

PRODUCTS:

    Airplanes

The Mooney Mite is the only production aircraft offered to
the homebuilder. The M—18 has set world distance and
speed records in Class 1a. First flown in 1948, still ahead of
its time. Retractable gear, flaps, steerable nose wheel, tricycle landing gear. You can build its experimental counter-
part the M—18X for less than $1,800. Kits and plans. Plans
sell for $35.00 (272 drawings).

Information packet $1.00

MOULD–N–MOUNT, INC.
Suite 200
First National Office Bldg.
Brownswood, Texas 76801

PRODUCTS:

Taxidermy

Utilizes a chemical dehydration process developed by Don
Jackson, a biologist at Howard Payne College. Insides of
animals do not have to be removed. Animal itself becomes
the final form. Simple, direct process works equally on
animals, fish, reptiles, birds, deer heads.

Brochure free

MOUNTAIN WEST ALARM SUPPLY CO.
4215 North 16th St.
Phoenix, Ariz. 85016

PRODUCTS:

Burglar/fire alarms, home or business

Over 350 items from more than 60 manufacturers and suppliers. A single source for every type of burglar/fire alarm
for home or business. Kits with instructions. Complete
systems, components, tools, books on security, etc. Many
hard-to-find items for the do-it-yourselfer as well as the
professional.

64 page illustrated catalog free

NATIONAL GREENHOUSE CO.
P. O. Box 100
Pana, Ill. 62557

PRODUCTS:

Greenhouses

NATIONAL GREENHOUSE CO. (Cont'd)

"National Eaglet" aluminum greenhouses come in lean-to, attached, and free standing models. All glass used is double-strength. Since the parts are prefabricated and the erection plans spell out each phase of building, the greenhouses are easily erected. Hobby sized though they are, these greenhouses are of professional quality. Heating, cooling and other greenhouse accessories are available.

6 page illustrated catalog free

NATIONAL LOG CONSTRUCTION OF MONTANA
Box 68
Thompson Falls, Mont. 59873

PRODUCTS:

Cabins/cottages   Vacation/leisure
Cabins, log   homes

55 models of log cabins ranging in price from under $2,000 to over $14,000. Complete materials package and plans. The Air-Lock logs used in the kits are hollow. Why bore the hole? Wood shrinks as it dries. A solid log must dry from the outside, while the inner part of the log retains its original moisture. As the outside dries, it shrinks. The center part of the log remains the same, and to relieve this differential shrinkage, checks and large cracks form. An Air-Lock Log is hollow and drying takes place from the inside as well as the outside. Seasoning is much more rapid and checking and cracking are minimized. Sizes range from small cabin retreats to lodge-like buildings. Also offers custom service.

64 page illustrated catalog with floor plans $2.00

180

NATIONAL PLAN SERVICE
1700 West Hubbard St.
Chicago, Ill. 60622

PRODUCTS:

CHILDREN'S THINGS
Playhouses

HOME CARE/IMPROVEMENT

Add-a-room projects	Office centers, home
Barns	Sewing centers
Fences	Workshop centers
Garages	

HOUSING

A-frames	Chalets
Apartments/income producing units	Vacation/leisure homes
	Year round homes
Cabins/cottages	

LAWN & GARDEN

Patio furniture	Storage/tool houses
Picnic tables/benches	Terraces

Publishes house plan books in magazine format for all types of houses. There are 16 such magazines, each emphasizing a particular type of house, for example, leisure homes, small homes, apartments/townhouses, etc. The magazines sell for $1.50 each. Blueprints are available for each plan. Also supplies Better Homes and Garden "guide-to" books, Popular Homes Handyman Plans, as well as other how-to books.

Publications list free

A. D. NELSON
Daniels St.
Franklin, Mass. 02038

PRODUCTS:

Inboards	Sailing, cruising
Outboards	Workboats/commercial
Runabouts	boats

181

A. D. NELSON (Cont'd)

Plans only for some 40 different boats from 20 ft. to 120 ft.
Plans range in price from $15.00 to $680.00. A. D. Nelson
and Associates is an informal association of independent
yacht designers who are offering their plans for sale in the
catalog. Each designer retains full ownership of his own
plans and is solely responsible for his own work. After sale
of the plans, the individual designer will take care of all cor-
respondence, alterations, advice, etc., relative to his own
plans. These plans are available on a stock plan basis.

42 page catalog and portfolio of designs $2.00

R. W. NELSON STRUCTURES, INC.
1700 S. Johnson Road
New Berlin, Wis. 53151

PRODUCTS:

Lifts, boat

Easy to assemble boat hoists. Model 500 lifts up to 500
lbs. and is especially designed for small sailboats and outboard motor boats. Model 1250 has a capacity of 1250
lbs. for boats up to 22 ft. long. No special tools are needed
for either model. Hoists may be taken out of or put into
water without difficulty.

Literature free

NETCRAFT, INC.
3101 Sylvania Ave.
Toledo, O. 43613

PRODUCTS:

Fishing lures/jigs/sinkers   Flytying kits
Fishing rods

182

NETCRAFT INC. (Cont'd)

Offers everything the fisher could want or need (except for the fish themselves). Net making, rod building, sinker casting, worm moulding, flytying, fish smoking, bait and lure components, tackle, gadgets and accessories.

170 page pocket-sized, illustrated, information-packed catalog free

NEWELL WORKSHOP
19 Blaine Ave.
Hinsdale, Ill. 60521

PRODUCTS:

Cane/rush furniture

Complete kits with step-by-step instructions for caning heirloom chairs or new ones.

Brochure free

NEWPORT ENTERPRISES
2309 West Burbank Blvd.
Burbank, Calif. 91506

PRODUCTS:

Clocks, decor   Clocks, period

Kits for decor and period clocks. No power tools are needed. Clocks can be assembled with a screwdriver and a pair of pliers. Also offers clock parts, faces, movements, case parts.

16 page illustrated catalog 25¢

NOMADICS – TIPI MAKERS
Star Route, Box 41
Cloverdale, Ore. 97112

PRODUCTS:

Tipis

Kits and instructions for making your own tipis. Manufacturers of tipis make them generally as a novelty. However,
the tipis designed by NOMADICS are meant to be lived in
and, in fact, are lived in. They are designed to withstand
the rigors of mother nature at her worst.

Information on the anatomy and philosophy of tipis and
the kits 25¢, to cover cost of mailing.

NORTH AMERICAN IMPORTS
2325 Cerro Gordo – P. O. Box N
Mojave, Calif. 93501

PRODUCTS:

Choppers (motorcycle)

Parts for choppers. Features the Brake-in-Wheel. This is a
slim front wheel brake for custom and competition use. No
external mechanisms detract from its slim configuration. It
is waterproof and will not fade under normal use. It laces
easily into any standard wheel rim or may be purchased as a
complete wheel assembly. Also offers spool wheels kits for
do-it-yourself lacing or spool wheels completed. Other custom parts and accessories are stocked.

12 page illustrated catalog free

NORTHERN PRODUCTS, INC.
Bomarc Rd.
Bangor, Me. 04401

PRODUCTS:

Cabins, log   Chalets

Kits and plans for 10 standard log cabins with individual options or custom service. Wall construction is of full 6 in. x
8 in. Northern Maine Timber. The logs are tongue and
grooved, and pre-shaped to provide a rustic appearance. The
logs arrive at the building site pre-cut, marked and ready for
easy assembly. Double roof construction. Separated by 3/4
in. strapping, double roof construction allows locked air
space which combined with log walls, eliminates the need
for costly insulation materials. Basic kits range from $2,530
to $9,060.

Illustrated catalog with floor plans $2.00

NOR-WES TRADING LTD.
1075 Marine Drive
North Vancouver, British Columbia
Canada

PRODUCTS:

Chalets

Kits and plans for chalets of Western Red Cedar. 10 models
from simple to luxurious, 645 sq. ft. to 2,558 sq. ft., complete packages from $5,383.00 to $23,038.00. Plans may
be purchased separately, and price may be deducted from
purchase price when kit is ordered. Plans range from
$200.00 to $400.00. (All prices are in Canadian dollars.)
Numbering is the key to the Nor-Wes pre-cut system. Except
for the shakes, decking and siding, practically all the lumber
that arrives is numbered in accordance with the plans. This
reduces construction time and complexity.

22 page color illustrated catalog with basic floor plans, $1.00

NUMRICH ARMS CORP.
Williams Lane
West Hurley, N. Y. 12491

PRODUCTS:

Rifles, antique

Kit for making a Hopkins & Allen muzzle-loading Kentucky
rifle. Sells in kit form for $99.50. Same rifle finished costs
$179.95. All metal parts are fully finished; no machine work
or power tools required; only a wood rasp and sandpaper
needed. Barrel is fully finished, but left unblued so it can be
either blued or browned. Booklet of complete finishing instructions and general muzzle-loading information and loading date included free. An interesting footnote, this is the
same company that manufactures the Thompson sub machine gun (Tommy gun).

Illustrated catalog $1.00

OAK HILL INDUSTRIES
1335 North Utah Ave.
Davenport, Ia. 52804

PRODUCTS:

Potter's wheels

Kits with instructions for assembling the Mark IV and the
Mark IV–SK potter's wheels. Parts are numbered for easy
assembly. Completed wheels are also available. Suitable
for craftsmen and institutions.

Illustrated brochure and price lists free

OCEAN ENGINEERING PRODUCTS CO.
5350 Strohm Avenue, Unit No. 3
North Hollywood, Calif. 91601

PRODUCTS:

Sails/sail gear

Offers a wide line of spars, rigging, fittings for the sailboat
from the deck up. Spars are available in either custom or Kit
form. In kit form you select precisely the parts you need
and assemble the mast. Each kit is shipped complete with
detailed assembly instructions.

15 page illustrated catalog free

OCEAN SHORE DESIGNS
P. O. Box 376
Millbrae, Calif. 94030

PRODUCTS:

Sailing, cruising

Plans only for 7 stock sailboat designs 18 ft. to 36 ft., plywood construction. One design, the 30 ft. Race-Cruiser,
is also available for welded aluminum. It is difficult to
state the cost of materials or number of man-hours required
for each boat due to the wide range of material costs as
well as the expertise of the home builder, but material costs
usually run about 1/3rd of the sale price of the boat. Just
check your local market to see the possible savings! For
example, an 18 ft. factory-made centerboard sloop is currently quoted at $2,200 and up, but the 18 ft. Bolide can
be built for about $650. Plans include consultation by mail
during construction. Designer is Robert E. Armstrong, Naval
Architect.

Portfolio of designs 50¢

OLD BEDFORD CLOCK CO.
555 Old Bedford Rd.
Westport, Mass. 02790

PRODUCTS:

Clocks, period
Weather instruments (thermometers,
barometers, hygrometers)

Basically sells finished clocks but also offers an "Old Bedford Clock" kit and a "Sheraton" barometer kit. Clockmaking materials and supplies. Also can custom design and supply drawings from a customer's sketch, and do wood turnings and hard-to-make parts from customer's sketch. Special school discounts.

Illustrated catalog 25¢

OLD SOUTH PATTERN CO.
Box 11143
Charlotte, N. C. 28209

PRODUCTS:

CHILDREN'S THINGS
Cradles, colonial | "Potty" rockers, colonial
FURNITURE
Beds/headboards | Chests
Benches, storage | Colonial style furniture
Bookcases | Corner shelves
Cabinets | Cupboards
Cabinets, collectors/curio | Desks
Cabinets, stereo/hi-fi | Dry sinks
Carts, hostess/tea | Hutches
Chairs | Lamps
Chairs, captain's | Lowboys
Chairs, Kang-Chi (oriental temple) | Mirrors
Chairs, Kang-Chi (oriental | Racks, gun/rifle
temple) |
Chairs, rocking | Racks, spice
Chest of drawers | Racks, spoon/silverware

OLD SOUTH PATTERN CO. (Cont'd)

Settles, fireside	Tables, coffee
Shaker style furniture	Tables, drop leaf
Spinning wheels	Tables, nest of
Stands	Tables, trestle
Stools	Toilet paper dispensers
Tables, cobbler's bench	

Plans only. Full-size plans based on authentic Early American and Colonial furniture designs. For the home craftsman, industrial arts instructor, and the woodworking shop operated for profit. More than 85 plans available from 50¢ to $16.00.

15 page illustrated catalog 25¢

BARNEY OLDFIELD AIRCRAFT CO.
(Formerly Great Lakes)
P. O. Box 5974
Cleveland, O. 44101

PRODUCTS:

Airplanes, biplane

Kits and plans for building the small "Baby Great Lakes" biplane. Tube fuselage, wood wings, fabric covering. Span 16 ft. 8 in., length 13 ft. 6 in., height 54 in., empty weight 480 lbs., gross weight 850 lbs., Continental A80 power plant.

Information packet $2.00

OLSON ELECTRONICS
260 S. Forge St.
Akron, O. 44327

PRODUCTS:

Burglar/fire alarms, home or business

OLSON ELECTRONICS (Cont'd)

Science fair projects

Parts, components, tools and equipment for the electronics hobbyist. Hi-fi equipment, burglar/fire alarms, P. A. systems, radios, ham equipment, casette players, etc. 66 stores across the country, or shop by mail through the catalog.

Illustrated catalog free

OSCO MOTORS
Souderton, Pa. 18964

PRODUCTS:

Marine engine conversions

Complete kits with instructions for marine engine conversions. All modern marine engines are conversions even when built by Chrysler, CrisCraft, Interceptor or any other builder. Do it yourself and save money. Parts, accessories, transmission kits.

40 page illustrated catalog with specifications and price lists 60¢

OSPREY AIRCRAFT
3741 El Ricon Way
Sacramento, Calif. 95825

PRODUCTS:

Amphibians

Plans only for a small amphibian, the "Osprey I". Specially designed trailer allows you to drive to any boat launching ramp, fold out the wings by inserting one pin at the rear

OSPREY AIRCRAFT (Cont'd)

spar, and you're ready to launch. Putting the "Osprey I" back on the trailer is easily handled by one person. Span 23 ft., length 17 ft. 3 in., height 5 ft. 3 in., empty weight 600 lbs., 90 H. P. Continental engine.

Brochure $3.00

OUTDOOR SPORTS
P. O. Box 1213
Tuscaloosa, Ala. 35401

PRODUCTS:

Canoes	Sailing, day sailers
Kayaks	Surfboards

Plans only for the smaller boat. Wide choice of kayaks: touring, white water, racing, from 11 ft. to 17 ft. 6 in. Kayak plans range from $7.00 — $10.00, 19 models to choose from. Day sailer boats from 11 ft. 6 in. to 17 ft.; four models. Two models of surfboards. Plans include instructions and materials list.

10 page illustrated catalog free

PACIFIC AIRCRAFT CO.
5942 Avenida Chamnez
La Jolla, Calif. 92037

PRODUCTS:

Gliders

Plans only. The D—8 sailplane is an all-metal single place high performance sailplane designed for the home builder. Its moderate aspect ratio — ten — is high enough to provide a good performance and yet is low enough to permit the

PACIFIC AIRCRAFT (Cont'd)

home builder to build the sailplane in the easiest way possible. The cost of materials and purchased parts to build the D—8 range from $200 to $500 depending on whether they are bought new or suplus. Plans are $29.95, with free advice to builder as construction progresses.

Information packet $1.00

PAIA ELECTRONICS, INC.
P. O. Box 14359
Oklahoma City, Okla. 73116

PRODUCTS:

ELECTRONICS
- Bird songsters, electronic
- FM —Dx-ers
- Noise pollution eliminators ("pink noise")
- Remote controls/switches
- Rotating speaker simulators
- Revolution counters (optical tachometer)
- Steam whistles, electronic
- Synthesizers, surf
- Synthesizers, wind
- Synthesizers, wind chimes

MUSICAL INSTRUMENTS
- Drums, electronic
- Attack delay units
- Ping pong effects (alternately routes musical impulses)
- Sustain units (compensates for decay of sound after instrument is struck)
- Waa-waa effects

TOOLS
Stud locators, electronic

Kits with instructions for an unusual collection of electronic projects. Some of these projects are unavailable anywhere else. Reprints of instructions may be purchased for 10¢ each. Please include a self-addressed, stamped envelope with requests for instructions.

18 page illustrated catalog free

192

PALMER AEROSYSTEMS
P. O. Box 1891
Coral Gables, Fla. 33134

PRODUCTS:

Airboats   Hovercraft

Plans and "critical parts" for airboats and hovercraft. Hovercraft uses a large diameter, low speed fan and propeller to reduce noise and increase efficiency. Powered by anything from two 3½ H. P. lawnmower or kart engines to a single 15 H. P. snowmobile engine. Payload is 200 to 400 pounds, depending on engine used. Simple tools and a torch, which can be rented, are needed. The airboat uses a 15 H. P. snowmobile engine with a payload of 250 pounds. The metal parts are assembled using brazing, which is as easy as soldering. No welding required.

Information packet $1.00

PAN ABODE, INC.
4350 Lake Washington Blvd. No.
Renton, Wash. 98055

PRODUCTS:

Garages   Vacation/leisure homes

Complete kits using dimensional Western Red Cedar lumber to simulate log construction. Surfaces, tongue and groove, corner joints are precisely pre-cut. Can erect a building from the blueprint with a minimum of experience and effort using these materials. While retaining the charm of the log structure, the walls and partitions of Western Red Cedar eliminate the difficulties associated with log structures. Starting with a 12 x 20 ft. garage that sells for $1,175, offers any of 10 models ranging up to a 31 x 62 ft. model 1600 ranch type for $9,260. Company will also cut materials to your

PAN ABODE, INC. (cont'd)

own floor plan at a cost of approximately $6.00 per square foot of floor space.

Illustrated catalog and information packet free

HENRY FRANCIS PARKS LABORATORY
P. O. Box 25665
Seattle, Wash. 98125

PRODUCTS:

AUTOMOTIVE EQUIPMENT
   Depth sounders   Windshield wiper controllers

ELECTRONICS
   Power suppliers, DC–AC   Ultrasonic cleaners
   TV Commercial eliminators

EXPERIMENTAL/SCIENTIFIC
   Geiger counters   Sleep inducers, electronic
   Science fair projects   Voice operated relays/switches

MUSICAL INSTRUMENTS/EQUIPMENT
   Amplifiers, guitar   Vibrato generators
   Metronomes

Plans only for electronic projects. Catalog lists over 180 projects, arranged for convenience by level of difficulty or skill required. Special designs are available. Established in 1933.

20 page catalog 35¢

VERNON PAYNE
Rt. 4, Box 319M
Escondido, Calif. 92025

PRODUCTS:

Airplanes

Plans only for 6 designs of the "Knight Twister" plane: the regular Knight Twister with the original 15 ft. top wing span called K. T.–85, a K. T. Jr., with 17½ ft. top wing span, a Sunday Knight Twister with 19½ ft. top wing span, the new K. T. Imperial with 17½ ft. top wing span, the K. T. T. 90 having a straight wing with more area (all other models are tapered wings), and the K. T. Co-ed 2 place. Recently made the K. T. with leading edge slots.

Information packets with three-view drawing $2.00

HAROLD H. PAYSON
Down East Dories
Pleasant Beach Rd.
So. Thomaston, Maine 04858

PRODUCTS:

Cruisers	Rowboat type (rowboats,
Inboards	prams, dinghies, etc.)
Outboards	Sailing, cruising
	Sailing, day sailers

Plans for 40 designs, 14 ft. to 45 ft., priced from $5 to $25. Boats are designed with the amateur builder in mind. Combination of fiberglass and plywood puts one afloat with a minimum of effort and time.

Portfolio of designs $1.00

PAZMANY AIRCRAFT CORP.
P. O. Box 10051
San Diego, Calif. 92110

PRODUCTS:

Airplanes

Partial kits and plans. The PL—1 was selected for fabrication by the Nationalist Chinese Airforce (45 already built),
and is under evaluation as a trainer by South Vietnam, South
Korea, and Thailand. The PL—2 is an advanced and simplified version of the PL—1. Partial kits, hard-to-make parts
for the PL—1, plans only for the PL—2. Also publishes two
books: "Light Aircraft Design" ($5.00), and "Light Air-
craft Construction" ($7.00). These are valuable guides
for the amateur aircraft builder.

Information packet $2.00

PEASE CO.
900 Forest Ave.
Hamilton, Ohio 45012

PRODUCTS:

Vacation/leisure homes

Three standard vacation homes are sold as plans or kits.
Walls are panelized, roofs made of trusses, joists are cut to
size. Wiring, plumbing, heating and cooling kits are not
available at this time. Standard homes may be individual-
ized to suit personal needs.

Illustrated catalog $1.50

196

PEM ENTERPRISES
16 Belmont Drive
Chelmsford, Mass. 01824

PRODUCTS:

Burglar alarms, automobile
Burglar/fire alarms, home or business

Burglar and fire alarms in both kits and completed units
for the home, small business, automobile, camper, etc.
Also supplies individual alarm components. Company offers to answer any question which pertains to burglar/fire
alarm equipment or installation problems. Address your
question to Dept. QA of PEM Enterprises, and provide a
stamped self-addressed envelope for the return answer. A 41
page illustrated manual "How To Build a Burglar Alarm" is
available for $2.00

Information on request

H. H. PERKINS CO.
10 South Bradley Rd.
Woodbridge, Conn. 06525

PRODUCTS:

Cane/rush furniture   Chairs, rocking
Chairs, ladderback   Stools

Kits and instructions for chair caning. "A chair is only as
good as the seat that is in it" – the company's motto! Company established in 1917.

Booklet explaining chair caning and reedcraft with price
lists, 25¢

PHASE CORP.
315-A Boston Ave.
Medford, Mass. 02155

PRODUCTS:

Audio generators	Time base generators
Calibration oscillators	Triggered pulse generators
Phase comparative analyzers	Utility function oscillators
Power suppliers, regulated/ variable	

Kits or factory assembled solid state electronic devices.
Save considerably by building from kits. For example, the
regulated power source (Model RPS–200) sells for $59.60
completed, $39.40 in kit form; the triggered pulse generator
(TPG 200) sells for $84.85 completed, $64.65 as a kit. Kits
come with instructions for assembly. Many of these kits are
unique and are unobtainable elsewhere.

Illustrated catalog free

PIERSON HOMES PREFABRICATORS
Rt. 1, Box 114
Eureka, Calif. 95501

PRODUCTS:

A-frames	Vacation/leisure homes

A-frames in redwood. The use of redwood provides rot-
resistant exteriors and interiors. Completely pre-cut, pre-
drilled and prefabricated for ease of construction by the
amateur builder. Basic shell ranges from $3,129.00 to
$9,068.00, four models to choose from.

Brochure $1.00

PLANS
P. O. Box 793
Fremont, Neb. 68025

PRODUCTS:

Bicycles, motorized   Karts   Mini-bikes

Plans and parts for karts, mini-bikes, mini-three wheelers and motor bikes. The last requires no welding, uses the frame of your existing bicycle. Plans are $2.00 each.

Illustrated brochure $1.00

PLASMA SYSTEMS
P. O. Box 3261
San Jose, Calif. 95116

PRODUCTS:

Flash units, electronic   Lasers   Stroboscopes

Kits, plans, parts for lasers and other devices using gaseous discharge principles. Plans may be purchased separately.

Illustrated catalog $1.00 (refundable)

POLYNESIAN CATAMARAN SAILBOATS
W. M. Cookson
1553 Armacost
Los Angeles, Calif. 90025

PRODUCTS:

Catamarans

Plans only for eight Polynesian catamarans designed by James Wharram. Boats from 16 to 51 ft., plans from

$15.00 to $200.00. Boats are simple to build, even the larger 46 and 51 footers.

Illustrated catalog showing basic designs and advantages of the Polynesian catamarans $2.00

POOLCRAFT
135 N. 9th Street
Zionsville, Ind. 46077

PRODUCTS:

Swimming pool filter systems

Swimming pool filter systems are expensive to buy for the smaller pool. No one wants to buy a 10 or 12 ft. pool for $10 to $15 and have to spend $40 on a filter system for it. What most owners of this size pool do is to dump, clean, and refill the pool every three or four days. This becomes expensive, what with high water bills, and also involves a lot of work. You can build an inexpensive (around $5) filter system from junk parts. Plans and instructions are $1.00

POPULAR MECHANICS, Dept. CO
Box 1014, Radio City
New York, N. Y. 10019

PRODUCTS:

AIRCRAFT

Airplanes

BOATS

Catamarans	Runabouts
Houseboats	Sailing, day sailers
Hydroplanes	Submarines

CAMPING
: Luggage carriers, car top

HOME CARE/IMPROVEMENT
: Barns   Garages   Sheds

HOUSING
: Vacation/leisure homes

SPORTING EQUIPMENT
: Gyms, family   Pool tables

VEHICLES
: Automobiles, midget (motorized)   Railroad engines, (midget, motorized)
: Trucking, off road

WOODWORKING
: Spinning wheels

Plans only for a wide range of projects. Also, photocopies of hundreds of past Popular Mechanics do-it-yourself articles. Books for the do-it-yourselfer.

31 page illustrated catalog 25¢

POPULAR SCIENCE PLANS DIVISION
355 Lexington Avenue
New York, N. Y. 10017

PRODUCTS:

BOATS
: Canoes   Sailing, day sailers
: Rowboat type (rowboats, prams, dinghies, etc.)

CAMPING
: Campers, folding

HOME CARE/IMPROVEMENT
: Add-a-room projects   Barns

HOUSING
: Geodesic domes   Vacation/leisure homes

POPULAR SCIENCE PLANS DIVISION (Cont'd)

LAWN & GARDEN
   Japanese teahouses

SPORTING EQUIPMENT
   Kites, man-carrying

VEHICLES
   Automobiles, antique   Sail cars

Plans only for a variety of projects developed by Popular
Science Magazine. Clear show-how drawings, written step-
by-step instructions, photos where helpful. Materials lists
are included if appropriate as well as suggestions about how
to obtain materials or parts you might have trouble finding
locally. All plans have been thoroughly pre-tested.

14 page illustrated catalog free

PROGRESSIVE EDU—KITS, INC.
P. O. Box 238
Hewlett, N. Y. 11557

PRODUCTS:

   Code, oscillators   Signal probes/tracers
   Radios, AM   Transmitters, phone/CW
   Radios, FM

"Edu-Kit" is basically an educational home training course
in radio and electronics. 20 radio and electronic projects
are built with the kits provided. Instructions, kits, tools.
For the individual student, a complete home study course.
For schools, this can be the nucleus of a well-rounded
course, to be supplemented by the instructor. Special
school discounts.

Information free

PROTECTO ALARM SALES
P. O. Box 357
Birch Run, Mich. 48415

PRODUCTS:

Burglar/fire alarms, home or business

Install your own burglar or fire alarm and save yourself up to 80%. Supplies quality name brand equipment. Also sells components and parts. Write for free design and equipment information.

48 page illustrated catalog and instruction manual free

QUICKSILVER BOATS
249 Warfield Avenue
Venice, Fla. 33595

PRODUCTS:

Canoes	Sailing, day sailers
Kayaks	Sails/sail gear
Rowboat type (rowboats, prams, dinghies, etc.)	

Kits as well as plans for the small boat: canoes, kayaks, skiffs — using oar or sail. Sail kits for these boats available.

Illustrated catalog free

RADIO SHACK
2615 West 7th St.
Fort Worth, Texas 76107

PRODUCTS:

Automotive equipment	Tachometers
Depth sounders	Timing lights
Engine analyzers	Windshield wiper controllers
Ignition, capacative discharge	

CHILDREN'S THINGS
Science toys

ELECTRONICS

Earphones/headphones

Intercoms

Motor/speed controllers

Radar detectors

Radios, AM

Radios, FM

Radios, short wave

RF signal generators

Signal probes/injectors

Stereo/hi-fi, amplifiers

Stereo/hi-fi, receivers

Stereo/hi-fi, speakers

Stereo/hi-fi, tuners

Telephone amplifiers

Transistor testers

Tube testers

VOM's

VTVM's

EXPERIMENTAL/SCIENTIFIC

Fiber optics

Lie detectors

Photoelectric relays

Science fair projects

Stroboscopes

Treasure/metal locators

HOME CARE/IMPROVEMENT
Burglar alarms/fire alarms,
home or business
Gas/smoke sensors

MUSICAL INSTRUMENTS/EQUIPMENT
Metronomes

OPTICS/PHOTOGRAPHY
Color organs   Psychedelic/light shows

SPORTING EQUIPMENT
Fish locators/spotters

Kits with instructions for electronics projects. Also carries tools, parts, components, test equipment. Stereo equipment, radios, tape recorders, automobile radios, and the whole range of consumer electronics products. 1500 stores in all 50 states. If a store is not nearby, you can order through the catalog. This year is the 50th anniversary of the company.

179 page illustrated catalog free on request at the stores

RAIN JET CORP.
301 So. Flower St.
P. O. Box 868
Burbank, Calif. 91503

PRODUCTS:

Fountains   Sprinklers, underground

Dozens of fanciful fountains from the smallest to the largest,
models for the backyard to the civic center. All parts and
accessories. Also a full line of underground sprinklers.
Kits, plans, instructions.

15 page color-illustrated catalog free

WM. P. RATAJAK HARPSICHORDS
300 East Ashland Lane
Ashland, Ore. 97520

PRODUCTS:

Harpsichords

 Kits for a harpsichord that adhere closely to historical prac-
tices of construction. Instrument is available either in kit,
semi-kit, or finished form. The kit form makes heavy de-
mands upon both the time and the woodworking skill of
the kit-builder. It calls for all the basic handworking tools.
The semi-kit requires only a few tools and a rather short
time to complete. Also sells harpsichords finished at the
shop. Cost for kit $800.00, semi-kit $1,500.00, finished
$2,800.00.

Information free

RAYJAY INDUSTRIES, INC.
2602 East Wardlow Rd.
P. O. Box 207
Long Beach, Calif. 90801

PRODUCTS:

Hot rod hardware

Turbocharger kits for VW   Bolt-on kit will double your VW
horsepower, when you need it, in day-to-day driving. Easy
to install without special tools.

Illustrated brochure free

HERB RAYNER
"THE CRATE FLYERS SQUADRON"
P. O. Box 572
Des Arc, Ark. 72040

PRODUCTS:

Airplanes, antique

Plans only for those great vintage planes from the early days
of flying, the "Crates", Rayner Curtiss type pushers. Two
models currently available at $10.00 a set, which include
both models.

Brochure free

RCA
415 So. Fifth St.
Harrison, N. J. 07029

PRODUCTS:

Science fair projects

Inexpensive kits with instructions for basic electronic and

experimental projects. These projects reflect the latest technology such as the use of integrated circuits. Company also publishes "Solid State Hobby Circuits" ($1.95), and "Silicon Controlled Rectifier Experimenter's Manual" (95¢). Kits and books are obtainable at most local electronics and hobby stores.

Brochure free

REDFERN & SON
Box "G"
Tekoa, Wash. 99033

PRODUCTS:

Airplanes, antique

Plans only for the World War I, Fokker Dr-1 tri-plane, more popularly known as the Fokker Triplane. This plane first saw action on the Western Front during the summer of 1917. Plans $50.00.

History and profile of the plane $2.00

REDWOOD DOMES
P. O. Box 666
Aptos, Calif. 95003

PRODUCTS:

Gazebos, geodesic dome	Greenhouses, geodesic dome
Geodesic domes	Sheds, geodesic dome

Kits with instructions for geodesic domes for utility purposes or living. No skills required for completing. Just match the color-coded ends with the corresponding hub colors, slide the bolts into the pre-drilled holes, and tighten

with a wrench. 14 ft. ($185 in fir, $220 in redwood);
20 ft. ($395 in fir, $470 in redwood); 26 ft. ($535 in
fir, $640 in redwood). Accessories and options are available. Plans may be purchased separately.

Illustrated brochure free

REIMANN AND GEORGER, INC.
P. O. Box 681
Buffalo, N. Y. 14240

PRODUCTS:

    Beacher marine railways   Lifts, boat
    Docks/piers

Boat lifts are designed as knockdown structures with easy
to assemble bolt-together angles and bars. Inboard lifts
with lifting hooks, outboard lifts with plastic slings, and
platform boat lifts. Docks/piers are also knockdown, but
without wood decking or pipe legs, since these are expensive to ship and can be locally bought with ease. Beacher
railways are also shipped knockdown. Full instructions
for assembly of all products.

Illustrated brochure free

PETER REIMULLER—GREENHOUSEMAN
P. O. Box 2666
Santa Cruz, Calif. 95060

PRODUCTS:

                  Greenhouses

Inexpensive do-it-yourself California Redwood greenhouses.
Free standing and lean-to models. "Pearl-Mist" line (3
free standing and 3 lean-to sizes) uses FILON panels, a

combination of fiberglass and nylon. These panels are shatter-proof and hailproof. "Crystal-Aire" line greenhouses are 84 sq. ft. in area, 7 ft. x 12 ft. Uses U. V. I. (Ultra-Violet Inhibited) 8 mil plastic film panels designed to withstand the deteriorating effects of ultra-violet rays of the sun. Greenhouses are simple to erect and come with step-by-step instructions. Accessories also.

Literature free

**REINFORCED PLASTICS DIV.,
REICHHOLD CHEMICALS, INC.**
**20800 Center Ridge Rd.
Cleveland, O. 41116**

PRODUCTS:

Patios

Plans for patios using Alsynite/Structoglas translucent fiberglass panels, as well as suggestions for other uses around the home.

Illustrated brochure free

RELCO INDUSTRIES
**P. O. Box 10839
Houston, Texas 77018**

PRODUCTS:

Treasure/metal locators

Kit with instructions for making your own treasure or metal detector, the No. 12T, "Trail Blazer". Save money by assembling. Kit sells for $19.95, $29.95 completed. Kits are also available for micro-coil search head and micro-tuner. In addition to a line of completed treasure locators, com-

RELCO INDUSTRIES (Cont'd)

pany offers accessories and books for the treasure or metal hunter.

40 page illustrated catalog free

RELIABLE INDUSTRIES, INC.
34403 Joel St.
New Baltimore, Mich. 48047

PRODUCTS:

Marine engines, steam	Stern-wheelers
Side-wheelers	Submarines, historic (the
Steamboats	"Monitor")
Steam engines, auto	Workboats/commercial boats

Seven models of steam power plants, 4 H. P. to 200 H. P. Modern and oldfashioned designs. Engines may be used for auto, marine, stationary applications. The kits are in castings form. A metal lathe, a drill press, and the necessary skill to operate power tools are required. Blueprints and plans may be purchased separately Boilers, condensers, feed pumps, and other accessories are also available. Plans only for 7 interesting steam powered boats of historic vintage, for example, side-wheelers, and even the Civil War submarine, the "Monitor"

20 page illustrated catalog-handbook $1.00

REPLICA PLANS
953 Kirkmond Crescent
Richmond, B. C. Canada

PRODUCTS:

Airplanes, antique	Airplanes, biplanes

Plans only. The SE–5 was designed for those who want a

REPLICA PLANS (Cont'd)

representative "antique" but who don't want to spend the
time or money on an exact reproduction. It looks like the
real thing and will impress all but the most discerning WW1
airplane fan. While conforming fairly well to the original
it features far simpler construction and the use of modern
and more readily available materials. The SE—5 is an all-
wood wire braced biplane. If you have no experience in
home building 24 months will probably do it. Costs will
vary widely but materials should not exceed $2,500 using
the C.85 engine. Plans and instructions $50.00.

Information package $3.00

RICKBORN INDUSTRIES, INC.
175 Atlantic City Blvd.
Bayville, N. J. 08721

PRODUCTS:

Flying bridges

Kits and instructions for self-fitting, one-piece fiberglass flying bridges. The five different sizes of flying bridges available from manufacturer will suit the needs, in most cases,
of any boat.

Illustrated brochure free

ROBBINS LIGHTNING PROTECTION CO.
P. O. Box 440
124 East Second St.
Maryville, Mo. 64468

PRODUCTS:

Lightning protectors

Lightning protection systems for home, farm, or business.

ROBBINS LIGHTING PROTECTION CO. (Cont'd)

Kits, plans, instructions. Also components and parts. Products are Underwriters' Laboratories inspected and approved.

Illustrated catalog free

ROGUE KAYAKS
P. O. Box 1281
Medford, Ore. 97501

PRODUCTS:

Kayaks

Complete kits for building 10 ft. to 15 ft. kayaks, from $59.50 to $84.75. Special discounts for schools, scout groups, etc. Kit includes all materials for a complete kayak except paint. Paint can be purchased locally where choice of colors can be selected. Kit includes all frame materials, heavy canvas, dope for canvas, liquid marine-tex for one coat, screws, nails, tacks, and tape. Diagramed instructions for assembling.

Literature free

ROHM AND HAAS CO.
P. O. Box 9730
Philadelphia, Pa. 19140

PRODUCTS:

Etageres, plastic	Tables, coffee, plastic
Pedestals, plastic	Tables, cube, plastic
Picture frames, plastic	Tables, double-X frame, plastic
Plastic furniture	Telephone centers/stands, plastic
Racks, magazine, plastic	Wine racks, plastic

Plans for making projects out of acrylic plastic sheets. Sup-

plies for projects must be bought locally through dealers.
(Company will send list of dealers on request.) Available at
the dealer free is a 15 page, illustrated pamphlet, "Do It
Yourself with Plexiglas Acrylic Sheet". This pamphlet
describes various projects you can make with Plexiglas plus
information on fabrication methods. You may also obtain
this pamphlet by writing to Rohm and Haas itself, but they
will charge 25¢ to cover the cost of mailing and handling.
A number of project plans have also been developed and
are sold at 50¢ each. Check with your dealer or write to
the company for the availability of these project plans.

Illustrated 15 page project catalog 25¢

ROMACK MARINE
P. O. Box 20481
Long Beach, Calif. 90813

PRODUCTS:

Cruisers	Sailing, cruising
Ferro-cement boats	Workboats/commercial boats

Plans only for ferro-cement sail and power boats from 23 ft.
to 65 ft. Eleven stock plans. Illustrated construction manual
sells for $12.50 plus 75¢ for handling. Study plans are avail-
able at $5.00 each, refundable on purchase of a full set of
plans.

20 page illustrated catalog $1.25

ROOSTER BOAT CO.
Hawthorne Rd.
Jamestown, R. I. 02835

PRODUCTS:

Rowboat type (rowboats, prams, dinghies, etc.)

ROOSTER BOAT CO. (Cont'd)

Sailing, day sailers

The ROOSTER is a 9 ft. 6 in. racing sailboat. The boat is
easily built by amateurs. When completed it makes an excellent all-weather sail boat, or it can be used as a row boat.
It is light in weight and can be easily car topped or fit into
a standard station wagon. Builders report a cost of between
$60.00 to $80.00 for everything but the sail, and man-hours
to build from 50 to 75 hours. No kits, only plans or finished
boats. Plans are $5.00. These plans include 11 pages of
drawings, a Bill of Materials, a set of building instructions,
and specifications. Completed boat including sails, $275.00.

Literature free

WILLIAM POST ROSS—HARPSICHORD MAKER
791 Tremont Street
Room 515
Boston, Mass. 02118

PRODUCTS:

Harpsichords
Virginals

Complete kits for making fine harpsichords and virginals.
Aim is to provide a musical instrument that is satisfying mu-
sically, has a good action, and is easy to build. Instruments
are patterned closely after antique instruments, with some
modern adaptations where indicated. May be purchased as:
(1) a Basic Kit. The basic kit is a woodworking task and
some power tools are desirable though not strictly necessary
if it is possible to obtain dimensional lumber to your specifications; (2) Cut-to-Fit. Here all wood parts are pre-cut
for you. (3) Assembled Case. This is essentially an assembly job. To compare costs the basic Virginal Kit costs
$345. Cut-to-Fit, $525, Assembled Case, $775. Harpsi-

chord Kits are approximately one-third higher than corresponding Virginal.

14 page illustrated catalog and manual free

ROTOCAST PRODUCTS, INC.
6700 N. W. 36th Ave.
Miami, Fla. 33147

PRODUCTS:

Pontoon boats

Kits with instructions for pontoon boats. The pontoons are made of high density polyethylene material which will not rust, corrode, or deteriorate from contact with salt water, acids, chemicals, fuels or solvents. Each pontoon section is 36 inches long with built-in mounting flanges for easy assembly. All necessary hardware is included, as well as accessories for completing pontoon boat as desired. Pontoons range from 17 ft. to 42 ft. Pontoons may be also used for docks, survey vessels, floats, work barges, instrument buoys, etc.

Literature free

RAYMOND C. RUMPF & SON
210 Krewson Terrace
Willow Grove, Pa. 19090

PRODUCTS:

Flytying kits

Everything needed for flytying kits, hundreds of items. Also books on flytying and flytying tools.

10 page catalog free

SAILRITE KITS
1650 Verde Vista
Pomona, Calif. 91767

PRODUCTS:

Sails/sail gear

Company specializes in kits and instruction manuals for the amateur sailmaker. Sails built from the kits are up to 50% cheaper than purchased sails and they are generally superior in quality to manufactured sails. Quite satisfactory for racing. Only tools required are a zig-zag sewing machine (portable is perfectly satisfactory) and a soldering iron or wood-burning tool (to cut the synthetic cloth). Also stocks sail supplies of all types for the sailmaker. Catalog lists sails by size and type as well as kits for many popular stock boats.

28 page illustrated catalog, $1.00

SAKRETE, INC.
P. O. Box 1
Cincinnati, Ohio 45217

PRODUCTS:

Barbecue pits	Planters
Patios	Pools, garden

Company which makes cement mixes offers free plans for 20 lawn & garden projects.

15 page illustrated brochure free

SAMSON MARINE DESIGN, LTD.
833 River Rd.
Richmond, B. C. Canada

PRODUCTS:

Cruisers	Ferro-cement boats

216

SAMSON MARINE DESIGN, LTD. (Cont'd)

Houseboats
Sailing, cruising

Workboats/commercial
boats

Plans and full size patterns for a wide range of ferro-cement boats. Sailboats from 29 ft. to 63 ft., houseboats from 32 ft. to 46 ft., powerboats from 29 ft. to 65 ft., workboats from 37 ft. to 53 ft. Over 50 plans, probably the largest collection of ferro-cement boat plans anywhere. Also supplies parts, accessories, fittings. Publishes superb books and manuals on ferro-cement boats and boatbuilding.

Literature free

SAN FRANCISCO PELICAN BOATS
203 Hawthorne Ave.
Larkspur, Calif. 94939

PRODUCTS:

Sailing, cruising

Sailing, day sailers

The "San Francisco Pelican" and Great Pelican sailboats are a unique combination of the famous Banks dory and the oriental sampan. The San Francisco Pelican is 12 ft. 2 in. in length. The Great Pelican, a larger version, is 16 ft. in length and is available with or without a cabin. The small cabin allows space for two berths and a head, yet still leaves a large cockpit for day sailing. Plans and instructional book for the San Francisco Pelican $7.00, for the Great Pelican $10.00.

Illustrated brochure 25¢

JERRY SANFORD
14636 16th, S. W.
Seattle, Wash. 98166

PRODUCTS:

Cabinets, stereo/hi-fi

217

JERRY SANFORD (Cont'd)

Plans only for an attractive stereo/hi-fi cabinet. Design can be changed easily to suit one's own ideas. Easy to add on shelves and other compartments. Plan costs $4.00.

SAVIN HANDICRAFTS
P. O. Box 4251
Hamden, Conn. 06514

PRODUCTS:

Cane/rush furniture	Chairs, rocking
Chairs, ladderback	Stools

Kits and instructions for making cane or rush furniture. Also seat and basket weaving kits and supplies. Books on seat and basket weaving.

Illustrated brochures free

SCAT ENTERPRISES
P. O. Box 4096
121 W. Hazel St.
Inglewood, Calif. 90302

PRODUCTS:

Hot rod hardware

Manufactures high performance kits and parts for the smaller car: VW, Datsun, Toyota, Pinto, Porsche, Vega, Opel, Capri, Corvair. Parts also for dune buggies and racing cars. Engine, transmission, body, chassis parts, plus interior and exterior accessories. Also manuals and tools.

55 page illustrated catalog with price lists $2.00

218

SCHMIEDER MOTORS
RD No. 1
Doylestown, Pa. 18901

PRODUCTS:

    Bicycles, motorized   Karts

Kits for go-karts. Also, plans only for motorizing your bicycle using either gasoline engine or electric motor. Go-kart
kit complete with wheels but minus engine, $19.95. Plans
for motorizing bicycle $2.00. Clutches and engines available.

Information 25¢

SCHOBER HARPSICHORDS, INC.
An Affiliate of the Schober Organ Corporation
43 W. 61st St.
New York, N. Y. 10023

PRODUCTS:

                Harpsichords

Complete kit for "Model 70" harpsichord. You do no saw-
ing and practically no measuring except to identify the
pieces. All pieces are furnished cut to exact size and shape;
you simply put them together and secure them with nails,
screws, and easy to use white glue (which is furnished).
While this harpsichord is built on the same principles as the
original instruments of the 17th century, its working parts
are made with the engineering knowledge and materials of
today. As a result, the instrument works far more reliably
than the original harpsichords ever did (and sounds as good
as or better than most of them). Save by building your own.
Kit costs $895.00, same instrument completed $1,550.00.

15 page illustrated catalog (containing an excellent history
and discussion of the harpsichord) free

SCHOBER ORGAN CORP.
43 W. 61st St.
New York, N. Y. 10023

PRODUCTS:

Organs

Complete kits for assembling electronic organs with easy to
follow, step-by-step instructions. Requires 50 to 175 hours
to complete depending on the model and your working
pace. Five models, in order of decreasing size: "Recital
Organ", "Theatre Organ", "Consolette II", "Spinet Organ",
"Studio Organ". Cabinetry may be purchased completed or
in kit form.   Organ accessories, tools, test equipment, books
and music books, records, and organ playing courses are
available. Catalog contains solid information on what to look
for in an organ and how to select one plus other helpful
hints on electronic organs.

24 page color illustrated catalog and price lists free

BOB SCHRIMSHER'S CUSTOM KNIFEMAKER'S SUPPLY
P. O. Box 11448
Dallas, Tex. 75223

PRODUCTS:

Knives, hunting/Bowie

Kits and supplies for making high quality knives. Makes a
strong point about not handling anything less than the finest
quality materials – at a reasonable price.

15 page illustrated catalog 50¢

220

SCIENCE & MECHANICS PUBLISHING CO.
Craft Print Division
299 Park Avenue South
New York, N. Y. 10003

PRODUCTS:

AIRCRAFT
               Airplanes, biplane

BOATS/BOATING EQUIPMENT

Canoes	Paddle-wheel boats
Houseboats	Pontoon boats
Hydrofoils	Rowboat type (rowboats,
Hydroplanes	prams, dinghies, etc.)
Iceboats	Runabouts
Inboards	Sailing, cruising
Kayaks	Sailing, day sailers
Outboards	

BOATING EQUIPMENT

Marine engine conversions	Trailers, boat

CAMPING

Campers, car-top	Tent campers
Campers, folding	

CHILDREN'S THINGS

Boats, children's	Toys

ELECTRONICS
               Selenium rectifiers

EXPERIMENTAL/SCIENTIFIC

Electrostatic generators	Treasure/metal locators

FURNITURE

Clocks, grandfather	Whatnot shelves
Racks, china/pewter	

HOME CARE/IMPROVEMENT

Room dividers	Ventilators, kitchen
Stairs, concrete	

LAWN & GARDEN
               Lawn/patio furniture

OPTICS/PHOTOGRAPHY

Stroboscopes	Telescope mounts

SPORTING EQUIPMENT
               Scuba scooters

TOOLS
               Bending brakes

VEHICLES

Automobiles, midget (motorized)	Pickup covers
	Snowmobiles
Ice karts	Tractors, garden/suburban
Karts	Trailers

Plans only for some 150 projects selected for outstanding design, utility value and ease of construction. The plans are $3.00 for most, a few higher. These projects have been compiled and selected by the publishers of Science & Mechanics Magazine.

15 page illustrated catalog $1.00

J. R. SCOVILLE
172 Cedarwood Terrace
Rochester, N. Y. 14609

PRODUCTS:

Airplanes

Formula 1 racers, the Stardust and the Stardust II. Plans and information only. Stardust pulled 6½ G's for F. A. A. flight test at over 300 m.p.h. Ailerons are 100% balanced and show no signs of vibrations at any speed. There is a 15 gal. fuel tank for racing type and rear end tip tanks can be used for sport flying. Plane cited in June's "All the World Aircraft, 1971–1972". Complete plans $35.00 plus mail.

Information packet $3.50

SEAFARER FIBERGLASS YACHTS, INC.
760 Park Avenue
Huntington, N. Y. 11743

PRODUCTS:

Rowboat type boats, (rowboats,   Sailing, cruising
prams, dinghies, etc.)   Sailing, day sailers

Full range of kits for fiberglass sailing yachts, 23 ft. — 48 ft., designed by top-notch designers. Kits may be purchased at any stage of construction. Company does that part of the job you do not want to do. You select and buy exactly what you need, when you want it, and as it suits you. Plans and instructions come with kits. Also kits for dinghies, sail or rowing.

15 page illustrated catalog free

SEECOM
P. O. Box 1274
Tustin, Calif. 92680

PRODUCTS:

Electric cars

Plans only for conversion of an internal combustion engine-powered car into an electric car. Most any automobile can be used, but weight should be limited to around 2,000 pounds, which unfortunately eliminates all American cars. Batteries specified are readily available and cost about $250.00. Conversion, using Loss-less series-parallel control, including batteries, but less car-body, can be achieved for about $600.00 or less. Plans include pictures, drawings, text, parts lists and sources. Plans $10.00.

Information free

SELVA COMPANY
487 Armour Circle, N. E.
Atlanta, Ga. 30324

PRODUCTS:

Clocks, cuckoo   Spinning wheels
Clocks, decor   Clocks, wooden wheel

Clock kits and instructions. Rustic and modern designs. Supplies and parts for clockmaking, Swiss musical movements, weather instruments, etc.

47 page color-illustrated catalog $2.00

SEMPLE ENGINE CO., INC.
Box 8354
St. Louis, Mo. 63124

PRODUCTS:

Engines, steam   Marine engines, steam

Marine steam engine kits for powering launches and houseboats. Burns either coal or wood. Engines are safe, dependable, economical, quiet, 5 to 10 HP. Engine kits are complete, not castings only. All the difficult machining work has been done. 95% of the remaining work can be done on a 10-inch lathe and drill press. Drawings are to the finest detail. Prices range from $213 to $474, as compared to $470 to $1,060 for the completed engine, a saving of over 50% by doing it yourself. Boilers and other steam power accessories available.

Information packet $1.00

SERCOLAB
P. O. Box 78
Arlington, Mass. 02174

PRODUCTS:

Science fair projects

224

SERCOLAB (Cont'd)

Inexpensive scientific projects and experiments for the student, teacher, schools.

Illustrated catalog free

SEVEN SEAS PRESS
32 Union Square
New York, N. Y. 10003

PRODUCTS:

Cruisers   Sailing, cruising
Ferro-cement boats

All the boating magazines publish designs every month, but to the person seeking a boat to suit his cruising needs, or to the person who just loves to study and file them, there just never seems to be enough. So, Seven Seas Press has embarked on a series of Plans Catalogs. Three catalogs are presently available, and more are on the way: "17 Designs From the Board of John G. Hanna" ($2.25); "20 Designs From the Board of Thomas E. Colvin" ($2.25); "29 Designs From the Board of Al Mason" ($3.00).

Literature free

SHAKER WORKSHOPS
P. O. Box 710
Concord, Mass. 01742

PRODUCTS:

Benches	Mirrors
Chairs, ladderback	Shaker style furniture
Chairs, rocking	Stools
Chests	Tables, drop leaf
Cupboards	Tables, trestle

Kits with instructions for Shaker style furniture based on authentic prototypes. Kits have everything you need. Only common tools such as a screwdriver and hammer are required for most pieces. Wood used is choice northern hardwoods and pine, carefully seasoned, knot-free. Also offers stains/paints/finishes, chair tapes, books and pamphlets, herbs, Shaker "Spirit" drawings, and Shaker designs in home accessories. Company specializes in Shaker designs and handles nothing else.

30 page illustrated catalog $1.00

SHEARD SCIENCE SUPPLIES, INC.
251 W. James St.
Columbus, Wis. 53925

PRODUCTS:

Science fair projects

While the company does not supply kits, it is a source of basic chemicals and laboratory supplies for the amateur or professional scientist. Also biology supplies, microscopes, telescopes, rocket models, etc.

38 page illustrated catalog 50¢

SHELTER–KIT, INC.
26 Franklin St.
Franklin, N. H. 03235

PRODUCTS:

Cabins/cottages   Vacation/leisure homes

Kits for modular designed housing. The basic unit is 12 ft. x 12 ft., or 144 sq. ft. Units may be combined to produce

SHELTER-KIT, INC. (Cont'd)

larger units when and as desired. Pre-cut, pre-drilled house kit. Assembly is easy and no professional or outside help is needed to accomplish the job. It is permanent in its parts, but can be taken down and put up elsewhere. Unit can be broken down into packages and two persons can carry it to any site. Kits include site preparation instructions and a construction manual. Basic unit sells for $1,630.00.

Illustrated brochure free

SHETTEL—WAY INNOVATIONS
P. O. Box 12
Twin Falls, Idaho 83301

PRODUCTS:

Dog houses

Kits with instructions for dog houses. There are two sizes: Model 27S, for medium to small dogs, having a 23 in. x 23 in. x 22 in. high den with a 25 in. floor, and Model 27L, for medium to large dogs, having a 28 in. x 28 in. x 26 in. high den with a 42 in. floor. Exteriors are plywood and floor and understructure are penta treated to resist decay and 2 in. x 2 in. skids give positive separation from the ground.

Literature free

SHOBER AIRCRAFT ENTERPRISES
P. O. Box 111
Gaithersburg, Md. 20760

PRODUCTS:

Airplanes, biplane

Plans only for the "Willie 11", a biplane. Designed as a two place open cockpit sport plans, it performs aerobatics well.

SHOBER AIRCRAFT ENTERPRISES (Cont'd)

The G leading has been computed at 9, plus or negative. The price of 16 sheets of drawings, photos and assembly instructions is $75.00, U. S. currency.

Information packet $2.00

SHOP SUPPLY HOUSE
476-A First St.
Encinitas, Calif. 92024

PRODUCTS:

Salt/pepper sets, wood

Kits for making salt and pepper shakers. Simple home workshop project or for the school shop.

Send stamped self-addressed envelope for brochure

SIDE STRIDER, INC.
15838 Arminta Unit 25
Van Nuys, Calif. 91406

PRODUCTS:

Sidecars, motorcycle

Did you ever want to put a sidecar on your motorcycle? Now you can. Offers a kit for adding a sidecar to your motorcycle. The frame is made of nickel-plated one-eighth inch mild steel. The hack body is one piece, virtually unbreakable fiberglass. Offers the chassis without body, or complete unit. Can be attached without welding in about one hour. After that the sidecar can be detached in a few minutes.

Brochure free

T. L. SINCLAIR, JR.
1443 Ahuawa Loop
Honolulu, Hawaii 96816

PRODUCTS:

    Cruisers   Rowboat type (rowboats, prams,
    Outboards   dinghies, etc.)

Plans only for 6 boats ranging from an 11 ft. utility to a 37 ft. sport fisher. Plans from $4.50 to $145.00, with a reasonable amount of consultation.

20 page portfolio of designs including a history of the Dory and the Sampan $1.00

SMITH MINIPLANE
1938 Jacaranda Place
Fullerton, Calif. 92633

PRODUCTS:

               Airplanes, biplane

Plans only for a small one-seat biplane. Suitable for home construction with the amateur pilot in mind. Length 15 ft. 1 in.; wing span — upper 17 ft., lower 15 ft. 9 in., empty weight 616 lbs. — gross weight 1,000 lbs. Detailed plans consisting of 33 plates of scale drawings and isometric views listing suggested material or possible substitute material — $25.00.

Brochure $1.00

JERRY SMYTH
RR No. 4
Huntington, Ind. 46750

PRODUCTS:

               Airplanes

JERRY SMYTH (Cont'd)

Plans and hard-to-make parts for the "Sidewinder". Other common parts and materials may be obtained from suppliers who specialize in the "Sidewinder" or through local suppliers. Can be built for $1,200 to $1,500. "1969 Outstanding Design" award at the 17th Annual International Sport Aviation Convention at Rockford, Illinois.

3-view sample drawing and 15 page illustrated brochure $2.00

SNUG HARBOR BOAT WORKS
10121 Snug Harbor Rd.
St. Petersburg, Fla. 33702

PRODUCTS:

Boats, children's   Sailing, day sailers

A small sailing boat, length 7 ft. 7 in., breadth 3 ft. 10 in. Suitable for children. Complete kit and instructions. The hull is already assembled, and work is therefore minimal. Kit sells for $124.95, including all parts and sails.

Brochure free

SOUND FOUR ENTERPRISES
4534 50th Street
San Diego, Calif. 92115

PRODUCTS:

8-track players conversion to
8-track players/recorders

Set of plans that gives complete instructions how to make an 8-track tape player into a player/recorder. It can be done for less than $25.00 and is a simple operation.

Information on request

230

SOUTHERN AERONAUTICAL CORP.
14100 Lake Candlewood Ct.
Miami Lakes, Fla. 33014

PRODUCTS:

Airplanes

Kits and plans for closed cockpit small sport/racers. The CAS-SUTT is powered by a Continental or Lycoming engine. It is professionally designed, and is one of the simplest designs to build of any homebuilt. It can be constructed for about $2,500 complete. The RENEGADE, also a sport/racer, is powered by either a VW 1600 or a FRANKLIN 20–120 engine. It is 14 ft. 2 in. long, with a span of 17 ft., chord of 54 in.; height 4 ft. 2½ in., airfoil NACA 23009. It is also a simple plane to construct. Estimated cost of building is $1,800 complete.

15 page illustrated information packet $1.00

SPEED PRODUCTS ENGINEERING (SPE)
3307 West Warner Ave.
Santa Ana, Calif. 92704

PRODUCTS:

Hot rod hardware

Quality engineered parts and components for dragsters and funny cars.

12 page illustrated catalog and price lists free

SPENCER AMPHIBIAN AIR CAR
8725 Oland Ave.
Sun Valley, Calif. 91352

PRODUCTS:

Amphibians

SPENCER AMPHIBIAN AIR CAR (Cont'd)

Plans and kits for the Air Car, the first four passenger home-built amphibian offered to the public. Plans comprise over 480 sq. ft. of blueprints with full size details for easy inter-pretation. Span 37 ft. 4 in., length 26 ft. 5 in.; height 9 ft. 6 in., wing area 184 sq. ft., powered by 260 H. P. Lycoming engine. Plans are $185.00.

Information packet $4.00

SPENCER BOATS, LTD.
1240 Twigg Rd.
Richmond, B. C. Canada

PRODUCTS:

Sailing, cruising

Fiberglass molded sailboats in 31, 35, 42, 44, and 51 ft. sizes designed by John Brandlmayr. Boats may be purchased in any stage of construction and finished by the do-it-yourself build-er. The more you do the less it costs.

Illustrated catalog of designs free

DOROTHY SPEZIO
211 Dennis Drive
Absecon Highlands, N. J. 08201

PRODUCTS:

Airplanes

Plans only for a folding wing, towable small airplane, the "Tu-holer". The wings can be readily opened for flight in about 15 minutes. Fuselage and tail surfaces are welded steel tubing. The wing ribs and leading edge are wood. The plans are geared to the "first time builder" and consist of 33 sheets, full size

232

DOROTHY SPEZIO (Cont'd)

wing drawings, and 22 construction photos. Plans are $40.00 for the set.

Brochure free

SPORTSCRAFT CO.
P. O. Box 636
Allentown, N. J. 08501

PRODUCTS:

    Canoes   Kayaks

Kits and instructions for wood/canvas canoes and kayaks. Kits are complete except for hull paint. 4 canoe models, 11 ft. to 17 ft. 3 kayak models, 12 ft. to 16 ft. Prices start at $25.00. Special school, youth groups discounts.

Literature free

SPORTSMAN MFG. CO.
444 11th St.
Clarkston, Wash. 99403

PRODUCTS:

                Pool tables

Kits for 4 x 8 ft. contemporary pool table. Plans may be purchased separately. Also carries billiard equipment and supplies. Table completed $349.00, kit $229.00, plans $10.00.

Brochure free

SPORTSTYL
P. O. Box 628
103 So. Main St.
Lewistown, Pa. 17044

PRODUCTS:

Mini-bikes

Three mini-bike kits, the SS–1, SS–2, SS–3. $69.95 and up
without engine, $119.95 and up with engine. Also makes com-
pleted mini-bikes. Parts and accessories for mini-bikes, motorcycles, karts.

53 page illustrated catalog $1.00

STANDARD HOMES CO.
P. O. Box 1900
U. S. Hwy. 169 and I–35
Olathe, Kan. 66061

PRODUCTS:

Apartments/income-
producing units

Garages
Year round homes

55 models ranging from 880 sq. ft. to 5,760 sq. ft., $5,358.00
to $27,356.00 with many options available. Partially assem-
bled and pre-cut parts make it easier and faster to build.
Many of the more difficult operations have been done in the
shop, so you don't need years of carpentry experience. For
example, wall panels come already assembled in units, and
similarly for gable ends. Year round homes, apartments/town
houses/garden apartments, and garages, all with individual
variations as desired. Building plans are not available separately. The company invites the public to visit its home display
center at the factory.

80 page color illustrated design catalog with price lists $1.00
if mailed, free at the plant.

234

STANLEY TOOLS
P. O. Box 1800
New Britain, Conn. 06050

PRODUCTS:

Beds/headboards	Cupboards
Benches	Desks
Bookcases	Dressers
Bookends	Dry sinks
Buffets	Hutches
Cabinets, stereo/hi-fi	Lamps
Carts, hostess/tea	Stools
Chairs, rocking	Tables, coffee
Chest of drawers	Tables, end
Chests	Tables, trestle
Clocks, grandfather	Toys
Clocks, grandmother	TV stands
Commodes	Valets

Plans only. Geared towards the school market. Plans come in packets of ten, with a variety in each packet, and cost $1.00. 95 plan set in a looseleaf binder for $2.00. 20 new plans are developed each year. These plan sets have been submitted for awards in Stanley Tools' National Scholarship Contest. Plans include easy-to-follow detailed drawings with full dimensions and list of materials. Also toy patterns, set of six for 25¢.

Catalog free

STEEN AERO LAB
3218 So. Cherry St.
Denver, Col. 80222

PRODUCTS:

Airplanes, biplane

Steen Skybolt is a 4 aileron symmetrical two place aerobatic trainer and competition biplane. 24 ft. span suitable for 125 to 260 H. P. engine. Ease of construction with excellent

235

drawings. Flight tested and stressed for aerobatic competition. Plans, fuselage and wing kits. Plans $50.00.

Information packet $2.00

STEPHENS AIRCRAFT CO.
832 N. Eldon Ave.
La Puente, Calif. 91744

PRODUCTS:

Airplanes

The Stephens AKRO is a single place cantilever mid-wing monoplane which was conceived and built specifically for competition aerobatics. The AKRO was designed for plus or minus 12 G's and has been tested to positive 7 G's and minus 6 G's. Plans, parts and components are available from the designer, Clayton Stephens.

Information packet $2.00

STEWART AIRCRAFT CORP.
Martin Rd.
Clinton, N. Y. 13323

PRODUCTS:

Airplanes

The "Headwind" is a small, easy to build, inexpensive airplane. It was the first VW powered airplane in the United States. Welded steel tube fuselage and tail structure, simple to construct wooden wing structure make it possible to build for approximately $990.00.

Information free

STOKES MARINE INDUSTRIES
505 East Chicago St.
Coldwater, Mich. 49036

PRODUCTS:

Marine engine conversions

Marine engine conversion kits. Also stocks completed marine engines, used marine engines, and a full line of parts and accessories. Established 1944.

48 page illustrated catalog free

STOLP STARDUSTER CORP.
4301 Twining, Flabob Airport
Riverside, Calif. 92509

PRODUCTS:

Airplanes   Airplanes, biplane
Airplanes, antique

Company builds, sells materials, parts, and plans for aircraft which take you back to the golden age of flying. Four biplane designs: The Starduster (one-place, open sport biplane); The Starduster II (two-place, open sport biplane); The Acroduster II (two-place fully aerobatic stressed to 9.0 G's both plus and minus); the V–Star, a new biplane. Also offers parts and plans for the Starlet, a small open monoplane. These aircraft are built using steel tubing, fabric, and wood with wire bracing. A modern aircraft for old-fasioned flying fun.

65 page illustrated catalog $1.00, refundable with first order.

THE STRING SHOP
8432 High Ridge Rd.
Ellicott City, Md. 21043

PRODUCTS:

Bancimers (dulcimer fretted banjos)   Psalteries
Banjos   Thumb pianos (West
Dulcimers   African instrument)

237

THE STRING SHOP (Cont'd)

Kits and instructions for making stringed instruments. Kits are easy to assemble and require no unusual tools. The "student dulcimer kits" are especially simple and inexpensive to build. Also sells finished instruments. Save at least 50% by building your own. Special school discounts. Books on folk instruments.

Illustrated catalog free

C. F. STRUCK CORP.
Cedarburg, Wis. 53012

PRODUCTS:

BOATS/BOATING EQUIPMENT

  BOATS

Canoes	Sailing, day sailers

  VEHICLES

All terrain cycles (ATC's)	Mini-bikes
All terrain vehicles (ATV's)	Mowers, riding
Automobiles, midget	Snowmobiles
(motorized)	Tractors, garden/suburban
Bulldozers, garden/suburban	Trail bikes

Kits and easy-to-follow plans and instructions for assembly. Plans may be purchased separately, $5.00 each, 2 for $7.50, $10.00 for 3. Kits come knockdown with all parts finished. This requires little skill and only the tools found in most home workshops. Company is the largest manufacturer of power equipment sold in kit (knockdown) form. Canoes and day sailers are fiberglass, ready for assembly with instructions.

46 page illustrated catalog $1.00

STURDY–BUILT MFG. CO.
11304 S. W. Boones Ferry Rd.
Portland, Ore. 97219

PRODUCTS:

    Gazebos   Greenhouses

A full range of greenhouses for home or hobby made of redwood. Lean-to models, attached models, regular styles (set on
base walls), glass-to-ground styles. Attractive, unique construction. Each unit is pre-fabricated to order so that can offer
highly personalized service. Kits and instructions.

11 page color illustrated catalog and informative pamphlet,
"Some Things to Consider in Selecting Your Home Greenhouse". $1.00

STURGEON AIR LTD.
36 Airport Rd.
Edmonton, Alberta, Canada

PRODUCTS:

    Airplanes   Airplanes, biplane
    Airplanes, antique

One of the largest suppliers of plans, parts, kits for home-
built aircraft. Kits and plans for the 2/3 WWII Mustang, for
the MJ–5 Sirocco, Baby Great Lakes, Emeraude 2-seater,
Minicab Hawk 2-seater, and more than a dozen others. Accessories, books, parts, basic supplies, etc. Brochures for
individual planes available at $4.00 each.

62 page illustrated catalog $3.00

SUPERCRAFT PRODUCTS
Perma Dock Marine Specialties
6 Cross St.
Monticello, N. Y. 12701

PRODUCTS:

BOATS
    Houseboats   Pontoon boats
BOATING EQUIPMENT
    Docks/piers   Rafts
    Ports, boat

Pontoon boats are based on the flotation lift of standard, inexpensive 55 gal. drums. Kit includes nose cones, outboard motor mounts., brackets, tie-rods for drums. Wood framing made from easily available lumber at any lumberyard. Rafts and pier kits, also using the flotation of 55 gal. drums. Bracket sets for non-floating dock kits using ordinary plumber's pipe are available. All kits come with instructions. Construction of these projects does not require the builder to go into water.

Literature packet free

TAFT MARINE CORP.
6512 Shingle Creek Parkway
Minneapolis, Minn. 55430

PRODUCTS:

BOATS
    Canoes   Rowboat type (rowboats,
    Catamarans   prams, dinghies)
    Ice boats   Sailing, day sailers
BOATING EQUIPMENT
    Sails/sail gear   Surf boards, sailing

Complete kits for the smaller boat, easily built. Most of the kits are class sailboats. The kits are made of quality marine plywood and meet all the rigid class specification. Recently added a new catamaran with 120 sq. ft. of sail in the main sail and 48 sq. ft. in the jib. The kit is 15½ ft. long and is of all fiberglass construction.

22 page illustrated catalog free

TAXIDERMY SUPPLY CO.
Box 5815
Bossier City, La. 71010

PRODUCTS:

Taxidermy

A complete line of taxidermy supplies. Also offers a taxidermy course at reasonable cost for home study.

25 page illustrated catalog free

T. C. INDUSTRIES
P. O. Box 71
N. Dayton, Ohio 45404

PRODUCTS:

Bird houses/feeders   Lamps
Cue racks

Kits with instructions for simple and useful projects requiring a minimum of skill.

Information on request

TECHNICAL WRITERS GROUP
Box 5994 State College Station
Raleigh, N. C. 27607

PRODUCTS:

AUTOMOTIVE EQUIPMENT
- Headlight dimmers, automatic
- Tachometers

ELECTRONICS
- Battery chargers
- Broadcasters, neighborhood
- 4-channel stereo adaptors
- Frequency meters
- Megaphones
- Multiplex FM stereo adaptors
- TV cameras
- TV remote controls

EXPERIMENTAL/SCIENTIFIC
- Clocks, digital
- Computers
- Frequency counters
- Holography
- Lasers
- Radar
- Remote writers
- Science fair projects
- Sound intensity meters
- Sound telescopes
- Sound transmission over
  light beams
- Tic-tac-toe machines
- Treasure/metal locators
- Weather stations

MUSICAL INSTRUMENTS/EQUIPMENT
- Echo units
- Fuzz boxes
- Vibrato generators

OPTICS/PHOTOGRAPHY
- Color organs
- Light/psychedelic shows
- Stroboscopes

PETS
- Dog houses, automatic heated

Plans only. Interesting collection of inexpensive and easy
to build projects for the amateur scientist, home experimenter, science fair project student. Plans include instructions, drawings and parts lists.

15 page illustrated catalog 25¢

242

TECHNI—KIT
Universal Electronics Co.
17811 Sky Park Circle Box 4517
Irvine, Calif. 92664

PRODUCTS:

Power suppliers, AC—DC   Power suppliers, regulated/
                                                        variable

AC to DC power supply kits with instructions, regulated
and unregulated. 450 models to choose from. Professional
design at hobbyist prices.

Illustrated catalog free

TEE—JON INDUSTRIES
38350 MacIntosh Ct.
Mt. Clemens, Mich. 48043

PRODUCTS:

Vacuum cleaners, built-in

Kits, fittings and parts, plans, step-by-step instruction mau-
ual for home built-in vacuum cleaning systems.

Illustrated catalog $1.00

THE TEENIE CO.
Box 3163
Pensacola, Fla. 32506

PRODUCTS:

Airplanes

Kits and plans for "Teenie Two", a small VW powered all-
aluminum home-built airplane. No special tools, jigs or
bending brakes. Span 18 ft., length 12 ft. 10 in., gross

weight 590 lbs. Featured in May, 1968 and May, 1971
"Popular Mechanics". Plans $35.00.

Information packet $3.00

TELESCOPICS
6565 Romaine St.
Los Angeles, Calif. 90038

PRODUCTS:

  Telescope mirror kits   Telescopes, reflector

Mirror making kits, 4½ in. to 12½ in., as well as mirror
making supplies. While the company does not offer complete telescope kits, it does offer amateur and professional
accessories and supplies needed to make or to upgrade reflecting telescopes. Highest quality optical goods only,
so-called "surplus" or "bargain" materials are not handled.

12 page illustrated catalog free

TENSION STRUCTURES, INC.
9800 Ann Arbor Rd.
Plymouth, Mich. 48170

PRODUCTS:

              Vacation/leisure homes

"O'Dome" structures which the company produces are circular, modernistic homes. The 15 ft. and 20 ft. O'Domes
are made of a durable wood fiber material with a Korad
acrylic laminated to the exterior for long wear and a white
linen vinyl material laminated to the interior. The 25 ft.
O'Dome is manufactured out of two very strong skins of
fiberglass completely encompassing a 1/2 in. slab of ure-
thane foam. This 1/2 in. of foam provides as much insula-

244

TENSION STRUCTURES, INC. (Cont'd)

tion as is found in 85% of the homes today. Structure can
be assembled in one day, is easily moved, easily stored.

Illustrated catalog $1.00

TEXAS DORY BOAT PLANS
P. O. Box 720
Galveston, Tex. 77550

PRODUCTS:

Cruisers   Runabouts
Inboards   Sailing, cruising
Outboards   Sailing, day sailers
Rowboat-type (rowboat-type boats,
 prams, dinghies, etc.)

40 plans, 15 ft. to 45 ft. Designs for fishing, surfing, sailing, power dories. Most designs use Marine Grade plywood
for construction, standard size sheets available anywhere.
Plans are from $5.00 to $25.00. 140 page design portfolio
including action photos and dory lore, as well as two plans
for the Gloucester Gull rowing dory and Morning Light
Surf 22, $5.00.

Brochure/photos 25¢

TEXAS GREENHOUSE CO., INC.
2717 St. Louis Ave.
Fort Worth, Tex. 76110

PRODUCTS:

Greenhouses

Over 120 models and sizes of greenhouses to choose from.
Pre-cut, pre-drilled parts, and easy-to-follow instructions.
From small lean to's to commercial greenhouses in red-
wood or aluminum, in double strength glass (1/8 in. thick

245

to withstand hail and wind) or fiberglass. Also carries
accessories for heating and cooling and anything else required for successful greenhouse growing.

15 page color-illustrated catalog free

THOMAS WOODCRAFT
1412 Drumcliffe Road
Winston-Salem, N. C. 27103

PRODUCTS:

    Clocks, wooden wheel

Full size plans only consisting of eight sheets for a wooden
clock. It is time only with no striking train. The clock has
a 39 inch one second pendulum with an hour, minute, and
second hand. The plans provide complete step-by-step
instructions. Hand tools are adequate, but power tools are
better. The finished clock is quite large and normally is
mounted un-cased on a pedestal. Plans sell for $4.00. Wood
suitable for the clock may be obtained from Albert Constantine and Son, Inc., 2050 Eastchester Road, Bronx,
N. Y. 10461.

Information free

TOTALTRON LABORATORY
36 Quirk St.
Watertown, Mass. 02172

PRODUCTS:

  Bell sensors, remote   Burglar alarms, automobile

The remote bell sensor allows you to hear the sound of
your bell chiming in any part of your home even if you
are outside the hearing range of your present chimes. The

pre-built sensor is easy to install and there is no fishing for wires. A unique product.

Brochure free

TPC (THEFT PREVENTION CO.)
Box AE
Cupertino, Calif. 95014

PRODUCTS:

Burglar/fire alarms, home or business

Professional kits and components not generally available to the public (consumer) for burglar and fire alarm devices and systems.

Illustrated catalog free

TRAILCRAFT, INC.
P. O. Box 606
Concordia, Kan. 66901

PRODUCTS:

Canoes   Kayaks

Kits for canoes and kayaks in choice of fiberglass, wood, or canvas. Boats from 12 ft. to 18 ft., 21 models and sizes to choose from. Prices $19.50 and up. All kits come with step-by-step instructions. Discounts for schools, church groups and youth organizations.

Illustrated brochure free.

TRAIL–R–CLUB OF AMERICA
Box 1376
Beverly Hills, Calif. 90213

PRODUCTS:

Campers	Trailers
Pickup covers	Van conversions to
	mobile home

Plans only for recreational vehicles: trailers, pickup campers, van conversions. Also books relating to every aspect of recreational vehicles, for the recreational vehicle traveler, for park operators and developers, for the would-be builder and owner of recreational vehicles, and even cookbooks for the recreational vehicle gourmet. This is the single best source of books and information on recreational vehicles.

Catalog free

TRI–STAR TRIMARANS
Ed Horstman, Naval Architect
P. O. Box 286
Venice, Calif. 90291

PRODUCTS:

Trimarans

Trimaran kits and plans designed by Ed Horstman, 16 models from 18 ft. to 65 ft. plywood construction. All plans have full-size frame patterns, with the exception of the Tri-Star 59 and 65. Plans include a 10-page bill of materials and over 30 pages of written instructions plus 50 basic construction photos on three 8 by 10 in. sheets to further clarify construction. Free consultation until launch time. Frame kits are of marine plywood and include plans, all hull frames, three laminated plywood bow stems, and three stern tran-

TRI-STAR TRIMARANS (Cont'd)

soms. Study plans available for $5.00, $2.00 for the 18 ft. Tri-Star.

24 page illustrated catalog $3.00

TRIGGER ELECTRONICS
7361 North Avenue
River Forest, Ill. 60305

PRODUCTS:

AUTOMOTIVE EQUIPMENT

Engine analyzers	Ignition, capacitive discharge

ELECTRONICS

Appliance testers	Radios, aircraft monitors
Battery testers	Radios, FM
Circuit testers	RF signal generators
Espionage/surveillance devices	Signal probes/tracers
4-channel stereo adaptors	Sine/square generators
Grid-dip meters	Stereo/hi-fi, amplifiers
Microphones, FM wireless	Stereo/hi-fi, preamplifiers
Motor/speed controllers	Stereo/hi-fi, receivers
Multi-signal tracers	Stereo/hi-fi, tuners
Oscilloscopes/vectorscopes	Transistor testors
Photoelectric relays	Tube testers
Power suppliers, DC–AC	VOM's
Power suppliers, regulated/ variable	Voice operated relays/switches VTVM's

HOME CARE/IMPROVEMENT

Burglar/fire alarms, home or business

OPTICS/PHOTOGRAPHY

Color organs	Stroboscopes

Electronic kits made by such well-known manufacturers as EICO and Dynaco. Also parts, components, tools, books for the kit builder, for the experimenter, and for the hobbyist. Hi-fi equipment, radios, tape recorders, ham equipment, radios, and so on.

67 page illustrated catalog free

STANLEY W. TULL CO., INC.
Sports Division
1620 Harmon Place
Minneapolis, Minn. 55403

PRODUCTS:

Karts

Does offer one kit for go-kart but basically this company is
large supplier of parts and accessories for mini-bikes, karts,
and snowmobiles.

154 page illustrated Mini-bike and Go-Kart catalog $1.50;
123 page illustrated Snowmobile catalog also $1.50.

TURNER AIRCRAFT AND ENGINEERING
P. O. Box 4582
Los Angeles, Calif. 90045

PRODUCTS:

Airplanes

The Turner T–40 series airplanes are folding wing aircraft,
all wood construction. The T–40 is a single place with conventional gear; the T–40A, two place with conventional or
tri-gear; the Super T–40A, with conventional or tri-gear,
tricycle retractable landing gear being optional. The Super
T–40A also has the folding wing structure, has a bubble
canopy, swept tail, 125 H. P. engine as standard, larger
wings, and higher gross weight than the T–40A.

Information packet $3.00

TURNER GREENHOUSES
P. O. Box 1260
Goldsboro, N. C. 27530

PRODUCTS:

Greenhouses

250

TURNER GREENHOUSES (Cont'd)

Pre-fabricated greenhouses for home or backyard use. Lean-to and free standing models. Framework is made of aluminized steel. Polyethylene series of greenhouses is the least expensive. Made of 6 mil film, it will last one year and must be replaced the next year. (Ultraviolet rays cause deterioration.) Cost of recovering is less than $15.00 per season. The fiberglass series is permanent but more expensive. The fiberglass panels are acrylic fortified and guaranteed for 15 years. Polyethylene greenhouses may be converted to fiberglass with a kit supplied by the company. Lean-to's range in price from $94 to $162 for polyethylene, and $228 to $404 for fiberglass. Free-standing range in price from $160 to $330 for polyethylene, and $435 to $875 for fiberglass. Accessories for greenhouse also available.

14 page color illustrated catalog free

U–BILD ENTERPRISES
Box 2383
15125 Saticoy St.
Van Nuys, Calif. 91409

PRODUCTS:

BOATS/BOATING EQUIPMENT
- Cruisers
- Houseboats
- Paddle-wheel boats
- Rowboat type (rowboats, prams, dinghies, etc.)
- Runabouts
- Sailing, day sailers

CAMPING
- Bike racks, car top
- Kitchens, camp

CHILDREN'S THINGS
- Boats, children's
- Cars/trucks, toy
- Cradles
- Cradles, colonial
- Doll furniture
- Doll houses
- Furniture, children's
- Hobby horses
- Kitchens, children's
- Playhouses
- Playpens
- Rocking toys
- Sandboxes
- Swings

251

CHILDREN'S THINGS (Cont'd)

Toy chests

Toys

Tricycles

Wading pools

FURNITURE

Bars

Beds/headboards

Benches

Bookcases

Breakfast nooks

Buffets

Cabinets, collectors/curio

Cabinets, gun/rifle

Cabinets, record

Cabinets, sewing

Cabinets, stereo/hi-fi

Cabinets, TV

Carts, hostess/tea

Chairs

Chairs, rocking

Chifferobes

Desks

Dining room sets

Hampers

Lamps

Office centers, home

Racks, gun/rifle

Racks, magazine

Racks, spoon/silverware

Shoe bars

Tables

Tables, card

Tables, cobbler's bench

Tables, coffee

Tables, dining

Tables, dressing

Tables, end

Tables, nest of

Tables, occasional

Telephone stands/centers

Valets

HOME CARE/IMPROVEMENT

Barns

Cabanas

Carports

Closets

Cupolas

Dens

Ironing centers

Kitchen islands

Room dividers

Shelving

Swimming pools

Wall units

Weathervanes

Window boxes

Workshop centers

HOUSING

A-frames

Cabins/cottages

LAWN & GARDEN

Barbecue carts

Barbecue dining sets

Barbecue pits

Caddies, garden

Christmas decorations

Connesota Wagon settees

Grist mills, lawn

Lamp posts

Lawn/patio furniture

Markers/signs/figures

Picnic tables/benches

Planters

Potting benches

Settees, outdoor

U-BILD ENTERPRISES (Cont'd)

LAWN & GARDEN (Cont'd)
- Swings, lawn
- Trash bins
- Tree seats
- Wheelbarrow planters
- Windmills, garden
- Wishing wells, garden

PETS
- Bird houses/feeders
- Dog houses
- Martin houses

SPORTING EQUIPMENT
- Cue racks
- Exercise machines
- Gyms, family
- Ping pong tables
- Tackle boxes

VEHICLES
- Campers
- Pickup covers
- Trailers

WOODWORKING PROJECTS
- Tool caddies
- Tool chests
- Utility chests

Plans, full size. Offers hundreds of projects for the home, lawn and garden, recreation. Projects are suitable for school, for the dedicated craftsman, or for the occasional build-it-yourselfer. All projects are taken from Steve Ellingson's syndicated do-it-yourself column, the world's largest.

83 page illustrated catalog $1.00

UNIVERSAL ELECTRONICS CO.
P. O. Box 4517
17811 Sky Park Circle
Irvine, Calif. 92664

PRODUCTS:

Power suppliers, AC—DC
Power suppliers, regulated/variable

Wide range of AC—DC power supply kits. Hundreds of

UNIVERSAL ELECTRONICS CO. (Cont'd)

models to suit every need. Schematics and instructions with every kit.

Illustrated brochure free

UNIVERSAL HOVERCRAFT
2611 182nd Place
Redondo Beach, Calif. 90278

PRODUCTS:

Hovercraft

Plans only for hovercraft, from the toy vehicle (6 ft.) powered by a model airplane engine to the 6 passenger high speed vehicle for sportsmen (18 ft.). Plans range in cost from $2.00 to $25.00. Vehicles designed and tested by aircraft engineers.

Illustrated catalog with explanation of what a hovercraft is and how it operates, $1.00

UNIVERSITY OPTICS, INC.
2122 East Delhi Rd.
Ann Arbor, Mich. 48106

PRODUCTS:

Telescope mirror kits   Telescopes, reflector
Telescope mirror testers

Kits with instructions for making your own reflecting telescopes. Kits also for mirror testers and for making mirrors from blanks. Company offers optical accessories of all types for the amateur or professional astronomer as well as books on astronomy. Completed telescopes are

254

UNIVERSITY OPTICS, INC. (Cont'd)

also available. Company specializes in and handles optical goods exclusively.

34 page color illustrated catalog free

URBAN SYSTEMS
1033 Massachusetts Ave.
Cambridge, Mass. 02138

PRODUCTS:

Pollution testers   Science fair projects

Designed by scientists from M. I. T. and Harvard. Allows the average person to test for pollution himself. Kits and instructions. Special provisions for schools.

Illustrated color catalog free

U–TAN CO.
28 Paris St.
Newark, N. J. 07105

PRODUCTS:

Tanning kits

Don't waste valuable hides – tan them at home. The basic kit consists of two key ingredients for tanning: a tanning agent and a hide liquoring or fat liquoring oil. The leather kit contains all the ingredients for hair removal without damage to the hide.

Information free

VANDESTADT & McGRUER, LTD.
Box 7
Owen Sound, Ontario   Canada

PRODUCTS:

Sailing, day sailers

The "Spindrift", a day sailer, comes either as kit or plans only. Length — 13 ft. 4 in.; beam — 5 ft. 2 in.; draft — 3 ft.; sail area — 100 sq. ft. Only 40 hours are required by the average builder to complete boat. Fiberglass hull comes ready-made. However, if you have time and enjoy wood-working, you can build from scratch out of plywood using plans. Kit sells for $870, plans for $20.00.

Illustrated brochure free

VAN DYKE SUPPLY CO.
Woonsocket, S. Dak. 57385

PRODUCTS:

Taxidermy

Kits, tools, and supplies for taxidermy and related subjects. Instructions are provided with some items. Taxidermy books.

72 page color illustrated catalog 50¢

VAN SICKLE CUTLERY CO.
P. O. Box 3688
San Angelo, Texas 76901

PRODUCTS:

Knives/hunting/Bowie

Parts with instructions for making your own custom hunt-ing knife. Offers a wide selection of blades, handles and

256

VAN SICKLE CUTLERY CO. (Cont'd)

hilts. Features "Hilt-Lok" kits which allow the blade and hilt piece to interlock to form a better union, eliminating the tedious job of handfitting the hilt. "Hilt-Lok" kits are available as a completed knife, as a blade with hilt blank silver soldered in place, or as a blade with hilt blank furnished separately. Instructions are included with each order. However, instructions may be purchased separately for $1.00. Ask for company's "Folder on Knife Making".

35 page illustrated catalog 50¢, $1.00 air mailed.

VENTURE AERO—MARINE
Box 5273
Akron, O. 44313

PRODUCTS:

Hovercraft

Kits and plans for hovercraft. Plans for hovercraft from small toy-like 6 footers, to 18 footers capable of carrying six passengers. Kit or completed for the HOVERBUG, an all-plastic ("Cycolac" by Borg-Warner) two passenger hovercraft. Also offers books and technical literature about every aspect of hovercraft. Supplies, parts and components for hovercraft or air cushion vehicles.

40 page illustrated catalog $2.00

VERMONT LOG BUILDINGS, INC.
Route 5
Hartland, Vt. 05048

PRODUCTS:

Barns	Garages
Cabins, log	Lean-to's
Chalets	Vacation/leusure homes

VERMONT LOG BUILDINGS, INC. (cont'd)

Kits and plans for 22 models of traditional log homes ranging from simple cabins to luxurious lodges. Prices from
$3,410 to $19,800. Logs of 8 in. to 10 in. are machine
barked (to retain their natural beauty), dried, pre-cut to
6 in. of exposed face, notched, grooved, and submerged in
the best wood preservative available. Four experienced men
can erect in four days with simple tools. Pre-cut materials
for easy erection. Blueprints at $15.00 a set may be pur-
chased separately, cost being applicable to the price if a
home is bought. Garages, lean-to's, barns made of whole
logs are also available.

Information packet and portfolio of designs $2.00

ALEXANDER W. VETTER
535 Park Blvd.
P. O. Box 376
Millbrae, Calif. 94030

PRODUCTS:

Cruisers   Inboards   Outboards

10 stock plans, 17 ft. to 45 ft. for offshore cruisers,
sportsfishermen, utility boats. Wood or wood with fiberglass covering. Designed by Alexander Vetter, Naval
Architect.

Design portfolio 50¢

VIKING CAMPER SUPPLY, INC.
99 Glenwood Avenue
Minneapolis, Minn. 55403

PRODUCTS:

Mobile home beautification
Mobile homes, conversion from buses

VIKING CAMPER SUPPLY, INC. (Cont'd)

Mobile homes, conversion   Pickup covers
from vans/trucks   Trailers

One of the largest suppliers of parts, equipment, accessories
to the do-it-yourself builder of recreational vehicles. Kits
and plans. Plans may be purchased separately. A pickup
cover can be completed for as little as $165, plus lumber
purchased locally. Pre-cut aluminum sheets. Easy-to-follow
plans.

72 page illustrated catalog free

VOLMER AIRCRAFT
104 East Providencia Ave.
Burbank, Calif. 91502

PRODUCTS:

Amphibians   Hang gliders

"Sportsman" amphibian, two-place, side by side, closed
cabins, high-wing monoplane amphibian boat. Blueprints
and some parts. Plans only for the Volmer VJ—11 hang
glider. Length 15 ft. 5 in., span 28 ft., wing area 225 sq.
ft. It is a controlled hang glider with ailerons, elevators,
rudder. The cost of materials to build is approximately
$200.00. Also plans only for the VJ—23 hang glider.
This glider is 17 ft. 5 in. long, 6 ft. high, with a wing span
of 32 ft. 7 in. and area of 179 sq. ft. Cost of materials is
approximately $400.00.

Three different illustrated catalogs, one for each plane,
$2.00 each.

WALMSLEY'S TACKLE
Box 202
Upper Darby, Pa. 19084

PRODUCTS:

Fishing lures/jigs/sinkers

Offers a full line of fishing tackle you can order by mail.

24 page illustrated catalog free

WARD CABIN CO.
P. O. Box 72
Houlton, Maine 04730

PRODUCTS:

Cabins, log   Chalets

Over 50 models of log cabins ranging from small cabins to
lodges, or will custom design according to your specifications. Wood usd is Northern White Cedar. Pre-cut logs
are numbered and labeled for easy assembly. No special
tools or skills required. Tongue and groove feature of logs
insures minimal maintenance. Prices range from $2,180
to $25,370.

Color illustrated catalog with floor plans and prices $2.00

BILL WARWICK
5727 W. Clearsite
Torrance, Calif. 90505

PRODUCTS:

Airplanes

One seater, all metal sportplane, the "Bantam W–3".
Powered by any suitable engine from 65 to 100 H. P., plane

260

BILL WARWICK (Cont'd)

has a fixed tricycle landing gear with space if desired for retracting. Span 18.5 ft., length 13 ft., 9 in., height 6 ft., empty weight 535 lbs. Set of plans consists of over 200 sq. ft. of detailed drawings at $55. Raw stock also available from company.

Specs and photos $2.00

WESTERN AIRCRAFT SUPPLIES
623 Markerville Rd., N. E.
Calgary, 62, Alberta, Canada

PRODUCTS:

Airplanes

Kits and plans for the "Monsoon", a two seat light sports aircraft. Span 25 ft., length 20 ft. 3 in., height 5 ft. 4 in., wing area 111 sq. ft., gross weight 1300 lbs. The kits supplied minimize the amount of tools required to build. Company also sells aircraft supplies.

Monsoon information packet $3.00; supply catalog $1.00

WESTERN WOOD PRODUCTS ASSOCIATION
1500 Yeon Bldg.
Portland, Ore. 97204

PRODUCTS:

FURNITURE

Benches	Desks
Cabinets	Picture frames
Cabinets, fishing gear	Sand boxes
Cabinets, gun/rifle	Toy chests

WESTERN WOOD PRODUCTS ASSOCIATION
(Cont'd)

HOME CARE/IMPROVEMENT

Closets	Paneling, wood
Decks	Room additions
Fences	Shelving
Garages	Vacation/leisure homes
Mobile home beautification	Wall units

LAWN & GARDEN

Barbecue carts	Patios
Gazebos	Storage/tool houses
Lamp posts	Sun traps
Lawn/patio furniture	Trellises

WOODWORKING

Wood turning projects

Plans only for indoor and outdoor wood projects. Plans are low priced. For example, 15¢ will bring a 25 page booklet: "Ten Build—It—Yourself Projects"; 25¢ will bring a 14 page color illustrated booklet: "Vacation Homes" of 12 plans for second homes. A bargain source for the home craftsman looking for a wide range of plans using wood.

Literature list free

WHEEL SPECIALTIES
2130 E. Orangewood Ave.
Anaheim, Calif. 92806

PRODUCTS:

Choppers (motorcycle)

Kits for chopper front ends, front brakes, wheel kits, intake systems, covers, etc.

Information packet free

J. C. WHITNEY & CO.
1917–19 Archer Ave.
Chicago, Ill. 60616

PRODUCTS:

Campers   Roadsters
Dune buggies   Trailers
Hot rod hardware

Company does not offer kits for making completed vehicles
as such, but it does carry hundreds of component and repair kits as well as parts and accessories for cars, antique
cars, customs, hot rods, pickup trucks, dune bugs, recreational vehicles, motorcycles, etc. Stocks over 100,000
parts with new lines being added all the time. Also do-it-
yourself books. A one-stop supermarket for parts by mail
for all types of vehicles. In business for over 30 years.

177 page illustrated catalog free

WHITTEMORE–DURGIN GLASS CO.
Box 2065
Hanover, Mass. 02339

PRODUCTS:

Lamps, Tiffany style

Kits with patterns and instructions for fashioning Tiffany
style and other stained glass lamps. Also offers a variety of
other stained glass projects. Stained glass making supplies,
tools, and materials. Company founded in 1925.

34 page illustrated catalog and price lists 30¢

LAUREN WILLIAMS SAILING TRIMARANS
P. O. Box 137
Mill Valley, Calif. 94941

PRODUCTS:

Trimarans

263

LAUREN WILLIAMS SAILING TRIMARANS (Cont'd)

Plans only for trimarans from 19 ft. to 50 ft. Boats are designed for the homebuilder without a full background in boating. Study plans and working drawings are available separately. The working drawings for these designs are large scale comprehensive drawings showing virtually every major joint in the boat. Included with the working drawings are: a step-by-step instruction booklet, a complete lumber list, full-sized stem patterns (full-sized frame patterns, too, for the W44 and W50), specific fittings list, a booklet of standard detail drawings, and a booklet of fiberglassing instructions.

18 page illustrated portfolio of designs and catalog $2.00, refundable with purchase of working drawings.

THE WILLIAMS WORKSHOP
1229 Olancha Drive
Los Angeles, Calif. 90065

PRODUCTS:

Harpsichords

Harpsichords based on historic museum piece models. Finished, semi-kit, or basic kit. As a semi-kit, all the casework is complete. This version is intended for people who do not have extensive woodworking experience and tools or who want to get on to playing in the shortest possible time. The basic kit is for people who have some woodworking background and tools and want to save money by using their own skills and time. The more you do, the less it costs. The single manual small Flemish-style harpsichord (modeled on a 1627 Ruckers) costs $1,250 completed, $580 in semi-kit form, and $240 in basic kit form.

Illustrated catalog and price lists free

WILSON–ALLEN CORP.
Box 243
Windsor, Mo. 65360

PRODUCTS:

Duck decoys

Make your own duck decoys using aluminum molds and expandable plastic. No tools are required. Place 1½ cups of expandable plastic in mold, heat in oven for 35 minutes, and paint. Decoys cost as little as 50¢ each to make so you can sell for profit or share the expense with your duck-hunting friends. Also molds for mourning dove decoys. Decoy paints also available.

Illustrated brochure free

J. WITCHER–ANCIENT INSTRUMENTS
P. O. Box 552
Forestville, Calif. 95436

PRODUCTS:

Clavichords   Hurdy gurdys
Harpsichords

Keyboard instruments are patterned after, and in many cases are exact copies of, instruments by famous makers of the 16th— 18th centuries. However, in the construction of the harpsichords modern engineering practice has been followed in the arrangement of the internal bracing. Kits, semi-kits, finished instruments. Also offers completed ancient stringed instruments, for example, the medieval gigue, cittern, gothic psaltery, as well as woodwinds, such as the Renaissance flute, the baroque oboe, etc.

Catalog free

WOOD—MOSAIC CORP.
P. O. Box 21159
Louisville, Ky. 40221

PRODUCTS:

Flooring, parquet

Teak parquet floors prefinished with durable seal. Rich, unique designs. Sold only through distributors. If no distributor is convenient to you, ask floor or lumber dealer to contact the company for prices and information.

Illustrated color catalog 25¢

YACHT CONSTRUCTORS
7030 N. E. 42nd Ave.
Portland, Ore. 97218

PRODUCTS:

Sailing, cruising

"Cascade" sailboats are 29 ft., 36 ft., 42 ft. Fiberglass hulls with at least seven layers in each lay up, more in larger boats. The basic kit is the hull and plans for completing the boat. Will also furnish hard-to-make items and accessories, such as a molded fiberglass cabin-cockpit-deck unit. On special order boat may be furnished in any advanced stage of completion. Approximate cost for components and materials to complete a basic boat (less sails) is $5,005 for the 29 ft., $9,720 for the 36 ft., and $13,670 for the 42 ft. This is at least a 50% saving over buying an equivalent sailing boat completed.

8 page illustrated catalog and price lists free

YANKEE BARNS, INC.
Box 1000
Boston, Mass. 02118

PRODUCTS:

Barn homes

Year round homes

Vacation/leisure homes

The classic 18th century Yankee barn is one of the great architectural treasures out of the American past. Instead of trying to renovate an old one, and they are difficult to find where and when you want it, or you are apprehensive of the cost of renovating one, the "Yankee Barn" is a modern adaptation of this classic structure. It uses elements, both old and new, to combine the best features of each. Options available. Full package for do-it-yourself assembly. Price range from $7,795 to $15,400 for full component package, 870 sq. ft. to 1,922 sq. ft.

Information package including specifications, plans, prices $2.00

YIELD HOUSE
North Conway, N. H. 03860

PRODUCTS:

CHILDREN'S THINGS

Doll houses

Rocking toys

CLOCKS

Clocks, cuckoo

Clocks, wooden wheel

Clocks, grandfather

FURNITURE

Bars

Benches

Cabinets, paperback

Book easels/stands

Cabinets, phonograph record

Bookcases

Cabinets, medicine

Cabinets, gun/rifle

Cabinets, recipe

Cabinets, stereo/hi-fi

YIELD HOUSE (Cont'd)

Cabinets, tie
Cabinets, TV
Cane/rush furniture
Cedar chests
Chairs, captain's
Chairs, ladderback
Chests, apothecary
Colonial style furniture
Cupboards
Desk organizers
Desks
Desks, rolltop
Display cases
Dressers
File cabinets
Hampers
Hutches
Lamps, Tiffany style
Log holders
Music centers
Racks, cosmetic

Racks, fishing gear
Racks, gun/rifle
Racks, magazine
Racks, spoon/silverware
Racks, towel/tissue
Racks, trouser
Sewing centers
Stools
Susans, stereo tape
Tables, cocktail
Tables, coffee
Tables, cribbage
Tables, dining
Tables, display
Tables, drop leaf
Tables, end
Tables, trestle
Telephone centers/stands
TV stands
Valets

HOME CARE/IMPROVEMENT

Closets

Cupolas

PETS

Martin houses

SPORTING EQUIPMENT

Cue racks

WOODWORKING

Pipes, smoking

Kits with easy-to-follow instructions in pine wood based on authentic early American furniture designs. These same kits are also available in finished form. Save by doing it yourself. A Chesapeake slant front desk completed sells for $115, in kit form for $75; a cedar lined chest completed for $84.50, sells for $56.50 as a kit. Other kits show proportionate savings. Some completed items need only finishing. Also carries accessories in harmony with the early American look. Items can be purchased by mail through the catalog or at five shops in North Conway, N. H., Pea-

YIELD HOUSE (Cont'd)

body, Mass., Meredith, N. H., Avon, Conn., and Hyannis, Mass. In business for 25 years.

75 page color illustrated catalog 25¢

THE YURT FOUNDATION
Bucks Harbor, Me. 04618

PRODUCTS:

Yurts

The yurt design has its origin in Mongolia where the prototype has, for thousands of years, been found to withstand the severe cold and violent winds of the steppes. This is an attempt to design a dwelling in harmony with nature. The design reduces the skill needed in building to a minimum and still have an inexpensive, permanent shelter which is aesthetically pleasing.

Plans $3.50

ZOMEWORKS CORP.
P. O. Box 712
Albuquerque, N. Mex. 87103

PRODUCTS:

Geodesic domes   Playground equipment, geodesic dome

Kits and plans for geodesic domes. Work is done with the customer to integrate their personal needs rather than by supplying uniform, set structures. Geodesic climbers for children come in a large variety of shapes and sizes, easy assembly.

Information free

DEFINITIONS

AND NOTES

AIRPLANES

The Experimental Aircraft Association (EAA) is the parent organization for enthusiasts who build their own aircraft. It is the largest organization of this type in the world with members in over 50 nations. EAA annually hold a week-long fly-in convention at Wittman Field, Oshkosh, Wisconsin — normally the first week in August. This is the largest sport aviation event anywhere. EAA also publishes a monthly magazine, "Sports Aviation", for its members. Membership in the EAA is $15.00 per year. Contact the Experimental Aircraft Association, 11311 West Forest Home Ave., Box 229, Hales Corners, Wis. 53130.

AIRPLANES, ANTIQUE

If you are interested in antique or vintage airplanes, you should know that there is an Antique Airplane Association whose motto is "Keep the Antiques Flying". It now has well over 5,000 active members in 26 affiliated-type clubs and 29 active chapters. It sponsors an annual antique airplane International Fly-In, the largest of its kind in the world, in Ottumwa, Iowa. The Association also maintains the Airpower Museum in Ottumwa. The Association publishes a bi-monthly magazine, the "International Antique Airplane Association News". Full membership in the Association is $15.00 per year, which includes a subscription to the News, the Quarterly APM (Airpower Museum Bulletin) and an Association Membership for one family member. Contact the Antique Airplane Association, P. O. Box H, Ottumwa, Iowa 52501.

BOATS

If you are interested in building your own boat, you might want to look into the International Amateur Boat

Building Society (IABBS). The IABBS publishes a magazine, "Amateur Boat Building", which reports on designs, building methods, boat building news and activities of interest to the amateur boat builder. The magazine is published bi-monthly and the subscription is $6.00 per year which includes cost of membership in the IABBS. Further information: International Amateur Boat Building Society, 3183 Merrill, Royal Oak, Mich. 48072.

GAZEBOS

The ancient gazebo was a turret or windowed balcony placed so that one could gaze at the surrounding scenery. Today the word refers to any small structure on a lawn or garden, with or without a view. The gazebo can be used for the scenery or for practical purposes such as a small greenhouse or a tool or garden shed.

GREENHOUSES

In selecting your greenhouse, there are a number of things to consider. First, you must select the type of greenhouse that will be best for you. There are free-standing models, lean-to models, attached models, regular style (set on base walls) and glass-to-ground styles.

The site for your greenhouse will dictate to some extent the type you should select. If you have a natural spot for a lean-to or attached type, you will find them to be the most convenient. The free-standing types, however, will give you the most growing room for your dollar.

Choosing between a regular and glass-to-ground style is mostly a matter of personal choice. The glass-to-ground models allow light under the benches for more growing space. The regular models are somewhat easier to heat, and they provide convenient out-of-sight storage space under the benches.

The exact site you select for your greenhouse, together with the type of greenhouse you select, should take into consideration the following:

1. How the placement of your greenhouse will best fit in with your home, garden, and general landscaping.
2. Exposure to sunlight, wind, and weather.
3. Convenience.

4. Physical ease of construction and installation.

The relative importance of each factor will vary, so there is never any pat answer for all situations. If everything else were equal, which is rarely the case, a southeasterly exposure is considered ideal; with east, south, and west exposures following in order. Adequate natural light, of course, is essential for successful greenhouse gardening.

An important reminder: check with your local housing or building office if a permit is needed to build a greenhouse. In many communities you may need one.

HANG GLIDERS

Hang gliders have no cockpits in which the flyer sits. The flyer hangs from the glider like a man with wings for short distance flights. Takeoff is from hills or other heights.

PSALTERIES

The psaltery is a small stringed instrument which is plucked with the fingers or with a plectrum. It is of medieval origin and can be considered as a simple form of the zither. In modern Kentucky adaptations it is often confused with the dulcimer.

VIRGINALS

The virginal is a member of the harpsichord family. The strings run parallel to the front edge of the keyboard. The sound is rich and resonant, not unlike an Italian harpsichord. The sound of the virginal blends very well with other instruments without either dominating or being submerged.

YURTS

The yurt is a primitive round house of Mongolian origin. Although simple in design, it is strong enough to withstand the rigors of nature at her worst. Like all great examples of folk architecture, it blends in with the environment in an easy, natural way.

Presents

the

Finder's Guide Series

CRAFT SUPPLIES
SUPERMARKET

FINDER'S GUIDE No. 2

Joseph Rosenbloom

A well illustrated and indexed directory of craft supplies. Thousands of products, including materials, kits, tools, etc., from over 450 companies, are analyzed from their catalogs.

224 pp, ill., August, 1974
LC 74-84298 $3.95

THE COMPLETE KITCHEN

FINDER'S GUIDE No. 3

Anne Heck

This book is a comprehensive guide to hard-to-find utensils, and describes the companies supplying such utensils as well as giving information about their catalogs. Many illustrations of unusual or interesting utensils.

96 pp, ill., September, 1974
LC 74-84299 $2.95

HOMEGROWN ENERGY

Power for the Home and Homestead

FINDER'S GUIDE No. 4

Gary Wade

This book offers the do-it-yourselfer a very complete directory to thousands of available products involved in the production of home grown power. Water wheels, solar cells, windmills, methane generators and other exotic equipment and parts are covered and indexed in depth.

96 pp, ill., September, 1974
LC 74-84300 $2.95

SPICES, CONDIMENTS, TEAS, COFFEES, AND OTHER DELICACIES

FINDER'S GUIDE No. 6

Roland Robertson

Answers difficult questions involved with finding and purchasing unusual ingredients, beverages and foods which are difficult to obtain locally. This illustrated and indexed directory is highly browsable, to say nothing of gastronomically stimulating.

288 pp, ill., October, 1974
$3.95

COUNTRY TOOLS

Essential Hardware and Livery

FINDER'S GUIDE No. 7

Fred Davis

Locates sources for the otherwise difficult to find tools essential to country living. This book covers everything from bell scrapers through goat harnesses to spoke shavers. An indispensible guide for the country resident working his land.

272 pp, ill., October, 1974
$3.95

⟨THE Scribner Library

America's Quality Paperback Series

CHARLES SCRIBNER'S SONS

Shipping and Billing Departments
Vreeland Ave., Totowa, New Jersey 07512

Order Blank

Dear Sirs:

I believe your new series "FINDER'S GUIDES" fills a definite need for information and I would like to order:

QUANTITY	TITLE	TOTAL
	copies of KITS AND PLANS @ $3.95 ea.	
	copies of CRAFT SUPPLIES SUPERMARKET @ $3.95 ea.	
	copies of THE COMPLETE KITCHEN @ $2.95 ea.	
	copies of HOMEGROWN ENERGY @ $2.95 ea.	
	copies of SPICES, CONDIMENTS, TEAS, COFFEES, AND OTHER DELICACIES @ $3.95 ea.	
	copies of COUNTRY TOOLS @ $3.95 ea.	
	copies of ALL OF THE ABOVE BOOKS ($21.70 Total)	